WHEN CRICKET AND POLITICS COLLIDED

Also by Richard Thorn and published by Matador,
an imprint of Troubador Publishing Ltd.

Shute: The engineer who became a prince of storytellers

WHEN CRICKET AND POLITICS COLLIDED

1968 – 1970 two years
that changed Test cricket

by

Richard Thorn

Copyright © 2021 Richard Thorn

The moral right of the author has been asserted.

Apart from any fair dealing for the purposes of research or private study, or criticism or review, as permitted under the Copyright, Designs and Patents Act 1988, this publication may only be reproduced, stored or transmitted, in any form or by any means, with the prior permission in writing of the publishers, or in the case of reprographic reproduction in accordance with the terms of licences issued by the Copyright Licensing Agency. Enquiries concerning reproduction outside those terms should be sent to the publishers.

Matador
9 Priory Business Park,
Wistow Road, Kibworth Beauchamp,
Leicestershire. LE8 0RX
Tel: 0116 279 2299
Email: books@troubador.co.uk
Web: www.troubador.co.uk/matador
Twitter: @matadorbooks

ISBN 978 1800463 790

British Library Cataloguing in Publication Data.
A catalogue record for this book is available from the British Library.

Printed and bound in the UK by TJ Books LTD, Padstow, Cornwall
Typeset in 11pt Aldine401 by Troubador Publishing Ltd, Leicester, UK

Matador is an imprint of Troubador Publishing Ltd

For Danusia
who has come to appreciate the unique tension
that a drawn Test match can generate

and

Barb, Sue and Chris
who still have that joy ahead of them

Contents

Author's Notes	ix
Prologue	xi

Part 1 – How Did We Get to This?   1
1. English Cricket is Absolutely Fine   3
2. Yet Another Ashes Series   14
3. A Friendship Under Strain   23
4. Cricket and Politics Clash   36

Part 2 – MCC Tour of Ceylon and Pakistan   55
5. Island Sojourn   57
6. Uncertainty   71
7. The First Test Match   86
8. The Second Text Match   103
9. The Third Test Match   117

Part 3 – From One Crisis to Another   127
10. It Might All Just Go Away   129
11. Stop the Seventy Tour   149

Part 4 – England v Rest of the World — 169
12. So What Now? — 171
13. The First Test Match — 181
14. The Second Test Match — 193
15. The Third Test Match — 208
16. The Fourth Test Match — 224
17. The Fifth Test Match — 240
18. After the Dust had Settled — 253

Selected Test Match Scorecards — 256
Selected Photographs and Credits — 274
Notes on Sources — 280
Acknowledgements — 300
About the Author — 302
Index — 303

Author's Notes

Test Match Status

The series between England and the Rest of the World in 1970 was advertised as five Test matches played under normal Test match conditions. In 1972 the International Cricket Conference (now the International Cricket Council) decided that these matches should be reclassified as first-class and no longer included in official Test match records.

To remain consistent with the terminology in use at the time they were played, in this book the matches between England and the Rest of the World have been called Test matches.

Change of Names

A number of countries and cities have changed their name since 1970. This book uses names in use at that time; those in use today are shown on the next page.

Name in 1970	Name in 2020
Bombay	Mumbai
Calcutta	Kolkata
Ceylon	Sri Lanka
Dacca	Dhaka
East Pakistan	Bangladesh
Lyallpur	Faisalabad
Rhodesia	Zimbabwe
West Pakistan	Pakistan

Prologue

An Unexpected Beginning
27 August 1968

It was a grey, damp day in South London. Even allowing for the fickle nature of the British weather, the summer of 1968 had been poor. For the cricket lover in particular it had all seemed so different four months earlier when the Australian side had arrived in England for a much anticipated tour, ready to compete again for the Ashes. As always, this oldest of cricketing rivalries was expected to be intensely combative but this time there had been genuine optimism among home supporters that England would prevail over an Australia team with a few perceived weaknesses.

Sadly, as the summer wore on, the Test series like the weather had been an increasing disappointment. England had been well beaten in the first Test match in Manchester, and although they had outplayed the tourists in each of the next three, the rain had intervened too many times and all had ended in a draw. The last Test of the summer had begun at Kennington Oval, South London on Thursday 22 August and by the beginning of the final day it looked as though England would finally win a Test, and at least draw the series. Needing to score an unlikely 352 runs to win, Australia had begun the day on 13 for 2, having lost the key wickets of Bill Lawry and Ian Redpath the previous evening. Realistically their only option would be to bat out the remaining 6 hours. By the end of the first session these hopes lay in ruins. Australia was 86 for 5, and an England victory sometime during the afternoon session seemed inevitable. England would have certainly been the happier of the two sides as the players left the field for lunch.

That mood changed, when 13 minutes before play was due to resume it started to rain. This was no short, sharp late summer shower, but a torrential monsoon like downpour. Very soon large parts of the ground were under water. When the rain finally stopped and the sun came out, the playing area looked more like a scenic water feature than a cricket ground; water rather than grass now covering large sections of the outfield.

The ground staff, with the help of many spectators mopped up the surface water using whatever means was available. The playing area was dried, the pitch declared fit for play and to the surprise of many the match restarted at 4.45 pm. The equation was now simple, England had 75 minutes to take the 5 remaining wickets, surely an improbability. When play resumed little happened immediately, and then almost unexpectedly a wicket fell. From a situation in which the batsmen had been defending quite comfortably, it now seemed that every delivery would take a wicket. The pressure built, wickets fell, and the last Australian batsman was out just 6 minutes before the close of play. England had achieved a victory against the odds, and deservedly drawn the series.

I was a 15-year-old student at the time. I had been a spectator on the second day, and seen my cricket hero John Edrich score 164 runs and more significantly for what was to follow, Basil D'Oliveira score 158. Like many other students I had a job during the summer vacation and so could not attend the match on the last day. However, like countless others across the country I was listening to the ball-by-ball commentary on BBC Radio 3 – mesmerised by the voices of John Arlott, Robert Hudson and Alan McGilvray. While not a great deal now remains clear in my memory about that Ashes series, or indeed the rest of the 1968 cricket season, over fifty years later I still imagine I can remember every one of those last 75 minutes play. As John Arlott once wrote about another Test series 'it was like looking down the wrong end of a telescope; everything was distant – yet wholly clear '[1] .

An Unexpected Beginning

With the Ashes series now over, attention turned to choosing an England side to tour South Africa during the coming winter. On the evening of the 27 August the MCC Selection Sub-Committee met at Lord's cricket ground to finalise the touring team. As a cricket obsessive, I had read much about England's upcoming tour to play what was then arguably the best cricket side in the world. There was the usual debate in the newspapers about who should be chosen and who should be left out.

What I did not know was that cricket and politics were about to collide, and start a chain of events that over the next two years would shake the very foundations of the world cricket establishment. Tours would be cancelled, a tour would be abandoned and ultimately one of the founding cricket playing nations banned from playing Test cricket.

Among this mayhem, replacement Test series between Pakistan and England; and England and the Rest of the World would be arranged at very short notice. For different reasons each was unique. The first was played in a country where law and order were disintegrating, with the tour schedule changing on an almost daily basis. The players were under enormous stress, their safety genuinely at risk, and even the government itself would soon be deposed.

The second series pitted England against the Rest of the World, opponents that many considered to be the strongest team ever assembled for an international match. There was the added problem that England was being led by a stand-in captain while the previous incumbent recovered from injury. Towards the end of the series both would be in the side going head to head to decide who would lead the winter tour to Australia and New Zealand.

It is worth looking back through the telescope, to revisit both the cricket and the extraordinary environment in which these matches were played. The illusion that international cricket could be isolated from the world of politics was finally being destroyed once and for all.

Part 1

April 1968 – December 1968

How Did We Get to This?

Part 1

April 1995—October 1996

How Did We Get to This?

1

English Cricket is Absolutely Fine
April 1968

The arrival of the *Wisden Cricketers' Almanack* in local bookshops at the beginning of spring has long been a signal to cricket enthusiasts that the start of the English cricket season is not far away. With its bright yellow cover and distinctive bulk, this 'cricket Bible', known to many simply as *Wisden,* has been published every year since 1864. It is in fact the longest running continuously available sporting handbook in the world.

In 1968, the 105th edition continued the tradition. The tried and tested format included a comprehensive record of cricket played across the world the previous year; pen portraits of five Cricketers of the Year; selected essays and the Editor's thoughts on the season just gone and the one ahead.

Even the Editor of *Wisden* could not have foreseen just how unusual the coming year would turn out to be; both on and off the field. It has since been called, with some justification, 'the year that shaped a generation' [2]. Politically, socially and culturally seismic shocks were occurring across many parts of the world. Freedom and liberalisation were the watchwords. The people (particularly the young) were disillusioned and no longer prepared to accept the status quo. Mass protests were increasingly being used to demand change. Often rallies became more serious using civil disobedience and unrest as valid forms of protest.

For example, in March 1968 a wave of rioting, burning and looting in cities across America had followed the assassination of the civil rights leader Dr Martin Luther King Jr. Protests against the Vietnam War were becoming increasingly violent and student riots in France, which would seriously threaten the very Government itself, were just a few weeks away.

In contrast, social change in Britain was also taking place but more peacefully. The Labour Government of Harold Wilson had been in power since 1964 and in that time done much to change the social makeup of the country. Legislation had been passed making abortion easier and legalising homosexuality, with new laws on divorce, family planning and censorship in the pipeline. The country's first Race Relations Act had become law in 1965, along with a new Rent Act. The Open University was being created and the death penalty abolished. Some would argue that during this period, by reducing the grip of the establishment, Britain had become a fairer and more humane place while others considered it a dangerous move to a more permissive society increasingly controlled by the working class.

The 1960's passion for reform did not extend to the game of cricket. In a decade in which there was so much rebellion the world of cricket seemed to remain untouched. Firmly rooted in the past, it was still viewed as a part of the establishment in which tradition and class were everything. The esteemed cricket writer Sir Neville Cardus encapsulated this perfectly when he wrote 'it is far more than a game, this cricket' [3].

In 1968, first-class cricket in the United Kingdom was effectively still owned and run by a private club, the Marylebone Cricket Club (MCC). From its headquarters at Lord's Cricket Ground in London, the MCC was responsible for the administration of all domestic first-class cricket. They also appointed the Test Selectors and organised England's overseas tours (known as MCC tours rather than England tours until 1977). Finally, they were custodians of the rules governing the game *The Laws of Cricket* [4]. Little could happen in the game without the agreement of the MCC Committee and its supporting structure of Sub-Committees, who were by nature generally conservative and cautious.

This MCC Committee comprised of the Club President, Treasurer, President Designate, three Trustees and eighteen Members elected by their fellow Members. In 1968 this Committee included an ex-Conservative Prime Minister, four ex-captains of England, seven peers of the realm, and fifteen past or future Presidents of the Club. Perhaps it was not so surprising that the status quo dominated.

First-class cricket in England and Wales revolved around the County Championship. This competition was contested by seventeen county cricket clubs, each having a representative on the MCC's Advisory County Cricket Committee. However, each club remained independent and was controlled by their own local committee and sub-committees. So for instance, Yorkshire County Cricket Club had a General Committee of elected and non-elected Members, and sub-committees covering areas such as finance and general purposes, public relations and junior cricket. All county structures were different but they had one thing in common, Members' subscriptions were vital to their financial survival. Unfortunately this was often not enough. At the end of the 1967 season Yorkshire County Cricket Club, which had again won the County Championship, still made a financial loss. With 13,000 Members they were one of the biggest clubs in the country. Membership subscriptions accounted for nearly 60% of the club's income, with gate receipts the other main contributor at just over 20% [5]. Sponsorship was in its infancy and hardly noticeable. The club was clearly very dependent on its own Members for financial survival, and so they had to be listened to, both by the club's General Committee and the MCC.

As for the players, they were part of what was in many respects was still a feudal system. A professional cricketer's county club decided each year whether they had work for the coming season or not, and the individual player had almost no say in their conditions of employment. The cricketers of today with their agents, long term contracts, freedom of movement and the Professional Cricketers' Association as a voice were light years away.

A career as a professional cricketer was neither lucrative or particularly secure. Individual success depended on many factors including sometimes just being in the right place at the right time. This can be illustrated by a photograph from the Surrey County Cricket Club Year Book for 1969 [6]. Showing playing staff from the previous season, there was the usual mixture of Test players, seasoned professionals who had played for the county for many years without making the England side and young hopefuls at the start of their career.

One of the best known faces in the Surrey team at that time was John Edrich. Although by then he had played 26 Test matches, his career was typical of the struggles that even those who made it to the top level had to face in order to sustain a career as a professional cricketer. Edrich came from a famous Norfolk cricketing family. Four of his cousins had played county cricket, the most famous of these Bill Edrich had also played 39 times for England, and was Captain of Middlesex from 1951 to 1957. By 1955 after gaining experience in club and Minor County cricket with Norfolk, John Edrich decided he was ready to take the next step and started to look for a county who would give him an opportunity. After being turned down by Lancashire, he was invited to Kennington Oval, London to trial for Surrey. Then like so many before him, he worked on improving his batting technique and learnt about the reality of county cricket by playing regularly for the Surrey 2nd XI. His career was interrupted by two years National Service before returning to Surrey in 1958.

He played just one game for the first team that season, but finally got his chance to play regularly for them in 1959. In this debut season he scored 1799 runs at an average of 52.91 with 7 centuries. In spite of this promising start, he had to continue to perform at this level for another three seasons before being selected to play for England against the West Indies in 1963. He was then chosen for the winter tour of India and the following summer's home series against Australia. In 8 Tests he had scored one century but his next highest score was only 41. When he was not selected for the 1964/65 winter tour of South Africa, or for the first two Tests again New Zealand the following summer be began to think that his Test career might already be over. He believed that 'I had been given my chance and had been rejected. It did not look as though I would be getting another opportunity' [7].

Fortunately, he was given another chance, and scored 310 not out against New Zealand in the third Test. By 1968 this dogged, left handed opening batsmen had played 26 Tests and could begin to consider himself an established member of the England team. In an era before protective helmets were worn Edrich had already faced some of the most hostile bowlers of the day in a Test career that would ultimately last thirteen years. In 1965 he had been badly injured by a Peter Pollock delivery playing against South Africa and in 1974/75 when England where being demolished by what became a legendary Australian bowling attack of Dennis Lillie and Jeff Thomson he would sustain two broken ribs when hit by a Lillee bouncer. Typical of the man, each time he returned and the following year against the same Australian attack at Lord's he scored 175. John Edrich finally retired from professional cricket in 1978 having scored 39,790 runs at first-class level and 5,138 in 77 Test matches. His twenty-year career could certainly be considered as successful.

While in 1968 Edrich was on the way to becoming an established member of the England team, others in the Surrey side were further down the ladder. Edrich's opening partner for Surrey most of that year would be Michael Edwards. A competent opening batsman and fine close to the wicket fielder, he had first played for the county while still at Cambridge University. He began appearing regularly as a member of the first team from 1964 and was capped in 1966. The following season, he scored 1413 runs at an average of 30.71. Now aged 28, he would have been clearly hoping to improve and catch the eye of the selectors. Although he managed 1408 runs at an average of 24.27 and 1428 at 36.61 over the next two seasons, Edwards never quite reached the level of consistency, or perhaps had the good fortune, necessary to be selected for the England side. In comparison, over the same period against the same bowlers but playing fewer matches for Surrey because of his England commitments, Edrich had scored 2009 at 44.64 and 2239 at 69.93. By 1971 Edwards' batting had begun to decline, and he retired from the first-class game in 1974 – a career of just a decade. He later returned to the Club as Director of Cricket Development, and also served terms as both Chair and Treasurer of the Professional Cricketers' Association.

Another of the Surrey playing staff, was less optimistic than Edwards at the start of the 1968 season. Roger Harman, the slow left-arm bowler, had experienced what can only be described as a meteoric introduction to county cricket. In 1964 after only three seasons at the club, he was given an unexpected opportunity to play in the first team following the decision of

Surrey's regular left-arm slow bowler, Tony Lock, to emigrate to Australia. In his first Championship match against Gloucestershire, Harman took 5 wickets for 37 runs in the second innings, and in the following game against Nottinghamshire at Trent Bridge 8 for 12. This was the beginning of an unbelievable debut for the 23 year old. He finished the season, second in the first-class bowling averages having taken 136 wickets at 21.01. Only the evergreen Derek Shackleton with 142 did better that year. Not surprisingly this had come at a cost, he had bowled 1131 overs by the time the season was finished, a large workload for such a young player. There was much talk of an England player of the future and the expectation that this would be the start of a long career in the Surrey first team.

The following season, for some unknown reason the wickets failed to come as quickly or as easily. Harman's confidence started to suffer and his performance declined quite dramatically taking just 63 wickets in 1965, and 50 in 1966. By 1967 he was no longer a regular in the first team, finishing with just 18 wickets that year; he may not have expected to have had his contact renewed but it was. There would though be no return to the form of that remarkable first season, and he finished 1968 having take just 48 wickets. This time there was no reprieve. He was not reengaged for the 1969 season, the Club's Annual Report noting that Harman had been 'sometimes brilliant, but all too often disappointing' [8]. He retired from first-class cricket, but in 2006 would return to Surrey as Chairman of Cricket.

Whether you were an established Test player like Edrich or a hopeful like Edwards or Harman your playing contract was awarded on a season-by-season basis, renewal depending on how you had performed the previous year.

Being selected to play for England was the pinnacle for most county cricketers. If the call came it was certainly not with a fanfare. Keith Fletcher described receiving a two page standard letter, which began:

> *'Dear Keith, The Board of Control Selection Committee will be glad if you will report to the England Captain on the ground at Edgbaston not later than 3 pm on Wednesday 10th July and be available to play for England v Australia if selected, on 11th – 16th July 1968'.*

The letter then contained a stern statement forbidding players from commenting publicly on any aspect of the match, followed by details of accommodation and other arrangements. Players received a match fee of £120 (Equivalent to £2,000 in 2020). The letter was stereotyped with a space left blank for the recipient's name to be hand written in. Another example of the almost feudal way in which players were still treated [9].

Even those at the top were still not guaranteed a very secure living. Ray Illingworth was a good example. By the beginning of 1968 the Yorkshire all-rounder had played 27 Tests and aged 36 was probably beginning to think that his professional career was coming to an end. Up until then he had spent most of his winters, when he was not touring, earning a living selling fireworks and Christmas cards. When approached by the MCC Selectors regarding his availability for the forthcoming winter tour of South Africa in 1968/9, he declined saying 'I must take a serious look at the future and a winter away from my job as a salesman would be a considerable setback. I can't afford to take the risk' [10]. At the same time, he also had what many in the traditional world of Yorkshire cricket had considered the impertinence to ask for a three-year contract rather than the traditional one year. This was bluntly refused with the forthright Chairman of the Cricket Committee Brian Sellers telling him he 'could go, and any other bugger who wanted could go' with him [11]. Illingworth moved on to have a successful second career with Leicestershire, steering the club to its first County Championship title in 1975 (with Yorkshire as runners up). He also led England for five years, and is now considered by many to have been one of England's best post-war captains.

The life of a professional cricketer was clearly unpredictable with few guarantees. Writing in April 1968, the well respected, long serving England and Surrey cricketer Ken Barrington, summed up what many felt: 'It is becoming increasingly difficult to keep good players in the game and the future is far from rosy. How can it be otherwise when the basic wage is low and it remains so difficult to get a worthwhile close-season job that four England players, Allen, Statham, Snow and Price, and several county cricketers were on the dole at various times in the last two winters?' [12].

No wonder players were beginning to seriously question whether they were receiving a fair reward for the job they did. Kerry Packer's World Series Cricket revolution was still a decade away, but the seeds of discontent were starting to grow [13].

From the start of the English cricket season at the end of April, a county cricketer could expect to be playing two three-day matches a week until mid-September. In such circumstances the cricket played could become mediocre, with captains reluctant to take risks and players occasionally just going through the motions. Uncovered pitches of variable quality had resulted in the growth of medium paced bowlers who often did not need to do much to take wickets. Batsmen quickly became jaded, with little opportunity for practice or to recapture their form if they had hit a bad patch.

When matches took place was also a growing problem. Hours of play were not designed to fit the working pattern of the average spectator. For example, the match between Yorkshire and Gloucestershire the previous season had been scheduled to take place from Wednesday 6 September to Friday 8 September, with the first two days play between 11.30 am and 7 pm and the final day 11 am to 4.30 pm (or 5 pm if a result was likely). In the end the match at Harrogate was over in just two days. On a turning wicket, Gloucestershire were bowled out twice in one day with Illingworth taking 7 wickets in each innings. In the second innings he ended with the remarkable bowling figures of 7 wickets for 6 runs in 13 overs. The match was over by 6.45 pm on Thursday evening. Attendance on the last day had also been remarkable with 10,000 watching Yorkshire win another County Championship [14]. This though was a special occasion, it could not hide the fact that normally these midweek matches would attract crowds of a few hundred not thousands.

For most cricket enthusiasts there was usually only one opportunity to watch first-class cricket and that was on a Saturday. However, cricket no longer had the day to itself. An increasing numbers of ways to spend leisure time at the weekend were being offered. It was not surprising that attendance at County Championship matches had fallen from nearly 2 million in 1950 to just over 500,000 in 1967.

One-day limited over cricket was in its infancy. In 1963 the first one-day limited over competition had been introduced. The Gillette Cup was a 65 over a side knockout competition (changing to 60 overs a side in 1964), which had proved to be hugely successful right from the start. Spectators were able to see a complete match in a day. In spite of its short history, the Gillette Cup Final, which was played at Lord's in the first week of September, had already become a key event in the cricket calendar. For both the players and spectators, like the FA Cup Final in football, it was a game that everybody wanted to be involved in. The 1967 Final between Kent and Somerset had been played before two fiercely partisan groups of supporters; the crowd of over 20,000 the biggest anywhere in England that season. This was only a brief diversion from the daily grind of county cricket, with a side needing to win a maximum of four matches to reach the final. It could also all be over after the first round, with the spectators having seen their side play just one limited overs game in the entire season.

Even though Sunday was usually a day of rest for most professional cricketers there was still something on offer for the enthusiastic cricket spectator. For the previous three seasons on Sunday afternoons, BBC2 had broadcast a 40 overs a side match between the International Cavaliers and a county side. Sponsored by Rothmans, the matches were usually in aid of a local cricketer's benefit, county development funds or a local charity. The matches were a great success. The previous season the average attendance at each match had been 7,000, while the television viewing audience each Sunday often approached one million. There was clearly a public appetite for Sunday cricket. However 1968 would be the last year such events were televised. In 1969 a new Sunday afternoon limited over competition, the Player's County League sponsored by John Player & Sons was due to be introduced (this soon became known as the John Player League). In return for financial sponsorship, much of which was to be returned to clubs in the form of prize money, it was agreed that counties would not permit any other matches involving their players to be televised on a Sunday. This effectively signalled the end for the International Cavaliers, but in a small way they were the forerunner for international limited over cricket competitions such as the Indian Premier League and Big Bash League in Australia that are played today.

It would be uncharitable to suggest that the game's administrators were unaware of the crisis that cricket was facing. Nearly every year since 1945 changes had been made to the *Laws of Cricket* in an attempt to increase the game's attractiveness. These had included limiting the length of the first innings of a match, limiting the length of a bowler's run up, placing restrictions on negative field placings and standardising the distance of boundaries. Opinion was split on whether this was just tinkering at the edges when more fundamental change was needed. Whatever adjustments were made, none had a substantial affect on spectator numbers.

By 1968, even the Government were beginning to take an interest in the cricket world. Following the election of the Labour Government in 1964, Harold Wilson recognising the increasing importance of sport to both the economy and everyday life had appointed Denis Howell as the country's first Minister of Sport. Howell championed the formation of a Sports Council to provide national bodies with funding for the development of sport. As a private club the MCC was not eligible to apply for funding, putting cricket at a serious disadvantage. Other sports such as football and athletics were already beginning to receive development grants.

Howell asked the MCC to propose a new national structure to oversee the development of cricket. This provided a dilemma since by definition any new national body could diminish the power of the club, which had controlled cricket for so long. While the MCC may have wished things to stay as they were, the hard truth was that it was becoming increasingly difficult to continue as the financial benefactor of the national game. The accounts for 1967 reported the biggest annual deficit in the MCC's history, and it did not seem as though things would improve any time soon. [15]

After a great deal of angst, in May 1968 the MCC Secretary, S. C. Billy' Griffith, announced a proposed new structure. From January 1969 cricket would be administered by three bodies. The Test and County Cricket Board (TCCB) would be responsible for the first-class game; the National Cricket Association (NCA) for all amateur cricket; and the MCC would remain responsible for the laws of the game. Each of these bodies would have representatives on an overarching 28 Member governing body the MCC Cricket Council.

At first sight it may have seemed that the role of the MCC had been diminished. However with the Chair and Vice Chair of the Cricket Council being the President of the MCC and Secretary of the MCC, and 18 of the other 26 Members of the inaugural Council either being nominated by the MCC or Members of the MCC Committee this was far from the case. As the club itself admitted 'that without intending that existing Bodies should lose their autonomy, the M.C.C. Council has taken every grade of cricket under its wing' [16].

At international level, Test cricket was overseen by a body known as the International Cricket Conference (ICC). Formed in 1909 the ICC was then known as the Imperial Cricket Conference. Consisting of representatives from the MCC, the Australian Board of Control and the South African Cricket Association its original role had been to organise an international tournament between the three Commonwealth nations.

In 1968 the ICC consisted of two Foundation Members (MCC and Australia), four Full Members who had by then been granted Test status (India, New Zealand, Pakistan and West Indies) and a number of Associate Members who had the potential to gain Test status such as the United States, Ceylon (now Sri Lanka) and Fiji. South Africa withdrew from the Commonwealth in 1961 and was no longer eligible to be a Member of the ICC, although it continued to send a representative as an observer. Now meeting once a year the main business of the ICC was to confirm future Test tours and oversee the regulations relating to Test matches and those entitled to play for a country. Since the Chair and Secretary of the ICC were by definition the President and Secretary of the MCC, and with the meetings being held at Lord's, it is not surprising that many viewed the ICC as a just another sub-committee of the MCC.

If a report on the health of cricket had been written at the start of 1968, it would have most probably concluded that overall everything was fine, with no need for any urgent change. There were no signs of a revolution in the cricket world. How wrong they would have been.

2

Yet Another Ashes Series
April – August 1968

On 27 April 1968, yet another English cricket season began with the traditional opening fixture between the MCC and previous season's County Champions, in this case Yorkshire. Maybe as a sign of what was to come, play was only possible on the first day. The other two days were washed out and the match abandoned and declared a draw. Not the best of starts, but for many this did not really matter. For most cricket lovers the coming season would be dominated by one event, and one event only, the arrival of the Australians to defend the Ashes.

As usual it had been four years since an Australian side had last visited England, and so when the tourists landed at Heathrow Airport on the morning of 27 April there was genuine excitement at the prospect of another Ashes series. There was also real hope among the home supporters that this time England could finally win a series and regain the Ashes that Australia had held since 1959. Even the normally parochial Australian press were not brimming with optimism, one cricket correspondent writing 'that this team hardly fills me with confidence' [17].

In 1967 Australia had been well beaten in South Africa, and so since then the selectors had looked towards a new crop of younger players to rebuild the team. The selection of the 1968 touring party had continued with this move towards the use of raw talent. The Captain Bill Lawry, Vice-Captain Barry Jarman and players Ian Chappell, Alan Connolly, Bob Cowper, Neil Hawke and Graham McKenzie had toured England before and provided an experienced core to the team, but for ten of the seventeen man party England was a new experience. There was always interest in the new faces, wondering who they were and what threat they might offer in English conditions. There was particular interest in the unorthodox leg-spin bowler John Gleeson, almost inevitably being described in the press as a 'mystery' spinner. The attacking young batsmen Doug Walters and Paul Sheahan were also the focus of much interest.

Test rankings did not exist, but England would have considered themselves at least as good as Australia at that moment in time. While this group of young players guided by their experienced captain had just beaten India 4-0 at home, they were aware that this had not been the toughest of challenges. The Ashes was a different matter and at his first press conference Lawry promised the very minimum that everybody back home would have expected, saying 'we'll play it hard … we hold the Ashes, that's what we're here to defend' [18].

The selection of the England captain and team for the forthcoming series was as usual the responsibility of the Selection Sub-Committee acting on behalf of the MCC. The 'on behalf' referred to the fact that the MCC Committee could in theory veto any decision made by the Selection Sub-Committee. As usual, the panel of four selectors for the coming year had been chosen by the MCC Advisory County Cricket Committee from a list of nominations provided by individual County Committees. In 1968 the four selectors, for the fourth consecutive year, were Doug Insole (Chair), Alec Bedser, Don Kenyon and Peter May. Insole and May were coincidentally also Members of the MCC Committee, while Kenyon had retired the previous season after a long career with Worcestershire both as player and captain. He did not know it but by the end of the season one of his former teammates would be a name on everybody's lips.

Being an England selector was often an unenviable role. Sometimes it seemed everybody had an opinion on who the England captain and team should be, and increasingly ex-players were being employed as 'pundits' in the national media. If the team did well, it was obvious but if they did badly they were calling for your head. This time though the choice of captain could not have surprised many. After leading England to a series win against the West Indies in the Caribbean it was almost unthinkable that the selectors would look past the then captain Colin Cowdrey. As expected, on the 12 May, Cowdrey was appointed to lead England again, not just for the first Test match but the whole series.

On 31 May the squad from which the England team to play Australia in the first Test match at Old Trafford would be chosen, was announced. It was no surprise that those who had performed so well against the West Indies less than six weeks before should be rewarded by selection, but it was a surprise that a squad of fourteen rather than the traditional twelve were named. Either the selectors did not know who their best team were or else they were trying to cover all possible pitch and weather conditions.

The top five batsmen would almost certainly be those who had played in all five Tests in the West Indies; Geoffrey Boycott, John Edrich, Colin Cowdrey, Ken Barrington and Tom Graveney. The only doubt seemed to be the fitness of Barrington for who Dennis Amiss was chosen as cover. Alan Knott was the only wicketkeeper in the squad and clearly now the first choice.

As far as the bowling was concerned, things were less clear. Only John Snow, who had been outstanding in the West Indies was an obvious selection. The other fast bowlers chosen were Ken Higgs and David Brown, with the spin bowlers Pat Pocock and Derek Underwood, and the all-rounders Tom Cartwright and Basil D'Oliveira making up the squad. With only four days to go before the opening Test match this uncertainty over who would actually play must have been unsettling. The situation was further exacerbated when a day later Barrington withdrew having not recovered from injury with his place being taken by an opening batsman, Bob Barber. This was a strange choice as Boycott and Edrich were the established openers, and also because of outside commitments Barber had only played two county matches so far that season.

One name among the English squad chosen for Manchester was that of Basil D'Oliveira. Born in South Africa with an Indian-Portuguese heritage, he was classified as a 'Cape Coloured' under the abhorrent apartheid laws in place at the time. A prolific cricketer in South Africa, he was ineligible for selection for the national team solely because he was non-white. Looking to further his cricket career, he had arrived in England in 1960.

With the help of John Arlott and the *Manchester Evening News* journalist John Kay, he had secured a job as the Professional for Middleton in the Central Lancashire League. After a shaky start, he adapted to playing in English conditions and topped the League's batting averages at the end of his first season – just ahead of a 24 year old Garry Sobers who was then playing for Radcliffe (mind you Sobers did achieve the double of 1000 runs and 100 wickets!).

D'Oliveira joined Worcestershire in 1964, and the following year scored 1691 runs and took 48 wickets. By 1966 his consistency was such that the national selectors could no longer ignore him and he made his England debut against the West Indies at Lord's in June 1966 – age 34 (although he claimed to be 31 at that time). He later admitted that even this may have been on the low side, writing 'If you told me I was nearer forty than 35 when I first played for England in 1966, I wouldn't sue you for slander' [19]. Since then he had played 14 Test matches and was beginning to establish himself as the batting all-rounder in the team. At the end of the summer the selectors would have to choose a side to tour South Africa, but it is doubtful if the difficulties that picking D'Oliveira could create had yet been fully appreciated.

The atmosphere on the opening day of the first Test of an English summer has always had a special feel about it, and when it is an Ashes series even more so. The 6 June 1968 was a little different, with the excitement of some in the crowd being tempered by the overnight news of the assassination of Senator Robert Kennedy in Los Angeles.

Rather disappointingly, and unusually for an Ashes opener, the ground was far from full with less than 10,000 present. The last time the Australians had played an Old Trafford Test four years before, nearly 110,000 had watched over the five days. Whether this was a reflection of the low ebb cricket was at in Lancashire or more worryingly for the authorities a decline in the interest for international cricket was not clear. Thankfully though at least the weather was fine.

Australia had chosen the attacking option, preferring an extra specialist bowler to a batsman. England on the other hand had done the opposite, unexpectedly omitting Brown, Underwood and Cartwright from their original fourteen. They were therefore going with a team of Boycott, Edrich, Cowdrey, Graveney, Amiss, Barber, D'Oliveira, Knott, Snow, Higgs and Pocock. By packing the side with batsmen and picking only three specialist bowlers, this looked to be a selection designed to try and ensure that they did not lose rather than going for a win. It was a strategy which looked even stranger when Lawry won the toss and decided to bat. If his side could bat well, it could quickly become advantage Australia.

So it proved, by lunch time on the fifth day Australia had won the match by 159 runs with time to spare. Many expected that Lawry's young side would now only get better as they became used to English conditions. For England, it seemed that their Ashes campaign was already in trouble.

Given the ease with which the supposedly young and inexperienced Australian side had won the first Test it was not a surprise that many in the press were calling for changes to the England team. The consensus of opinion was that the selection had been wrong and that by starting the match with only three specialist bowlers, England had been asking for trouble. While D'Oliveira and Barber had batted reasonably well, they were batsmen who could bowl. Having both in the team was a luxury that England could not afford when they needed at least four specialist bowlers.

The selectors it seemed did not agree. For the second Test at Lord's they dropped Amiss, Barber and Higgs from the fourteen that had been chosen for Manchester and selected the swashbuckling Northamptonshire batsman Colin Milburn. A hopefully fit again Barrington was also bought back into the squad.

Team selection was again thrown into disarray when a day later Cartwright withdrew with a knee injury, to be replaced by Barry Knight. A medium-fast bowling all-rounder, the Leicestershire player was something of an enigma. He had first been capped for England in 1961 and then in a stop-start international career only played in 22 Test matches since then. He would play one or two Test matches and then be dropped, seemingly in the category of good enough for the occasional game but not good enough to be worth a permanent place. On his day he could clearly play, at least at county level. He had already achieved the double of 1,000 runs and a 100 wickets in a season four times. This was something that

Cartwright managed only once in his career and D'Oliveira not at all. When Leicestershire had played the Australians earlier in the tour, Knight had taken 5 wickets in their first innings including Redpath, Walters and Chappell. Knight himself was not surprised at his call up as he later said 'They picked me quite often at Lord's. I did well there. I knew the slope, had bowled on it for years' [20]. He also believed that both he and D'Oliveira would play.

Knight and many others were wrong. On the morning of the match a team of Edrich, Boycott, Milburn, Cowdrey, Barrington, Graveney, Knight, Knott, Snow, Brown and Underwood were named. D'Oliveira and Pocock, two of the best performers at Old Trafford had been left out. In his autobiography written in 1980 D'Oliveira remembers that on the morning of the match when Cowdrey broke the news that he was twelfth man he told him 'Bas, I'm sorry but I have to make you twelfth man. We need Barry Knight as the extra seamer. I know you did very well up at Old Trafford, and that you're disappointed, but before the season is out you'll be back'[21]. England was already one down, in the five Test series and it is doubtful whether the selectors were thinking as far ahead as the tour to South Africa. Cowdrey's reasoning was that while D'Oliveira had bowled tidily at Manchester, he was not the incisive third seam bowler that would be required for the Test at Lord's. In his view they had to choose the best team for the conditions on a Test by Test basis [22].

D'Oliveira himself was less certain. Once you lost your place it was often hard to get back quickly, and for him time was running out. Given his age, he knew that the winter tour of South Africa would be his one and only chance of realising a dream and playing Test cricket in the country of his birth. In a one sided game Australia were bowled out for 78 by an English seam attack of Snow, Brown and Knight, the later taking 3 for 18. Only the weather saved Australia from a heavy defeat.

Things did not look good for D'Oliveira. He was not picked for either the third or fourth Test matches, both of which ended in draws, again with the weather and team changes a prominent feature. D'Oliveira's chances were not helped by his county form. After being left out from the England side at Lord's he returned to play for Worcestershire, but in 13 innings managed a score of over fifty only once, and failed to reach double figures seven times. He was having a bad run at exactly the wrong time.

When the England side for the fifth and final Test of the summer was announced on 18 August, few could have been surprised that D'Oliveira was not in it. The England twelve this time were Colin Cowdrey, John Edrich, Roger Prideaux, Colin Milburn, Ted Dexter, Tom Graveney, Alan Knott, Ray Illingworth, Derek Underwood, David Brown, John Snow and Ken Higgs. Again injury had caused problems, with important players such as Boycott and Knight missing, and Illingworth now taking the all-rounder's spot for the second Test in a row. Barrington being dropped for a game England needed to win seemed inexplicable to many. He had scored 49 and 46 not out in the last Test and the Oval was his home ground.

In keeping with a summer in which there had been so many late changes, two days after announcing the England side Roger Prideaux withdrew suffering from pleurisy and severe bronchitis. In many ways this was a risk for Prideaux. He had made his debut for England in the fourth Test at Headingley. He had top scored with 64 runs in the first innings but only scored 2 in the second. Would this be enough to secure his place on the forthcoming tour of South Africa? The replacement for Prideaux was not another specialist batsman but a batting all-rounder; Basil D'Oliveira. A door which had seemed firmly shut was now at least a little ajar.

On the morning of the final Test match the selectors did indeed decide on D'Oliveira, leaving out Higgs from the twelve. Although Australia had retained the Ashes, England could at least come away with a draw in the series if they could win this game. Cowdrey won the toss and, with fine weather forecast chose to bat. While the Australians would have been firmly focused on winning, or at worst not losing the Test, some of the England side must have also been thinking about the winter tour to South Africa. Of the eleven who started the game, Dexter and Illingworth had declared themselves unavailable. Only Cowdrey, Edrich, Graveney, Knott, Snow and Underwood could have been confident of a place on the tour. Milburn, Brown and D'Oliveira were almost certainly playing for their places, and in D'Oliveira's case because of his age, possibly his Test future.

At the end of the first day, England were a comfortable 272 for 4, with Edrich having ridden his luck a little to reach 130 not out and D'Oliveira a confidant 24 not out. The following morning when D'Oliveira had reached 31 he edged a delivery from the part-time leg spinner Chappell, and was dropped by Jarman behind the stumps. If that catch had been taken, it is probable that international cricket would have been saved from much of the turmoil that was about to occur.

Edrich was finally out for a solid 164, and with fate smiling D'Oliveira went on to score 158 in an impressive England total of 494. At the close of day two Australia were 49 for 1 and already facing a huge challenge to save the game. D'Oliveira's innings was his first hundred of the season, and as one cricket correspondent observed 'Basil D'Oliveira's superb and phlegmatic Test innings yesterday means – by all cricketing standards – that his MCC place for South Africa is assured '[23.]

By the start of the final day it looked as though England would finally win a Test and at least draw the series. Needing to score an unlikely 352 in their second innings, Australia had begun the day on 13 for 2 having lost the experienced Bill Lawry and Ian Redpath the previous evening. Realistically their only option would be to bat out the remaining six hours in order to avoid defeat. By lunch they were 86 for 5 with the game seemingly lost. Then the rain came and chances of escape improved. To the delight of the home crowd, the rain stopped, the playing area was dried out and the game resumed at 4.45 pm. In a nail biting finish, the last Australian wicket fell with just 6 minutes to go before close of play. England had achieved a victory against the odds, and deservedly drawn the series. See the Appendix for the match scorecard.

That evening the MCC Selection Sub-Committee were due to meet at Lord's to finalise the team for the winter tour of South Africa. Up until the week before many would have been surprised if D'Oliveira was one of those being considered. However his contribution to the match that England had just won was significant, 158 runs in England's first innings and a crucial wicket on the final afternoon. Surely now he had to be picked for the tour.

A conflict which had been building ever since D'Oliveira had first been selected to play for England in 1966 was now unavoidable. South Africa's stance on multiracial cricket had been circumvented or ignored over many years, but this time things were different. Cricket and politics were about to meet head on, and nobody should have really been surprised. The warning lights had been flashing for a long time.

3

A Friendship Under Strain
May 1948 – August 1968

England and South Africa had first played Test cricket against each other in 1889, but it was not until the late 1950s that politics started to become a factor in these encounters. By the time the England selectors sat down to choose a side for the 1968 tour of South Africa, politics had become more than a factor, to many it was now the number one issue.

The England cricket team had last visited South Africa in the winter of 1964/5 to play a five match Test series which they had won 1-0 (with 4 drawn Tests). The Republic of South Africa was then governed by the National Party led by Prime Minister Dr Hendrik Verwoerd. Since its surprise win over the English speaking United Party in 1948, the Afrikaner based United National Party had increased its majority at every election. In 1951 it merged with the smaller Afrikaner Party to form the National Party.

In a country in which only around 20% of the population were white, there had long been unease among the Afrikaners and English about the possibility of the non-white majority gaining power. While this was somewhat hypothetical, as only whites could vote, none the less legislation which limited the rights of non-white South Africans had been part of Government policy ever since the country had gained independence from Britain in 1910. As early as 1913, the Native Land Act had prohibited black

South Africans from buying land in over 90% of the country. This and other legislation created over the following years was however somewhat ad-hoc rather than the part of any grand plan.

Following the General Election of 1948, this all changed. In line with their manifesto pledge, the Afrikaner based Government of Dr Daniel Malan immediately started to develop and implement a strict system of racial segregation known more widely as apartheid. The foundation stone of apartheid was the Population Registration Act of 1950 under which all South Africans were classified as white, coloured (including mixed race) or native. In the original Act, a native was defined as someone from any aboriginal race or tribe of Africa. Indian was added as a fourth group later. A large number of further parliamentary Acts were then quickly passed which determined an individual's rights depending on this racial classification. For example the Group Areas Act 1950 defined where different racial groups could live, while the Native Building Workers Act 1951 defined the type of work each group was allowed to perform. Sexual relationships or marriage between white and non-white were strictly prohibited. In every way the life of non-white South Africans was increasingly being controlled and suppressed.

Hendrik Verwoerd, who had been Prime Minister since 1958, was totally transparent about his reason for apartheid; to ensure the minority non-white population kept control of South Africa. He had bluntly expressed this view in Parliament in 1963 saying 'We want to make South Africa white ... Keeping it white can only mean one thing, namely white domination, not leadership, not guidance, but control, supremacy' [24].

Given the Afrikaners growing interest in sport, particularly rugby union and cricket, there were those who hoped that this might be an area in which pressure could be applied from outside the country to relax apartheid. In 1965, in a speech to mark the opening of the Loskop Dam, Verwoerd quashed any grounds for such optimism, making it clear that 'racially mixed sports would not be allowed among South Africans, nor would mixed teams from abroad be permitted to visit the Republic' [25].

Apartheid most definitely also applied to cricket. Although each of the three non-white groups had their own competitions, they could also play each other in representative matches. White cricketers could not play against non-white, and only white players could be selected to represent South Africa's national side.

Facilities available to the different racial groups varied widely. For instance, D'Oliveira remembers playing matches on a piece of open land catering for anything up to 25 games at the same time. Being hit by a ball from an adjacent game was not uncommon, while the pitches were unpredictable matting which the players themselves had helped to roll and water earlier in the day. In comparison the manicured grounds and carefully prepared grass pitches available to white cricketers was a world away.

The policies of Verwoerd and his Government were abhorrent to much of the rest of the world. Apart from words of condemnation, in practice foreign Governments did little to try and persuade South Africa to change its apartheid policy. Finally on 21 March 1960 the world was forced to take action. In the township of Sharpeville, just outside Johannesburg, South African police opened fire on a group of unarmed black South Africans protesting against the Government's restriction of non-white travel. 69 men, women and children were killed and approximately 200 injured.

The British Government wrestled with the issue of how to respond. The United Kingdom still had significant emotional and financial ties with South Africa but public opinion had been moved by these events and expected a response. In the end they, like much of the world community, sat on the fence. On 1 April the United Nations took its first formal action on South Africa. A weak motion calling for change in the broadest of terms was proposed by the Security Council [26]. Nine Members voted in favour, with France and the United Kingdom abstaining. The response from South Africa to this and subsequent actions from the United Nations and other international organisations was to develop a siege mentality. Facing expulsion, in March 1961 the country resigned from the Commonwealth and in May 1961 became the Republic of South Africa.

Internally the attitude was different, the majority of white South Africans were fully behind their Government. At the General Election in March 1966 the National Party had increased its number of representatives to

126 in the 170 seat House of Assembly. Only whites were still allowed to vote.

Then on 6 September 1966 an event which could have caused major turmoil in the country occurred; Hendrik Verwoerd was assassinated. A parliamentary messenger repeated stabbed Verwoerd just after the Prime Minister had taken his seat for the start of the day in the House of Assembly. In spite of immediate help from medical staff in the House, he died on his way to hospital. The assailant Dimitri Tsafendas was of mixed Greek/Mozambique heritage with a history of mental health problems. At subsequent court proceedings, he was considered to be unfit to stand trial, and detained in a secure mental institution for the rest of his life. While there were various accounts of what Tsafendas had shouted when he attacked Verwoerd, the motive for the murder was never fully explained.

To the surprise of many in September 1966 Verwoerd was replaced as Leader of the National Party and Prime Minister by 50 year old Balthazar Johannes (John) Vorster. As Minister of Justice, Police and Prisons in Verwoerd's Government he had been considered the National Party's strongman. He had a long record of extreme right-wing affiliations, and had been interned during the Second World War by the Government of General Smuts for being a leading member of the pro-Nazi Ossewabrandwag Organisation.

The British Government were certainly not optimistic about a future under Vorster. In a confidential memo the Foreign Office and Commonwealth Office described him as 'dour and stubborn' and 'anti-British', concluding that his election 'was unlikely immediately to involve any significant changes in South Africa's internal and external policies. But the outlook for the future must be reckoned worse than it was under Dr Verwoerd' [27]. Other diplomatic observers were more optimistic, believing that Vorster was far more moderate and flexible than his public image so far had suggested. All were agreed that, as an Afrikaner born and bred he would be a strong willed leader, and unlikely to permit dissent.

This seemed a reasonable prediction when in a speech outside Parliament immediately following his unanimous election as Prime

Minister, Vorster in an uncompromising mood stated 'I believe in the National Party and its principles and the full implementation of them in every respect, whatever the consequences' [28]. It was clear, that under him white South Africans alone would decide the country's destiny.

Three months before Vorster became Prime Minister of the Republic of South Africa, Basil D'Oliveira had played his first Test match as an England cricketer. When the side to play the West Indies in the first Test at Old Trafford, Manchester was announced on the 30 May 1966, it contained two uncapped players; Colin Milburn and Basil D'Oliveira. There was as much interest among the cricket writers in the hard hitting opening batsman Milburn, as in D'Oliveira. There was surprise from some that D'Oliveira had been picked after only one full season in county cricket, but also support for a player who had come up the hard way. He was 34, an age at which cricketers would normally consider retirement rather than playing their first Test for England. During the 1965 season he has scored 1691 runs at 43.35, and taken 38 wickets. The current season was only a few weeks old, but he had already scored a century against Nottinghamshire.

D'Oliveira was batting in a one-day Sunday game in aid of his Worcestershire colleague Roy Booth when the England team was broadcast over the ground's public address system. The game stopped so that the players could hear the announcement, D'Oliveira was in the side. There was genuine pleasure for what he had achieved. At the close of play he was carried off the field on the shoulders of team mates Norman Gifford and Martin Horton, applauded by his fellow players and the crowd. He later described this as 'one of the greatest days of my life' [29].

Only a small number worried about the future implications of his selection. One of these was the cricket correspondent of *The Times* who noted that D'Oliveira's selection 'is politically ironic and may in time become politically contentious, if he is still in the picture when the MCC next go to South Africa' [30]. While he thought D'Oliveira was worth a try, he doubted whether he would make it as a Test batsman or Test bowler. At the end of the five match series against the West Indies, D'Oliveira had shown that he had the potential to make it as a Test batsman while also taking useful wickets. He had played in four of the Test matches, scoring 256 runs at an average of 42.66, and with his medium paced off-cutters taking 8 wickets at 41.12. In comparison the other new player, Milburn had also played in four of the Tests, scoring 316 runs at an average of 52.66, with one century. As the 1966 English cricket season came to a close, D'Oliveira must have been happy with the start of his career as an England cricketer. With no winter tour scheduled, he would have also been aware that his future in the side was still far from guaranteed.

He had fulfilled one boyhood dream by playing Test cricket, the second would be to play Test cricket in the country of his birth. Although England's tour of South Africa was still over two years in the future, with Vorster now in charge, the chances of achieving this did not look promising.

By the end of 1966, the disruption and cancellation of international sporting events with South Africa had become an increasingly common form of protest by organisations opposed to the country's apartheid structure. The assumption was that the Government would eventually have to make changes to their racial sports policy, rather than face complete international sporting isolation. This strategy had already led to South Africa being banned from the 1964 Olympic Games in Tokyo and 1966 FIFA Football World Cup in England, but so far the Government had remained steadfast, refusing to change what it called a sports policy based around separate development.

In Britain in the early 1960s, organisations such as the Campaign Against Race Discrimination in Sport and the Anti-Apartheid Movement were in their infancy. Some voices in the world of cricket, such as the journalist and commentator John Arlott spoke out publicly against apartheid, but these voices were in the minority. The mantra that politics and cricket were separate worlds still prevailed. When the South Africa cricket team arrived in Britain in April 1960 the possibility of anti-apartheid demonstrations was already such that the MCC felt it necessary to appeal to the sporting public to make the visitors welcome, adding that it was 'wholly unjustifiable to identify members of the team with politics' [31]. The tourists were met by a small group of placard waving demonstrators when they arrived at London Airport, and although they were present to a greater or lesser extent outside the grounds of many of the matches during the five-month tour, no play was disrupted.

The most high profile protest from a current cricketer had been at the start of the tour when the Reverend David Sheppard (later Lord Sheppard of Liverpool) announced that he would not captain the Duke of Norfolk's XI against the South Africans in the traditional opening tour match, or play for his county Sussex against the same team. As an ex-Cambridge University and Sussex captain, occasional England batsman, England captain for two Test matches in 1954 and Member of the MCC Committee, such publicity could have caused the cricket establishment some discomfort. The Assistant Secretary of the MCC declined to publicly discuss Sheppard's decision, making it clear that nothing had changed and that the MCC would continue to welcome the South African team as cricketers and guests.

Test series between England and South Africa had always been arranged by the MCC and the South African Cricket Association (SACA), who were on the best of terms and shared the common belief that politics had nothing to do with cricket. SACA maintained that they had never objected to playing against non-white cricketers on overseas tours but that teams visiting South Africa had to respect the laws of their country. For its part the MCC believed that it was only by keeping sporting contacts with South Africa open that dialogue, and ultimately change might be possible.

When the South African cricket team captained by Peter van der Merwe arrived again in Britain in June 1965 for a three-month tour, the issue of apartheid had moved further up the political agenda with more people taking an interest. The Anti-Apartheid Movement was now better funded and more professionally organised. There were leaflets, posters, car stickers, balloons all displaying anti-apartheid slogans, ready for use by supporters at demonstrations outside the grounds to be used during the tour. The publicity was having some effect as following advice from the Government; the Queen declined the traditional invitation to attend the Saturday of the Lord's Test Match.

Whether sport should be used as a means of changing a country's political views, was still debated. The Conservative leaning *Daily*

Telegraph showed that the cricket supporting establishment had certainty not changed. In an Editorial they criticised the famous West Indian cricketer Sir Learie Constantine for joining demonstrations against the tour, calling such tactics 'a discourteous, clumsy, and ineffective way of showing distaste for apartheid'. They also believed that 'there is no evidence that the South African cricketers are supporters of apartheid' and thought 'there is very little doubt that they would themselves be delighted to play against, or with, West Indians, East Indians or anyone else' [32].

The Labour leaning *Daily Mirror*, perhaps unexpectedly, had a similar view. Commenting after the first day's play of the Lords' Test Match, Peter Wilson thought both the play and the anti-apartheid demonstrations outside the ground were both 'lukewarm'. He concluded that 'the English who are basically a tolerant nation, cannot really equate what the so far anonymous characters do on a cricket field with what their government cruelly does six thousand miles away' [33].

Most England players selected to tour South Africa rarely commented publicly about what they had seen on tour. They argued that the politics of the country was the role of politicians. Players were also bound by a clause in their contract forbidding them from making public comments about the tour without prior permission of the tour Manager or Secretary of the MCC. The respected Warwickshire professional Tom Cartwright was a member of MCC tours to East Africa in 1963/64 and South Africa in 1964/65 and probably spoke for many when he wrote 'I thought it was good to go out there to make contact with people, to make them aware of what the rest of the world was like. I'd met a lot of people on my two trips there and I thought that was important. It was only in 1968, with all the things that happened with the selection for that tour, that I changed my mind' [34].

Another person to change his view, but in a more public way was Mike Brearley. A future England captain, he was a colleague of Cartwright's on the MCC tour to South Africa in 1964/65. Still at Cambridge University, he approached the tour with an open mind, keen to see as much as he could while in the country. He was soon to realise that bridge building via sport was not a viable strategy, and would become a prominent member of the group who would eventually challenge the might of the MCC itself over its handling of cricket relations with South Africa [35].

With no England winter cricket tour scheduled, Billy Griffith visited South Africa during Christmas and the New Year of 1966/67. As Secretary of the MCC he had been invited by SACA on a all expenses paid trip to watch the first two Tests of the Series between South Africa and Australia. His verbal report to the MCC Committee on his return may well have been detailed, but the minute was very brief, giving no specific detail other than noting that discussions had been interesting. [36]. It did though note that the South African Cricket Association were keen to rejoin the International Cricket Conference. Griffith was more open in a discussion with the *Daily Telegraph's* cricket writer Michael Melford, believing that South Africa should be readmitted as a full Member of the International Cricket Conference [37]. As for England teams containing non-white cricketers touring South Africa, he thought it was something best left until the situation arises.

Griffith was not the only person to visit South Africa during the English winter of 1966/7, Basil D'Oliveira was also there. He had arrived in Cape Town at the beginning of October, and was greeted like a hero, with a Mayoral reception and large enthusiastic crowds. This was the start of a tour sponsored by Rothmans to coach non-white cricketers. Although he was now an international cricketer, D'Oliveira's coaching clinics and lectures were still restricted to non-white facilities. Over the next four months wherever he went there was the same enthusiastic response.

There was of course pressure on him to make comments on political aspects, and predict what might happen if he were picked to represent England on a future tour of South Africa. To his credit he steadfastly refused to become entangled in what he realised could be a political minefield.

During the trip there were not surprisingly continual frustrations having to readjust again to segregation laws, many of which seemed so barbaric after six years in England. For instance, in one match in which D'Oliveira took part, the Indian organisers were threatened with prosecution for allowing a mixed non-white crowd to watch. There were also problems at an award dinner towards the end of the tour at which D'Oliveira was to be presented with South Africa's 'Non-White

Sportsman of the Year' trophy. It had originally been planned to hold the function in a private room of the Langham Hotel, Johannesburg at which non-whites could be present with Government permission. The audience was to include dignitaries such as the Mayor of Johannesburg, and cricketing luminaries such as Richie Benaud, Denis Compton and Roy McLean. The Government continued to delay granting permission for the mixed gathering, and so at the last moment it had to be moved to the editorial offices of *The Post* on the condition that the guests were offered a stand up buffet rather than a sit down dinner. In his acceptance speech on receiving the award D'Oliveira made some fairly broad observations about the differences in opportunities for non-white cricketers in South Africa and England. In spite of the encouragement for him to do so, during the evening he 'maintained his attitude of saying nothing about the controversy that had broken out in Britain over him' [38].

On the 22 January 1967 the issue of whether D'Oliveira would be allowed to play in South Africa as a member of an England side suddenly became big news in both countries. Under the banner headline 'Minister Adamant: "Dolly" Will Not Tour S.A.' [39] a *Sunday Express* reporter in Johannesburg claimed South Africa's Minister of the Interior Pieter le Roux had made it clear D'Oliveira would not be allowed to tour South Africa as a member of any MCC team. Although le Roux later stated in Parliament that the reporter had misinterpreted his remarks, he then went back on his statement somewhat by saying that D'Oliveira would still not be allowed in. The statement, and the massive publicity it received, lit the blue touch paper in Britain. What up until then had been a somewhat hypothetical issue, had become real now that le Roux had linked the name of D'Oliveira to it. As a member of the Foreign Office in Cape Town observed 'There are many people in South Africa and of course in Britain who are not given to worrying themselves much about apartheid but whose interest in cricket has forced the issue on them as a result of the D'Oliveira case' [40].

This was certainly true in the British House of Commons where a motion calling on the MCC to cancel its tour to South Africa gained cross-party support from 150 MPs almost immediately. There was an equal frenzy of activity in the press.

Both the British Government and MCC were cajoled into issuing statements in response to le Roux's comments, perhaps rather sooner than they would have liked. The MCC tour of South Africa was still nearly two years away and it was by no means certain that D'Oliveira would be selected for the team. He had, after all only played four games for England so far.

Even so, on the 30 January, Denis Howell the Secretary of State for Education and Science with special responsibility for sport, told a cheering House of Commons that he was sure that a MCC tour to South Africa would be cancelled if any member chosen for the touring side was rejected by the South Africa Government. In prior discussions with Griffith he had indirectly applied pressure by stating that while the Government would not interfere in MCC affairs, if they chose to cancel the tour they would of course receive Government support [41].

This put Griffith, who according to Howell (and many others) was a man 'whose integrity was beyond any question' [42], in a very difficult position. He had been Vice-Captain of the England team which toured South Africa in 1948, and witnessed apartheid at first hand. Like John Arlott who was also there, he was appalled at many of the things he had seen [43]. However as Secretary of the MCC he had to be careful about expressing a personal view. Under pressure (and now with advice!) from the Government, and much to the consternation of some on the MCC Committee, he also issued a statement stating that 'once we have chosen the team it will be up to the South African authorities to let us know if they are prepared to accept it in its entirety. Should they say "No" then there would be no question that the tour would have to be cancelled' [44]. The let us cross that bridge when we get to it tactic was no longer an adequate response.

The next day most of Britain's major newspapers reported Howell's speech (and the MCC statement) on their front pages. The *Daily Mirror* had the headline 'MCC Say 'No' to Colour Bar' [45] occupying most of the page. Whether the MCC liked it or not it seemed that others were now driving the agenda.

Rumour suggested that Prime Minister Vorster was far from happy with le Roux's statement. There was a belief that the new regime had been looking at ways of improving its image abroad, and maybe even softening its approach as far as the composition of visiting teams was concerned. So when it became known that Vorster was to make a statement at the beginning of April on his Government's sports policy, there was hope from those opposed to apartheid that change was in the air.

Vorster's statement in the House of Assembly on 11 April 1967 was uncharacteristically cautious and at times convoluted. For those looking for change, the beginning was certainly not promising. Restating the country's apartheid sports policy, he made it absolutely clear that threats from outside would not force the Government to change, no matter what the consequences as far as sporting contacts were concerned. After discussion of many hypothetical cases where non-whites might be allowed into the Republic as part of a visiting team, he then went on to say that the Government's policy on the make-up of visiting teams was that 'our Government does not prescribe whom you may select because our Government is not your selection committee' [46]. This could have been interpreted as a change in existing policy, although Vorster went to great lengths to insist this was not the case, it was just an explanation of interpretation. He did though add some important caveats, most likely to placate the right wing of his party who were completely against any change at all. Firstly this policy would only apply to countries with which the Republic already had sporting ties, so that for instance it did not mean that the Indian cricket team would now be allowed to visit. Secondly, if anyone tried to make political capital from a visit, or internal calm could be disturbed then permission to enter would be refused.

Vorster, maybe with D'Oliveira in mind, also made it very clear that it was not helpful to 'name an individual long before a tour was to take place, and to say "Will you or will you not receive him?'. He thought that this was 'the type of question which is asked purely to cause difficulties where no difficulties exist' [47].

There were then signs of hope, but in reality it seemed each case would be considered on its merits, and if Vorster was unhappy, permission would be refused. The door allowing D'Oliveira to play as an England cricketer in South Africa was opening slightly – possibly.

Back in England in the spring of 1967, like many others Basil D'Oliveira was preparing for a new English cricket season. Through no fault of his own, in less than six months he had gone from being a new cap for England to the central figure in a debate on apartheid in sport. His immediate concern was to continue to play well for his county Worcestershire and keep his place in the England side. As he observed 'The pressure will be on me. It won't be so easy for me to do well' [48].

This proved to be an understatement. However, by August 1968 a combination of a determination to succeed, some luck and of course an outstanding innings at the Oval had forced D'Oliveira to the front row of those being considered for the upcoming tour of South Africa. His dream of playing Test cricket in the land of his birth was now within reach.

4

Cricket and Politics Clash
August 1968 – December 1968

Up until 1977, when the England cricket side travelled overseas for a winter series, they did so under the auspices of the MCC. For international matches on the tour the side was named England, at all other times they were the MCC. Once the last Test match of an English summer was over, the MCC Selection Sub-Committee would meet to finalise the side for the winter tour as quickly as possible. Tuesday 27 August 1968 was no different in that regard. Following the conclusion of the fifth Test match between England and Australia at the Oval, the members of the Committee, most of who had been at the match, hurried across London to Lord's cricket ground ready to begin their deliberations at 8 pm.

With most names already pencilled in, the meeting would normally concentrate on filling the last few places, something that could usually been done fairly quickly. This time the meeting did not finish until 2 am, it had clearly been anything but a straightforward selection process. In fact it was the beginning of what quickly became one of the most controversial and divisive issues that the MCC had ever encountered; now known to most around the world as 'The D'Oliveira Affair'.

What took place that August evening has become the source of an almost endless stream of speculation. Over fifty years on it is a subject, which still has the power to arouse passionate debate. There have been numerous conspiracy theories, suggestions that minutes of the meeting were never written or went missing and even that one of those present was passing information back to the South African Cricket Association.

Much that has been written and spoken about the D'Oliveira Affair (particularly the final selection meeting), can only be conjecture. All of those who were present at this meeting, as well as D'Oliveira himself, are now dead. Few with first hand knowledge ever commented publicly about the discussions that took place. All that now exists as a record of that evening is a single page confidential minute.

The meeting and its consequences have generated hundreds of thousands of words in newspapers, magazines and books ever since. Of course like all stories with a political dimension, even if there is agreement on the facts, interpretation of events and conclusions can be different. D'Oliveira himself wrote three books [49], while Michael Melford's article in *Wisden* [50] is considered one of the best summaries of events written at the time. The more recent books by Oborne on the life of D'Oliveira [51], and Murray and Merrett on the broader issues of politics in South African cricket [52] are both excellent, and have benefited from access to Government records in Britain and South Africa which were not available earlier. In spite of all that has been written, the D'Oliveira Affair still has the potential to warrant further analysis [53].

At first sight it seemed that the selectors were faced with the same task as those of their predecessors, to choose a group of players to represent England on an overseas tour. As usual that morning many of the cricket correspondents in the national press had made their predictions, and not all had agreed. When the final touring party was announced there would of course be disappointments and maybe some surprises, but that was the nature of these things.

So why should this particular meeting have been so contentious? The answer is that since Basil D'Oliveira was one of those being considered for selection, then this was no longer purely a cricket issue but now also a political one. The question that will never be answered for certain, is to what extent did the fact that D'Oliveira's selection would have almost certainly led to the cancellation of the tour influence the choice of the team that evening? Was D'Oliveira left out on cricketing or political grounds? While the MCC might have often declared that cricket and politics should be kept separate, on this occasion whether they liked it or not the two were inextricably linked. The tragedy of the situation is that they either did not recognise this or did not want to recognise this. Ultimately the D'Oliveira Affair was not really about cricket, it was about international politics. Reflecting on the decision of the selectors, the cricket commentator John Arlott wrote 'The final thought on it, however, must be one of sadness and that in the selection MCC have stirred forces – for both good and evil – whose powers they do not truly comprehend' [54]. In this he proved to be totally correct.

The Selection Sub-Committee who assembled in the Committee Dining Room at Lord's consisted of the four national selectors Doug Insole, Alec Bedser, Don Kenyon and Peter May; the President and Treasurer of the MCC, Arthur Gilligan and G. O. B. 'Gubby' Allen; and the Secretary and Assistant Secretary of the MCC, S. C. 'Billy' Griffith and Donald Carr. The final two present were Colin Cowdrey who had been chosen as captain of the tour a month previously, and Les Ames who had been appointed Tour Manager. Griffith and Carr were there for administrative purposes and would not have had any voting rights.

There were no hard and fast rules as far as the selection of the touring party was concerned. The objective was to choose a group of players with the best chance of beating South Africa in their own country in a five Test series. Of course current form came into the decision, but so did the suitability for playing in non-English conditions.

Many of the selection committee had experience of South Africa, some more recently than others. Griffith had been vice – captain and Bedser a player of the MCC tour in 1947/48, while May had been captain, Insole vice – captain, and Cowdrey a player on the 1956/57 tour. Donald Carr had been the most recent visitor, and to some extent got nearest to the reality of everyday life in the country, having been manager of the 1964 tour. Although the movements of touring parties were carefully controlled, most would have seen apartheid at work during their tours of the country.

It was common practice for overseas tours to select a group of sixteen players, generally (or though not always) six or seven batsmen, six or seven bowlers, two all-rounders and two wicketkeepers. It was also usual for three of the batsmen to be specialist openers, with one of the wicket keepers being a batsman/wicketkeeper rather than a specialist wicketkeeper.

As far as the bowlers were concerned the breakdown between seam bowlers and spin bowlers would depend on the conditions they were expected to face. For instance for the 1964 tour of South Africa four seam bowlers, two off-spin and one leg-spin bowler had been chosen. The selectors would also consider batsmen who could bowl a bit to supplement the bowling attack. There was a rumour that pitches in South Africa had changed since the MCC had last toured there, now perhaps greener and more suited to D'Oliveira's medium paced out-swingers.

During the series against Australia, which had just finished, eleven different batsmen had been used. Of these Colin Cowdrey, Geoffrey Boycott, John Edrich, and Tom Graveney were certainties. So the selectors faced the problem of who to leave out. The question was whether D'Oliveira was the right person to take one of the remaining three batting places, one of which would be filled by a specialist opening batsman. While at county level he could be classed as an all-rounder, at Test level he was more realistically a batsman who could bowl a bit. His Test record so far seemed to confirm this. He had now played sixteen Test matches, scoring 972 runs at a average of 48.60 with two centuries and seven fifties. As a bowler he had only taken eighteen wickets at an average of 46.94.

As always headline statistics do not tell the whole story. Five of D'Oliveira's Test appearances had been in England against relatively weak teams from India and Pakistan, playing on pitches better suited to his bowling. His only overseas tour at that stage had been the recently completed series against the West Indies, here the statistics were less flattering. He had played in all five Test matches, scoring a total of 137 runs at an average of 22.83. As far has his bowling was concerned he had only taken three wickets at 97.66. Of course, every player can have a bad series, and it was against one of the strongest sides in the world at that time, but the selectors had to consider whether his bowling was likely to be effective in South Africa. If not, was he worth a place purely as a batsman who could maybe bowl the occasional over.

There was though another issue which had arisen during the West Indies tour, D'Oliveira liked a drink and a party. As Oborne noted, there were two groups in the Worcestershire county team at that time, 'the heavy drinkers and the light drinkers' [55]. D'Oliveira was in the first group (as was his Test colleague Graveney). When the MCC arrived in the West Indies, D'Oliveira was the member of the team it seemed everybody wanted to meet, and he found it hard to say no. In his autobiography, D'Oliveira himself later admitted that he had 'accepted far too many invitations to dinner parties and receptions' and that he 'was wrong to try and please everybody when the invitations kept flooding in… all I got in return was more pressure' [56]. Despite rumours to the contrary he was adamant that he had not been fined for his behaviour, and received the full £150 bonus (Equivalent to £2,600 in 2020) at the end of tour like other players. Unfortunately the Manager and Captain's Report for the tour are no longer in the MCC archives.

The question for the selectors then was that if D'Oliveira had struggled in the West Indies because of off field distractions, how would he cope in South Africa where he would without doubt be the centre of attention. Cowdrey and Ames who had been captain and tour manager in the West Indies were due to perform the same roles in South Africa, and this must have been something that had crossed their minds .

The above issues were essentially cricketing and management ones, typical of those selectors had always had to deal with. This time there was also the political dimension. John Vorster's statement on the sporting policy of South Africa in April 1967 did not stop the media discussing what had now become 'the D'Oliveira Affair'. The MCC themselves were sufficiently unsettled, that on 5 January 1968 Billy Griffith wrote to the Secretary of the South African Cricket Association to confirm that the selection of the touring party would be a matter for the MCC Selection Sub-Committee alone, and not subject to any external criteria [57].

Receiving no response, the MCC Committee had then asked Sir Alec Douglas-Home to intervene. Douglas-Home was Shadow Foreign Secretary and had previously been Prime Minister and a President of the MCC. He was visiting Rhodesia (now Zimbabwe) and South Africa during the spring of 1968 and at the MCC's request took the opportunity to raise the issue of the forthcoming tour during a meeting with John Vorster. On his return to the UK, he reported on his meeting with Vorster at a MCC Committee on 21 March 1968. He advised the Committee not to press for an answer to their letter of 5 January, and that the chances of the tour going ahead with D'Oliveira in the team were slightly better than even (he actually gave odds of 5/4). It was agreed that arrangements for the forthcoming tour should go ahead, with the assumption that the selected team would be acceptable to the South African Government [58].

At around the same time, Viscount Cobham was also in South Africa. A previous President of the MCC, Cobham had strong family and business connections in the Republic. During his visit a number of friends had asked if he would like to meet the Prime Minister. Delighted to do so, a meeting was eventually arranged for 13 March, a few hours before Cobham sailed for home. During this short unofficial meeting with Vorster, Cobham also raised the topic of the tour, but this time asked a more direct question about D'Oliveira. The result was much less optimistic. When asked if D'Oliveira would be acceptable, if selected by the MCC, Vorster had been blunt saying 'Anyone else. D'Oliveira – no' [59]. Contrary to many newspaper reports at the time Cobham was clear that Vorster did not ask for this message to be passed back to the MCC [60].

There is uncertainty as to how, and in what form Cobham's message was passed to the MCC. What is certain though is that when it reached Griffith, he showed it the MCC President (Arthur Gilligan) and MCC Treasurer (Gubby Allen) and it was decided not to pass this information onto the MCC Committee or selectors. In a statement released in April the following year, after rumours in the press of a conspiracy of silence, the MCC said the reason for this action had been so as to not influence the two members of the MCC Committee (Insole and May) who were also

Test selectors. The advice from Cobham was of course also less optimistic about the tour going ahead than that from Douglas-Home. Peter May later told a journalist that 'It's not for me to say whether MCC was right not to tell me of Lord Cobham's report. How can I tell whether it would have prejudiced me against D'Oliveira? I suppose it might have affected my feelings' [61].

So when the selectors met that Tuesday, some were aware of the reports from Douglas-Home and Cobham, some of just Douglas-Home's and some of neither. All though must have been aware of public opinion, most of which was strongly behind D'Oliveira. The *Daily Telegraph's* cricket correspondent had spoken for many when a few days earlier, after D'Oliveira's innings of 158 at the Oval, he had written 'it is hardly conceivable that he will not find a place on merit when the party is named next Wednesday' [62].

The official record of what occurred that evening is brief. The one page minute only has five items. These were: (i) a list of the three players who had declared themselves unavailable for the tour (Dexter, Illingworth and Higgs); (ii) a list of the sixteen players who had been selected for the tour; (iii) the action that should be taken to test the fitness of the bowler Jeff Jones; (iv) a statement that the Chairman and the captain should discuss reserves and submit to the Committee in due course; and (v) the decision that once on tour the selection committee should comprise the captain, vice-captain and tour manager with the authority to add others as required [63].

The minute does not include any record of the discussion that took place to determine the final team, and it is not signed or dated. The author is unknown but was most likely Donald Carr, the Assistant Secretary of the MCC.

After nearly six hours of discussion, with a few short breaks, the selectors finally reached a decision on the sixteen players who would go on the tour. The minutes of the meeting do not record the results of any votes taken when there was a disagreement over particular choices. There has been a great deal of conjecture over the years about who voted for and who voted against D'Oliveira being chosen. The truth is that nobody will ever know. For example in the case of Gubby Allen, one source suggests that Allen abstained while another that he was against. All that is certain is that when the final sixteen were chosen, D'Oliveira was not among them (Although even this has now been questioned). The final list of players were:

1. M.C. Cowdrey (Captain) – Batsman, Age 35, 101 Tests
2. T. W. Graveney (Vice Captain) – Batsman, Age 41, 75 Tests
3. K. F. Barrington – Batsman, Age 37, 82 Tests
4. G. Boycott – Opening Batsman, Age 27, 35 Tests
5. D. J. Brown – Medium/Fast Bowler, Age 26, 19 Tests
6. T. W. Cartwright – Medium Bowler, Age 33, 5 Tests
7. R. M. H. Cottam – Medium/Fast Bowler, Age 23, 0 Tests
8. J. H. Edrich – Opening Batsman, Age 31, 31 Tests
9. K. W. R. Fletcher – Batsman, Age 24, 1 Test
10. A. P. E. Knott – Wicketkeeper, Age 22, 9 Tests
11. J. T. Murray – Wicketkeeper, Age 33, 21 Tests
12. P. I. Pocock – Off-Spin Bowler, Age 21, 3 Tests
13. R. M. Prideaux – Opening Batsman, Age 29, 1 Test
14. J. A. Snow – Fast Bowler, Age 26, 18 Tests
15. D. L. Underwood – Slow/Medium Bowler, Age 23, 8 Tests
16. To be filled by a fast bowler once the fitness of I. J. Jones is known.

That afternoon at 3.45 pm, the full MCC Committee met to consider and approve the decision of the MCC Selection Sub-Committee [64]. There was discussion on the team that had been selected, and the best way to deal with the obvious interest that would arise from the media once the team was announced. It was agreed that the Chairman of the Selectors, Doug Insole, and the MCC Secretary Billy Griffith should act on the Committee's behalf. It was also agreed that no voting figures relating to the selection of the team should be released to the media.

The ex-England Captain, Mike Brearley, has recently written that in 2016, a then 90 year old Insole had confided in a Member of the MCC that contrary to the previously accepted version of events in fact 'D'Oliveira was in the squad initially selected; but the decision was rescinded by 5 p.m. on 28 August', either before the team chosen by the Selection Sub-Committee was presented to the MCC Committee or at the MCC Committee Meeting itself [65]. If this were the case then the Minutes of the Selection Sub-Committee that currently exist are an amended version of what took place. Like many conspiracy theories, nobody will probably ever know for certain.

Whatever did or did not happen, what is certain is that at the end of the MCC Committee Meeting, D'Oliveira was not a member of the touring party. Following the meeting, Griffith and Insole had the unenviable task of facing the waiting press. Before the team was read out by Griffith, Insole emphasized that no pre-conditions on the selection of the touring party had been set by the South African Cricket Association and that 'the team had been picked solely on the basis of providing the best players in a cricketing sense to beat the South Africans' [66]. What Insole and his colleagues did not know was that the previous day the Premier John Vorster and his Cabinet had met in South Africa, and already decided that 'if D'Oliveira is chosen the tour is off' [67].

In explaining why D'Oliveira had been left out, Insole suggested that given the nature of the conditions they would be playing in, that D'Oliveira had to be considered as a batsman rather than an all-rounder. The two openers selected were the established pair of Boycott and Edrich, with Prideaux as a reserve. Two of the next four batting places would be taken by the Captain Cowdrey and Vice-Captain Graveney. So D'Oliveira was in a list alongside Barrington, Fletcher, Milburn, and Alan Jones of Glamorgan competing for the two remaining batting places. In the end the selectors went for Fletcher who they thought was one of the most promising middle-order batsmen in the country, and Barrington. Ken Barrington had not had a good season, but had vast experience having played 82 Test matches with an excellent record on overseas tours. His leg-spin bowling would also be a useful asset. The team did not include a single genuine all-rounder, something almost unheard of. In an unusually frank discussion with the press, Insole also commented that he expected both D'Oliveira and Don Wilson of Yorkshire to be coaching in South Africa during the winter, and therefore they would be candidates for call-up as replacements if required.

There is little doubt that the MCC would have expected some adverse reaction to D'Oliveira being left out of the touring party, but they surely could not have foreseen the torrent of outrage that would occur.

Apart from those reading the late editions of the London evening newspapers on their way home, the first chance most people across the United Kingdom had of learning who had been selected for South Africa, would have been from the BBC evening sports bulletin at 6.32 pm. D'Oliveira was playing for his county Worcestershire against Sussex at the time. He had just scored a century and was back in the dressing room crowded around a transistor radio with some of his team mates waiting for the news. When he realised that he had not been selected, D'Oliveira was stunned. Writing over ten years later he remembered 'I was numb struck. You could have heard a pin drop in the room. I don't know how long I stood there but the first thing I recall was Tom Graveney swearing bitterly and saying 'I never thought they'd do this to you Bas''[68]. Outside among the spectators there were shouts of 'shame' when the team was read out over the ground's public address system. The decision was the lead item of the BBC late evening television news, and this was just the beginning.

The next morning the news of D'Oliveira's omission made the front page of every national newspaper in the United Kingdom – even the *Financial Times*. There were many aspects of the team selection worthy of discussion. For instance why pick Fletcher when he had only played one Test match?; why not choose Milburn instead of Prideaux as a back-up opening batsman?; if the team had been chosen on merit, where was David Green who had scored more first-class runs than any other English batsman that season?, and was Cartwright a risk as he was currently injured and had not performed well in South Africa in 1964/65?. These were all valid cricketing questions, but it seemed all the newspapers wanted to talk about was D'Oliveira. The two best selling tabloids made it absolutely clear what they thought of the matter with the *Daily Mirror* proclaiming 'This Despicable Affair'[69] and the *Sun* 'Hero D'Oliveira is Left Out'[70]. A few days later the *Observer* perhaps captured most succinctly the feelings of many with the headline to Alan Ross's article 'This Sad Illusion That Cricket Is Only a Game'.[71]

Every newspaper had a view on the tour party that had been chosen. Some believed that as well as D'Oliveira, Milburn had also been badly treated while others thought the decision to leave out D'Oliveira was correct on cricketing grounds. The cricket correspondents of the three big broadsheets covered the full spectrum. John Arlott in the *Guardian* wrote with passion that 'MCC have never made a sadder, more dramatic. or potentially more damaging decision' [72]. E. W. Swanton in the *Daily Telegraph* also disagreed with the omission of D'Oliveira but was more cautious, writing 'I think the omission of D'Oliveira substantially weakens the strength and balance of the side' [73], while John Woodcock in the *Times* thought 'They have, I think though made the right decision though there will be those, no doubt, who accuse them of either prejudice or cowardice' [74]. Woodcock was later to change his opinion.

One of the few professional cricketers playing at the time, willing to go public was Ted Dexter. He had played alongside D'Oliveira in the fifth Test at the Oval, which as it turned out was Dexter's sixty second and last Test in a long England career. Writing for the *Sunday Mirror* he was completely unambiguous saying that assuming he was in good form, D'Oliveira 'has always been my first choice to bat number six for England' [75]. He also made the point that if selecting D'Oliveira against South Africa was likely to cause a problem, why had the selectors brought him back into the England side for the final Test match against Australia [76]. Whatever the view of the press in England, many in both the Government and cricket administration in South Africa, must have greeted the news of the team with a sigh of relief. The tour was still on.

Over the coming days, the decision not to select D'Oliveira remained on the front pages and if anything the negative reaction grew. There were demands for the tour to be cancelled, a call from a MP for the Race Relations Board to investigate, and the resignation of a number of MCC Members. Others outside of cricket also got involved. The television chat-show host, and journalist, Michael Parkinson wrote an article in the *Observer* castigating the MCC for dodging the real issue and suggested that the decision should have been not to tour at all no matter what the composition of the party. He believed the building bridges with cricket strategy was no longer viable [77].

There were also letters to newspapers. Social media was far in the future, and so if you wanted to express your view publicly about something you wrote to the national press. Many people did just that. The *Guardian* had an unusually large postbag on the issue, receiving 236 letters in the first two days alone. Of these only three supported the MCC selectors' decision. Opinions were strong on both sides. A letter to the *Times* supporting the selectors ended 'It is incredible how self-righteous liberalists so persistently attribute unworthy motives to those who don't do what they want' [78], while from the other side a letter to the Guardian ended 'I have been a cricket supporter all my life. Never have I felt such a deep sense of shame as I feel today' [79]. This outpouring of emotion was far more than just a few people disagreeing with the selectors' decisions.

Some at the MCC, unused to being in the spotlight, were becoming unsettled by the intensity of this public outcry. There was though more trouble in store. On 4 September the Personnel notices in the *Times* [80] contained an advertisement titled 'D'Oliveira Case' calling for MCC Members unhappy with the Club's handling of matters related to tour selection and cricket relations with South Africa to ring a Mr Barr on the number in the notice. Discontent among some Members of the MCC, normally such a private community, was beginning to be aired in public.

The rising tide of public anger had also affected the England Captain. On 8 September, Colin Cowdrey felt it necessary to issue a statement clarifying his position. He made it clear that he had been 'assured by the MCC Committee that the team would be selected on cricketing ability alone' [81]; if a replacement was necessary D'Oliveira could be considered; and that South Africa would be responsible should the tour need to be cancelled. He also added that while he was against apartheid that sport was still one of the best ways of building bridges. What Cowdrey did not say was whether he supported decision to leave D'Oliveira out.

The MCC hastily arranged another full Committee Meeting on the 12 September to try and head off a Special General Meeting being proposed by some of its Members and discuss ways of dealing with it, should it go ahead [82].

Naturally the person above all most wanted to talk to was D'Oliveira. He kept a dignified silence during the increasing storm, expressing disappointment but little else. He also now had an agent, Reg Hayter, to advice, guide and protect him in dealings with the media. This turned out to be a wise move, as pressure was now coming from many directions. In mid-August, M. J. 'Tienie' Oostuizen who was employed by a South African tobacco company, had made D'Oliveira an offer on behalf of the South African Sports Foundation. He was offered £40,000 over ten years (equivalent to approximately £700,000 in 2020) to coach non-whites in South Africa during the winter, as long as he declared himself unavailable to tour before the fifth Test at the Oval began. D'Oliveira had turned down the offer, but he was no longer just the focus of attention for the British media.

Although he would now no longer be going to South Africa during the winter as a member of the MCC touring party, he would still be there. Spotting an opportunity the *News of the World* had offered D'Oliveira a job as a cricket correspondent. This was not without precedent as they had done the same to Brian Close the previous winter, after he had been sacked as England captain and Cowdrey had replaced him for the tour of the West Indies. The news of D'Oliveira's new role did not go down well with Vorster, who was already suggesting that he may not get a visa to enter the country as a journalist. It was though soon not to be an issue.

The Selection Sub-Committee still had to meet one more time before their role in the winter tour was finished. They had to decide whether Jeff Jones was fit to take his place in the side, and consider reserves for the tour. In light of the news coming out of South Africa that D'Oliveira would not be accepted as a journalist, there were those who now wanted assurance from the South African Government that D'Oliveira would be allowed in, if he were named as a reserve. It began to look as though whatever happened at the final Selection Sub-Committee, there would be trouble. There was indeed trouble, but the initial source was not D'Oliveira but one of the original selections, Tom Cartwright.

Few would dispute that Cartwright had been a fine bowler for his county Warwickshire over the last ten years. A right-arm medium pace bowler, he was capable of bowling long spells with metronomic accuracy. He had taken over 100 wickets in a season six times, and the previous year had taken more wickets than anybody else in county cricket. He had though, only played five Test matches for England, and at 33 was beginning to suffer increasing injury problems. He had in fact only played in less than half of the County Championship matches for Warwickshire that season, but still taken more wickets than anybody else on the playing staff.

Cartwright had been injured when the team to tour South Africa had been announced but was still included in the squad, subject to fitness. Having received treatment from a specialist orthopaedic surgeon in London, he had a final chance to test his fitness before the tour left for South Africa. He played in a 50 over a side match between the winners of the Gillette Cup that season (Warwickshire) and a Gillette Invitation XI on 14 September. Sadly rain ruined the match and there was only time for the Invitation XI to bat for their 50 overs. In did though give Cartwright the chance to bowl his allotted 10 overs, during which he took the wicket of the England captain. Cowdrey was keen to see Cartwright in action. While he felt all right after the match, the next day the damaged shoulder was sore. Returning to the specialist on the Monday Cartwright was given a stark choice. He could go to South Africa and try and play, but if he damaged his shoulder further he might never be able to play again. Alternatively he could have an operation and spend the winter recuperating. Cowdrey asked him to at least start the tour and see how things went, but the final decision would be his. Cartwright decided to withdraw from the tour party.

When the MCC Selection Sub-Committee reconvened on 16 September, they expected the meeting to be short. The unexpected withdrawal of Cartwright quickly put an end to such hopes. The minutes show that Jones was passed fit and invited to join the touring party, and that four reserves were named. As far as a replacement for Cartwright was concerned this was more problematic. The selectors agreed that no direct replacement for Cartwright was possible, and although they were aware that the balance of the touring party would be altered, Basil D'Oliveira was invited to join the tour [83]. There were other seam bowlers who could have been chosen as a replacement for Cartwright and the inconsistency in the selectors' thinking did not escape the press, but it was doubtful if D'Oliveira was worried – he was now in the team.

The same day, even before the selectors had met, Vorster told the United Kingdom's Ambassador, Sir John Nicholls, that while he would have accepted D'Oliveira as a member of the original touring party, now things were different [84]. Vorster believed that if D'Oliveira now came either as a journalist or as a replacement in the original team he would become a target for politically motivated agitation. If there was any doubt, the next day Vorster made his position absolutely clear. In a speech at a National Party Meeting in Bloemfontein the huge crowd of Afrikaans supporters cheered and applauded when they were told 'we are not prepared to receive a team thrust on us by people whose interests are not the game but to gain political objectives which they do not even attempt to hide' [85]. This view was of course not one held by all in South Africa. A clearly bitter Editor of the *South African Cricket Annual* would later write that he could not 'subscribe to the view that the 2,000 odd hysterically cheering people who acclaimed the fateful pronouncement constitute the 'voice' of genuine sportsmen and sportswomen in this country' [86]. The most important 'voice' though was that of the Government, and they had now spoken.

Many doubted whether Vorster would have really accepted the original MCC touring side if it had included D'Oliveira. Now that was purely hypothetical, MCC's change of selection had given Vorster a way out, while at the same time keeping the right-wing of his Party on side.

There was now no room for manoeuvre from either side. Vorster had made it clear that he would not accept a touring party containing D'Oliveira, while the MCC had publicly stated that if any member of their side were rejected by the South African Government then the tour would be cancelled.

On 24 September the MCC Committee met yet again, to discuss the tour [87]. Two members of the South African Cricket Association were present at the meeting, although they accepted that the matter was now out of SACA's hands and that their attendance was more about protecting future relations between SACA and the MCC. The MCC Committee unanimously agreed that the tour to South Africa should be cancelled,

The letter formally cancelling the tour was sent to the South African Cricket Association the following day [88]. It seemed that one of the most contentious episodes in English cricket was now at an end.

This though was not a normal year, and the MCC still had two items of unfinished business to attend to. With the cancellation of the tour to South Africa now confirmed, there was the immediate problem of whether it was possible to arrange a replacement.

The schedule for future Test series' was normally agreed by the International Cricket Conference (ICC) years in advance. For instance, the July 1968 meeting of the ICC had a calendar going as far forward as 1977, when Australia was due to visit England. Even if a tour could be arranged at such short notice there were not many options. The West Indies and New Zealand were coming to England during the 1969 season, and England were already scheduled to visit Australia and New Zealand again at the end of 1970.

Realising that the tour to South Africa might be in jeopardy, the MCC had though already made preliminary approaches to India and Pakistan. Responses so far had been mixed. India had offered to host a three match Test series while Pakistan had responded that the matter was under consideration, and a decision would be made soon [89]. There had also been requests from two ICC Associate Members, Ceylon (now Sri Lanka) and Malaysia. Both were keen for a tour of their countries to be added to any tour of India and/or Pakistan. They were eager to gain experience to enhance future claims for Test status.

Without waiting for the destination of the tour to be finalised, it was agreed that all players that had been selected for the South African tour should be invited to join its replacement, and that payment should be the same even though the new tour would be shorter. Responsibility for arrangements was then passed to the Overseas Tours Sub-Committee. By the normal standards of the MCC Committee this pace of decision making must have seemed almost reckless.

Also on the agenda that day was the preparation for a Special General Meeting. For only the second time in its two hundred year history the competence of the MCC's elected Committee was being publicly challenged by its Members. The response to the advert from Charles Barr which had appeared in the Personal Notices column of the *Times* on 7

September had been an informal meeting of MCC Members unhappy with the Club's recent handling of the South African tour selection. Seeking an alternative to resignation as a way of making their voices heard the decision to call a Special General Meeting had been agreed. Aware of the controversy their action might unleash, the group were conscious of the need for a high profile name to lead them. The Reverend David Sheppard was contacted and gave his whole hearted support to the venture [90]. With the signatures of the twenty Full Members required under the rules of the MCC a Special General Meeting to discuss the Club's handling of the tour selection and future cricket relations with South Africa was formally requested.

The MCC Committee did not take this challenge lightly and had already put significant effort and resources into trying to persuade the protest group from going ahead with its action. At an earlier meeting on 12 September, Sheppard, a future England captain Mike Brearley, and four other members of the protest group had been confronted by the full MCC Committee chaired by Sir Alec Douglas-Home. Even the Club's solicitor had been present. Their aim was simple, to pressurise the group into dropping its action. At what was clearly a tense meeting Brearley later remembered that Douglas-Home, then Shadow Foreign Secretary, had been 'glacial in conveying the message that we were naive and childish' [91]. This though was all to no avail, and so planning was now underway to ensure that the MCC would not be defeated at the Special General Meeting.

In the meantime, there was still the problem of the replacement winter tour to cope with. By mid-November the plan of a tour to Ceylon (Sri Lanka), India and Pakistan was beginning to unravel. Despite the original positive response from the Indian Cricket Control Board, the Indian Government were now unwilling to release the £20,000 (equivalent to £350,000 in 2020) financial guarantee required to underwrite the tour. By 26 November there was no alternative but to give up on the idea of a tour to India and revise the schedule. There were those who were beginning to question the point of a winter tour at all.

The date and location of the Special General Meeting was finally fixed for Thursday 6 December at Church House, Westminster. All 10,000 full

MCC Members were then sent details of the resolutions that would be debated on the day along with a voting slip which could be completed in advance.

On the day itself the venue was completely full by the time the meeting began at 6.30 pm. The overflow was accommodated in an adjoining room. Aware of the potential for trouble from anti-apartheid protest groups, attendance was strictly monitored to ensure that only full Members gained admission to the meeting.

The three motions debated that evening were i) regretting the MCC Committee's handing of the selection of the team for the intended tour of South Africa; ii) a proposal that there be no further tours to and from South Africa until there was evidence of progress towards multi-racial cricket; and iii) that the MCC set up a Committee to report on progress by the South African Cricket Association towards multi-racial cricket.

When the meeting came to an end three and a half hours later, all three resolutions had been soundly beaten. As the *Daily Telegraph's* E. W. Swanton observed 'It is one thing for members to say among themselves, as so many certainly have, that the committee have made the wrong decision' [92] but to criticise them in public was something different altogether.

The D'Oliveira Affair and its aftermath had caused a bitter rift between many in the cricket world. Sheppard himself was conscious of personal friendships that had been broken, some of which would never be repaired [93].

Watching from the side-lines, the Government's official line was unchanged. The decision regarding any future cricket tours to or from South Africa was a matter for the MCC alone. From the club's perspective, the Special General Meeting had been an unnecessary diversion, but none the less a battle which they had won. Sport and politics were still separate worlds but there where were those at the Foreign and Commonwealth Office who believed the MCC should be aware of the consequences of their decision in the real world [94].

The destination of the winter tour, still had to be resolved. With India now out of the question, the only option seemed to be a short tour of

Ceylon and Pakistan. Finally on 20 December a seven week tour of these two countries was announced. After the turmoil of the D'Oliveira Affair there were many in the MCC who were desperate to see the end of 1968, hoping that the New Year would a bring a return to normal business.

What they almost certainly did not know was that on the 7 November there had been a demonstration of 2000 college students in Rawalpindi, West Pakistan. In the clashes with authorities that followed, one student had been killed, 3 buses burned, four police wounded and schools and colleges closed [95]. While not widely reported at the time, this small demonstration was the start of a nationwide uprising, which would grow rapidly and less than five months later culminate in a military coup and overthrow of the country's President. The MCC had unwittingly just agreed to tour a country which was beginning a slide into anarchy. A return to normality in the world of English cricket was already looking a forlorn hope.

Part 2

January 1969 – March 1969

MCC Tour of Ceylon and Pakistan

5

Island Sojourn
January 1969 – February 1969

The year began with the inauguration of Richard Milhous Nixon as the 37th President of the United States of America. Without doubt, the most important of the campaign pledges he had made was to bring an end to the divisive Vietnam War. Increasingly clear that this was a conflict America had little hope of ever winning, most people now just wanted their country's involvement to end.

1969 would also be remembered for the moon landing. Eight years earlier the Soviet Cosmonaut Yuri Gagarin had made headlines around the world when he became the first man in space. American public opinion now demanded that the USA should win the race to the moon.

In Britain, Harold Wilson's Government was also embroiled in a war, but this was a domestic one with the Trade Unions. The use of a voluntary incomes policy to help manage the economy was failing, strikes continued to grow and there seemed to be no way of controlling them. Wilson was now proposing to use legal means to reform industrial relations and control the power of the Trade Unions. To achieve this, Barbara Castle the feisty Secretary of State for Employment and Productivity developed and published the White Paper *'In Place of Strife'* [96]. Both the Trade Unions Congress and much of the Cabinet and Parliamentary Labour Party fiercely opposed this controversial legislation. Months of unrest were to follow. The challenges that the English cricket administration had been dealing with over the last months must have seemed mild in comparison to the industrial turmoil faced by the Government.

The year also marked the creation of a new structure for the administration of cricket across the United Kingdom. At its inaugural meeting at Lord's on 21 January, the MCC Cricket Council voted unanimously to approve the tour of South Africa to England in 1970. They also made it clear that 'any team chosen by the South African Cricket Association' would be welcome. No constraints were placed on the racial composition of the South African team. The Council Secretary S. C. 'Billy' Griffith confirmed that they had not consulted the Government regarding this decision, and repeated the mantra that its policy 'was to play and foster the game as widely as possible' [97]. In spite of the massive upheaval that had been caused by the D'Oliveira Affair, it seemed that little had changed or been learned.

The day before, an innocuous looking item had appeared in the 'In Brief' section of the Times [98]. The few lines of news noted that the African Commission of the National League of Young Liberals were threatening to disrupt the tour that the MCC Cricket Council were about to approve. Peter Hain an unknown eighteen-year-old engineering student had submitted this item. His would soon be a name that many in the world of cricket would come to know, and in some cases loathe.

January in Britain was a month in which football, rugby and horse racing rather than cricket dominated the newspapers' sports pages. This was not the case on the other side of the world, where a Test series between Australia and the West Indies was in progress. The young Australians, still led by Bill Lawry, were now about to start the fourth Test match against an ageing West Indies. Many in the West Indies team were now past their best but because they had been iconic names in a winning side for so long it seems the selectors were reluctant to drop them. Results could not lie, and Australia were already 2-1 up in the series and getting stronger. The West Indies were going the other way.

Just after midday on the 21 January the MCC touring party, which itself was facing problems of ageing, finally took off from Heathrow Airport for a short tour of Ceylon (now Sri Lanka) and Pakistan. To some, this seven week hastily arranged tour with three Tests against Pakistan may have seemed a poor substitute for a seventeen week tour of South Africa with a five match Test series against what was then arguably the best team in the world. It is possible that the England Captain Colin Cowdrey had similar feelings since in his autobiography written in 1978 he does not give the tour a single mention [99].

The sixteen chosen for the cancelled South African tour the previous August, had all been invited to take part in its replacement. Unfortunately, almost immediately two of those selected had to withdraw, in both cases for health related reasons. On 7 October, Geoffrey Boycott declined the invitation to tour. In a letter to the selectors he gave a full account of the reasons for this decision. He explained that removal of his spleen during childhood had made him more susceptible to certain types of infection. Wary that the implied issues of hygiene could offend the host countries, the MCC decided to withhold this information. [100].

Two weeks later another key member of the batting line up withdrew. While Boycott's absence was only expected to be short term, the loss of Ken Barrington was a different thing altogether. He had suffered a heart attack during a cricket competition in Australia in mid-October, and although rest and recuperation meant that he was expected to make a full recovery, his international career was over.

Since first being selected for England in 1955, Barrington had been a key part of the batting line-up. He had played 82 Test matches and only Walter Hammond, Colin Cowdrey and Sir Leonard Hutton had scored more than his 6,806 runs. Occasionally criticised for his risk free approach to batting and at times slow scoring, Barrington had once been dropped for taking too long to score a century. Even so, he was often the player around which many of England's matches had been won or saved over the last decade [101]. His ability to take wickets with his part-time leg-spin bowling was an often underestimated bonus. While not in the best of form the previous season, an overseas tour without Barrington in the side would take some getting used to. John Arlott summed it up with the heart felt phrase 'Kind as they have ever come: there were better batters – but not many if they were playing for your life – but sure, none was so liked by so many' [102].

No new batsmen were added to the squad to compensate for the loss of Boycott and Barrington, but Robin Hobbs the Essex leg-spin bowler was called up to strengthen the spin bowling. In addition Colin Milburn, now playing for Western Australia was named as a reserve, should it be needed. The party of fifteen now on their way to Colombo were:

Batsmen
M. C. Cowdrey (Captain) – Batsman, Age 35, 101 Tests
T. W. Graveney (Vice Captain) – Batsman, Age 41, 75 Tests
J. H. Edrich – Opening Batsman, Age 31, 31 Tests
K. W. R. Fletcher – Batsman, Age 24, 1 Test
R. M. Prideaux – Opening Batsman, Age 29, 1 Test

Bowlers
D. J. Brown – Medium/Fast Bowler, Age 26, 19 Tests
R. M. H. Cottam – Medium/Fast Bowler, Age 23, 0 Tests
R. N. S. Hobbs – Leg-Spin Bowler, Age 26, 5 Tests
I. J. Jones – Fast Bowler, Age 26, 15 Tests
P. I. Pocock – Off-Spin Bowler, Age 21, 3 Tests
J. A. Snow – Fast Bowler, Age 26, 18 Tests
D. L. Underwood – Slow/Medium Bowler, Age 23, 8 Tests

All-Rounder
B. L. D'Oliveira – Batsmen/Medium Bowler, Age 37, 16 Tests

Wicketkeepers
A. P. E. Knott – Wicketkeeper, Age 22, 9 Tests
J. T. Murray – Wicketkeeper, Age 33, 21 Tests

In additional to keeping the membership of the tour party as close as possible to that originally selected for South Africa, an early decision was also made to offer the same salaries, expenses and bonuses even though the new tour was much shorter. Each player therefore received the following [103] (£100 equivalent to £1,750 in 2020)

> Salary – £700 plus £25 for each major tour previously completed
> Kit Allowance – £125

Expenses – £1 5s a day (£1 25p)
Bonus – Up to a maximum of £125

Just before the touring party left London both Colin Cowdrey and Leslie Ames talked to the press. Cowdrey was as you would expect positive promising 'entertaining cricket' [104] and hopeful that the team would do well. Ames was less confident, he was concerned whether a side which had been chosen for South Africa would also be suitable for Pakistan. In particular he was worried that the slow pitches would 'take the sting out of fast bowlers' and that with four in the party, and also now without Boycott and Barrington that the side was unbalanced [105]. He understood though that it would have also been unfair to drop half the side just because the destination had changed. Whatever the misgivings and uncertainties, a tour that had already experienced a few twists and turns was finally underway.

Located off the southern coast of India, the island of Ceylon (now Sri Lanka) had long been a popular stopping off point for MCC tours on the demanding journey by ship to Australia for an Ashes series. It provided the players with a chance to experience dry land for a while and play some matches against the cricket loving islanders. Even when the journey switched from travel by ship to aircraft the tradition remained. In the most recent tour to Australia and New Zealand in 1965/66, Mike Smith's side had stopped over to play two one day games in Colombo before flying onto Perth for the start of the main event.

In the 1960s many in the United Kingdom would not have automatically associated Ceylon with the game of cricket. Far more likely the island would be thought of as an exporter of tea or rubber, or as a destination for exotic holidays.

As with many other British colonies, Ceylon had started on the road to independence at the end of the Second World War. While the island's population comprised of at least forty different ethnic groups, two dominated. The Sinhalese accounted for 66% of the population, and the Tamils 20%. Although there had been periods of conflict since colonisation by Britain in 1815, Ceylon's diverse cultures had generally managed to coexist by living separately. Over time the Tamils had migrated to the north and east coast of the island with the Sinhalese dominant in the west, south and south-west [106].

On 4 February 1948, the Dominion of Ceylon was established when *the Ceylon Independence Act 1947* came into force. Ceylon became an independent Member of the British Commonwealth of Nations. This gave the island significant but not total independence from Great Britain. A Governor-General still represented the British Monarch, and agreements on defence, external affairs and the appointment of certain public officials were written into the Independence Act in order to protect Britain's interests. Parliament followed the two tier Westminster model with the House of Representatives (equivalent to a House of Commons) and the Senate (equivalent to the House of Lords). To ensure that Britain still had a say, half of the members of the Senate were appointed by the Governor-General.

The political structure that evolved was from the start dominated by two parties; the right wing United National Party and the left wing Sri Lanka Freedom Party. Initially, and perhaps not surprisingly, both the political parties and the administration were controlled by a small English educated elite. An enclosed society in Colombo (similar to the Westminster bubble), they did not really represent the locally educated Sinhalese and Tamil population. As the locally university educated began to find their voice, then so the political landscape changed.

Discontent between the two main ethnic groups continued to grow, the economy faltered, and the political parties seemed to be trying to pull the country in fundamentally different directions. Even so, at the beginning of 1969 the country was considered to still be a safe place for a tour. Few would have believed that a twenty-six year civil war that would tear the island apart, lay in the future.

Cricket was popular in Ceylon and the visit of an MCC touring side was always a much anticipated event. In spite of the enthusiasm for such visits, the truth was that Ceylon was not a Test playing country, and they were some way off achieving this. Even the most partisan supporters of Ceylonese cricket would have reluctantly admitted, that with a few exceptions, most of their players were at best good club cricketers. It was difficult to know how many were capable of going further, as opportunities for regularly playing teams at a higher level were still hard to come by. Many would have found it difficult to imagine that in just over twenty seven years a Sri Lankan national team would thoroughly beat Australia in the final of the cricket World Cup.

The first side officially representing the MCC visited the island in 1927 at the end a tour of India. The side which was captained by A. E. R. (Arthur) Gilligan (coincidentally he was President of the MCC at the time of the D'Oliveira Affair) played thirty four matches on an arduous four month tour [107]. During their stay in Ceylon the MCC played three two-day games and one three-day match against All Ceylon. The tourists were no second rate side that had been put together for a holiday. The side contained a number of the very best England players of the era such as A. 'Andrew' Sandham, R. E. S. 'Bob' Wyatt and M. W. 'Maurice' Tate.

International teams from England, Australia, India and Pakistan continued to visit the country, usually on their way to or back from an overseas tour. Private clubs such as the State Bank of India, Hyderabad Blues and Pakistan Eagles also became regular visitors, all helping increase the island's experience of playing first-class cricket.

Whether a country's standard of domestic cricket and supporting infrastructure had reached the level necessary for it to be classified as a Test playing nation was a decision that lay solely in the hands of the International Cricket Conference or ICC (known today as the International Cricket Council).

At the beginning of 1969 there were six full Members of the ICC; Australia, England, India, New Zealand, Pakistan and the West Indies. These countries all had a cricket governing body recognised by the ICC and a representative team qualified to play official Test matches. South Africa had withdrawn from the ICC in 1961 when the country became a Republic and left the Commonwealth. In theory international matches between South Africa and full Members of the ICC should then have no longer been classified as Test matches. However, fixtures involving South Africa continued to be designated as Test matches in *Wisden*.

In the ICC meeting held in July 1966 the Maharajah of Baroda, representing India, pointedly observed that 'it appeared South Africa had suffered no loss in cricket prestige through being omitted from membership of the conference' [108]. By 1969 this was still the case. England (and the MCC) certainly expected that the international matches between England and South Africa due to take place in 1970 would be classified as Test matches.

Recognising that there were a number of countries who aspired to Test status but who needed help to achieve this, in 1965 following a suggestion from Pakistan, the ICC had created a class of Membership known as Associate Member. This was for countries whose cricket was organised and governed in an appropriate manner but who had not yet reached the level necessary to play official Test matches. Ceylon, along with Fiji and the USA, became the first countries to be admitted to this new class of membership. Even so, Ceylon were still some way from achieving full membership and therefore Test status. Part of the reason for this was the lack of opportunities for a national side to go on overseas tours, and the reluctance of major Test playing nations to make Ceylon more than just a stopping off point for one or two games.

As well as limited chances to play overseas opposition, Ceylon's domestic cricket structure did not provide its cricketers with much of an opportunity to play regular first-class cricket. By definition, a first-class match was accepted as being 'a match of three or more days' [109] duration between two sides of eleven players officially judged first-class. In 1969, cricket in Ceylon did not meet these criteria.

The domestic cricket season was centred around two competitions. A three tier cricket league, in which the ten teams in Division One competed for the Saravanamutti Trophy, teams in Division Two competed for the Donovan Andree Trophy and those in Division Three the Daily News Trophy. The bigger clubs had a team in each division, and matches were played over two days on Saturday and Sunday.

In addition to the league competition, there was an annual knockout competition usually played in December between the leading clubs on the island. The Robert Senanayake Trophy had three rounds of three-day matches but did not take place in December 1968 as members of the Defence Services team were needed to respond to a general strike by public servants underway in the country [110].

Colin Cowdrey and his colleagues arrived in Colombo on the 22 January. It had been a 21 hour flight, with three refuelling stops and a change of aircraft at Karachi. Though tired, they could not help but be lifted by the warmth of the welcome waiting for them. The captain of Ceylon, Michael Tissera led the reception committee, as the visitors receiving garlands of jasmine flowers with a drum band playing in the background. The hot, humid weather must have already seemed a world away from the grey damp skies they had left behind in London just the day before.

Describing the location as 'idyllic', Tom Graveney later summarized his time in Ceylon as 'played a bit of golf, played a bit of cricket (against players better than most people would credit), did a bit of swimming' [111]. Graveney could afford to be relaxed, after all he had more experience of playing on the subcontinent than most of his colleagues. He had played his first matches in Ceylon in 1952. As a member of an MCC side he had experienced the extremes of the game in his two matches. In the first against a Commonwealth XI he was bowled for 0, and in next against Ceylon he scored 102 not out [112]. For some of his colleagues it was different. For instance, John Snow, the man who was likely to lead the fast bowling attack had not played on the subcontinent before, while another of the bowlers Bob Cottam had never even played outside of England. Bowling long spells in temperatures of over 30°C and 80% humidity on slow pitches would take some getting used to.

The cricket part of the schedule that lay ahead over the next twelve days comprised three one-day matches and a three-day match. The full scorecards of all of these matches can be found on CricketArchive.com [113]. While it was generally accepted that the standard of cricket in Ceylon was improving, MCC were still expected to win all four of these matches with something to spare. The real test would come during the second part of the tour in Pakistan.

Four days after their arrival, MCC began their tour with a one-day match against a Ceylon Board XI at the Colombo Oval. Played under Gillette Cup rules, it was an opportunity for the selectors to assess the fitness and form of the players, in particular the fast bowlers. Normally the opening match of a tour was a relaxed affair, almost like a benefit match, giving the tourists an opportunity to stretch their legs and blow away cobwebs. For the local Ceylonese players it was a different matter altogether. Any match against overseas opposition was a chance to test themselves against higher quality players and maybe catch the attention of overseas clubs. Opportunities to play in league and occasionally county cricket in England were increasingly possible.

Played in front of an enthusiastic crowd of 7,000, the Ceylon Board X1 was led by the experienced and popular M. H. (Michael) Tissera. He had been captain of Ceylon since 1964, and in his first match they had beaten a Pakistan A side. A year later he had led Ceylon to an even more famous victory; beating India in a four-day unofficial Test match in Ahmedabad [114]. Such victories were still rare, but it showed that on their day Ceylon were capable of an upset. The element of surprise was also on their side. When the Ceylon Board XI lined up against the MCC on Saturday 25 January, both the players and what they might be capable of were a complete unknown to most of their opposition.

As the MCC party only contained six batsmen they all played, while Cottam, Jones, Hobbs and Pocock were the first chosen from the seven bowlers to be given the chance to make a claim for a place in the Test matches ahead.

The Ceylon Board XI won the toss and decided to field, possibly to avoid the chance of batting first and being bowled out cheaply, resulting in a short day's cricket for the spectators. For the MCC the innings was satisfactory, with the batsmen using the opportunity first and foremost to get some batting practice, rather than play flamboyant but risky shots in pursuit of a massive score. The match had originally been scheduled as 50 overs per side, but at lunch MCC were 110 for 2 with only eleven overs of their innings left. The tour manager Les Ames agreed to a proposal from Ceylon cricket officials to extend each innings to 60 overs in order to give the spectators a chance to see more of the visiting batsmen in action. Such a unusual decision reflected the friendly atmosphere in which the match was being played. Although some of the batsmen took longer to adapt to the conditions than others, in the end all of the top six batsmen scored runs, and MCC ended their 60 overs on 236 for 6.

The Ceylon Board XI started their innings with care, but the openers Reid (a doctor by profession) and Fernando (a tea taster), quickly grew in confidence and put on 121 for the first wicket. The MCC bowlers looked rusty. Jones, in particular, who was returning after a long absence with injury, looked well below par. The middle order batsmen continued where the openers had left off, with the leg-spinner Hobbs proving expensive. The local side seemed on course for a famous win, when unfortunately after 56 overs the match had to be halted because it was literally just too dark to continue play. At that point, the Ceylon Board XI had scored 234 for 7, and were just 3 runs from victory with three wickets left.

Most of the spectators went home assuming the result of the match to be a draw. However following a meeting between Cowdrey, Tissera, the tour manager Les Ames and the umpires, it was decided that under the regulations agreed at the beginning of the match, the Ceylon Board X1 had won on a faster scoring rate. This was a generous concession by Ames and Cowdrey who had not tried to alter the regulations when the number of overs per side was increased part way through the match.

The remaining two one-day matches against another Ceylon Board XI in Colombo and a Central Province X1 in Kandy, were both won by the MCC but not as impressively as they might have hoped. On the plus side all of the top order batsmen had scored runs and demonstrated that they were adjusting to the pitches, heat and humidity.

For the bowlers, the picture was less straightforward. Hobbs had played in all three of the one-day matches, been expensive in all, and in the last Rajaratnam a local university student had treated his bowling with disdain hitting him for five increasingly big sixes in eight deliveries, on the way to a cavalier 50. In the same match, the experience of a team mate of Rajaratnam illustrated the fine margin that can exist between success and failure. The scorecard records the number four batsman as 'D Amerasinghe Retired Hurt 1'. Playing his first game for a Central Province XI and no doubt eager to impress, he tried to hook a bouncer from Cottam, mistimed the shot and directed the ball into his face. That night he was being operated on as surgeons tried to save the sight in the injured eye. Amerasinghe did not play representative cricket again [115].

Sadly the match against the Central Province XI also marked the end of the career of another player. The form of Jeff Jones had been a worry since the start of the tour. On paper he looked all right with bowling figures of 9-2-0-24 and 10-3-2-30 in the two matches he had played. In practice though, things were far more serious His delivery was laboured and he was well short of the pace and accuracy that would be needed in a Test match. A few days later the news was even worse. He had suffered the reoccurrence of an elbow injury that had kept him out of cricket for most of the previous season. Unable to play any further part in the tour, he was sent home for examination and treatment by a specialist. It soon became clear that the career of this genuinely fast, left-arm bowler who had already taken 44 wickets in 15 Test matches was now in real doubt. At only 27, Jeff Jones would never play cricket for England or his county Glamorgan again [116].

With the three one-day matches out of the way, the MCC returned to Colombo to prepare for a three-day match against an All Ceylon side, their only first-class match on this leg of their tour. Beginning on 30 January, this was the nearest thing Ceylon had to a Test match as that stage in their international cricket development. The MCC were certainly not underestimating the opposition as they fielded what most would have considered to be a full strength Test team. Edrich, Prideaux, Cowdrey, Graveney and Fletcher were the specialist batsmen, D'Oliveira an all-rounder, Knott the wicketkeeper, and a bowling attack of Snow, Brown, Pocock and Underwood.

Although the respected cricket writer Michael Melford believed that there were a number of the Ceylonese players 'who could hold their place in a county side if they so wished' [117], only James Piachaud from the eleven that lined up against the MCC that morning had any county cricket experience. Piachaud had played briefly for Hampshire after graduating from Oxford University. Unfortunately Michael Tissera had to withdraw just before the match began with a knee injury, and so his place as captain was taken by B G (Buddy) Reid. The career of Buddy Reid was typical of the limited opportunities that most Ceylonese had to play first-class cricket at that time. He made his debut for Ceylon against Bob Simpson's Australian side in August 1964 and played his final game in February 1970 against Tony Lewis' MCC team (top scoring for Ceylon in both innings). In the intervening 6 years Reid only played 10 first-class matches. The opportunity to captain his country for the first time on that January day must have been one of the highlights of his career [118].

At the end of the first day on a lifeless pitch, All Ceylon had reached 191 for 5, ground out over 92 overs. It was a day in which the Ceylonese were unwilling to take risks and the slow pitch made wickets hard to come by. Typical of the slow cricket was the innings of Anura Tennekoon who had so far scored 71 runs in 282 minutes, with only three fours.

On day two, 22 year old Tennekoon batted with far more enterprise in front of a capacity crowd of at least 12,000. Within 45 minutes he become the first batsman to make a hundred for Ceylon against the MCC. A tobacco company executive by day, this was the third century of his brief career, the other two having been achieved while still at school. All Ceylon declared on 283 for 9, the highest score Ceylon had so far scored against the MCC. Edrich and Prideaux started the reply cautiously, and at the close of play had reached 143 for the loss of Prideaux who was run out.

On the final day MCC showed their class against what was at times average bowling. Edrich reached his century in almost exactly four hours, and was eventually out for 177, more likely due to a combination of heat and fatigue rather than the skill of the bowler. The highlight of the day though was undoubtedly the innings of Tom Graveney. The 41 year old quickly decided that with the temperature out in the middle in the mid thirties, boundaries were to be much preferred to running between the wickets. He reached his 100 in just over two hours, hitting 13 fours and 2 sixes. His century was greeted by delighted spectators setting off a series of thunder flashes around the ground. With just over an hour and a half play left in the day, Cowdrey declared the innings closed on 406 for 4. In a relaxed final session the match then drifted towards the expected draw, with Reid and Fernando both scoring 50s as the All Ceylon side finished on 118 for 0.

During the three-day match, Les Ames had other things on his mind. Since their arrival in Ceylon, the news from Pakistan had become increasingly more worrying. After ten years of President Ayub Khan's authoritarian rule, the opposition had at last found a voice. Dissatisfaction, which had been smouldering for so long, finally erupted. Civil unrest was growing, with riots and disturbances spreading across both West and East Pakistan. The day before the match against All Ceylon began, the MCC had been advised that the East Pakistan section of the tour scheduled for the 4 to the 14 February was cancelled [119].

The MCC Secretary released a statement to say 'we have advised Les Ames, the manager, to proceed to Karachi on Sunday when the Ceylon part of the tour ends' and that 'the British High Commission advises us that there is no danger to individuals in Karachi' [120]. This seemed to be at odds with the news in the *Times* the day before that six people had been killed in clashes between security forces and demonstrators in Karachi, with fifteen lorry loads of troops needed to restore order and hundreds being arrested [121]. The proposed venues for the three Test matches; Dacca, Lahore and Karachi were also now all subject to a dusk to dawn curfew. The situation was not exactly designed to build the confidence of any of the MCC touring party concerned about their safety.

It was proving extremely difficult for Les Ames to get an accurate picture of the situation in Pakistan. Communication with the Board of Control for Cricket in Pakistan (BCCP) in Lahore and the MCC in London was unreliable due to an on-going strike of overseas telegraph and telex operators, and the telephone was proving a poor means of negotiating changes to the tour schedule. The clear disconnect between the cricket administrators in London and the rapidly changing situation in Pakistan, meant that in practice Ames and Cowdrey were being left in effect on their own to make decisions which could have unforeseen political consequences.

With this increasingly gloomy news about the deteriorating situation in Pakistan, it was not surprising that some of the players were beginning to think that once the three-day match against All Ceylon was over that they should be going home [122].

Nonetheless, on 2 February the MCC flew out of Colombo bound for Karachi. It was still not clear what the cricket schedule would now be in Pakistan, or indeed whether there would be any more cricket at all.

6

Uncertainty
2 February 1969 – 17 February 1969

The MCC tourists arrived in Karachi on the afternoon of the 2 February. The mood among the players was apprehensive. They were now in a country in which law and order was breaking down, to play a series of cricket matches where not even the location of the first one was still yet certain. Keith Fletcher playing his first Test series abroad was later to write 'I doubt whether any cricket tour has ever been as unpleasant as our 1969 visit to Pakistan' [123]. What followed over the next five weeks certainly more than justified such a statement. Perhaps the turbulence and bloodshed that had already occurred in a country with such a short history should have been a warning.

The creation of Pakistan first became a possibility, when on 20 February 1947 the British Government announced its intention to leave British India. In reality the campaign for independence, which had been led by the Indian National Congress, was no longer one, which Britain had either the manpower, money or even willpower to keep suppressing.

The objective was simple enough; to transfer the responsibility for governing this vast area with a population of 400 million back to Indian hands by June 1948. The British could then depart and focus on the many post war problems they had to deal with closer to home. As was the case with other parts of the British Empire it seemed that once the decision had been made to leave that often 'the plan was to catch the first boat home regardless of the consequences in their former colonies' [124].

It was not that simple. By May 1947 Clement Attlee's Government had already concluded that the transfer of power to a single Dominion of India was out of the question. Although 70% of the population was Hindu, the significant Muslim minority no longer believed that they would be protected by a one state solution. The Muslim League, led by the astute Muhammad Ali Jinnah, now wanted nothing less than a separate Muslim state.

The last Viceroy of India, Lord Louis Mountbatten, then increased the pressure by declaring that the date for handover would be bought forward a year. It seemed that everything was being done in undue haste. On the 3 June, Mountbatten made a radio broadcast to the Indian people in which he revealed the decision to partition British India, although he did not mention Pakistan. It was also announced that the final position of the boundary between the two new states would not be disclosed until after the new Dominions of India and Pakistan had formally come into being.

Remarkably, the task of defining the boundaries of the two new Dominions was given to Sir Cyril Radcliffe, a British judge with a sharp legal mind, but with no experience of India. He set foot in the country for the first time on the 8 July. He was to lead two Boundary Commissions, which would decide where the dividing line would be across British India in order to create two new states. The terms of reference were imprecise and statistical population data provided was out of date. In addition, the Indian National Congress had insisted that in return for agreeing to Partition, the highly contentious provinces of Bengal and Punjab were also to be divided. Understandably, Radcliffe had little awareness of the many complex cultural issues that Partition would ignite, and little time to learn about them. He was given a mere five weeks to complete a task, which would have profound and tragic effects for years to come.

British rule in India formally ended on midnight of the 14/15 August 1947 when the Dominions of India and Pakistan were created. However, the actual boundaries between these two new Dominions were not publicly announced until 17 August, a period of uncertainty, which resulted in further rumour, violence, and unnecessary loss of life.

The new Pakistan consisted of two regions; West Pakistan and East Pakistan separated by the massive 3.1 million square kilometres of India. The contentious division of Bengal and the Punjab meant that Calcutta (now Kolkata) remained part of India while Lahore was now part of Pakistan. A further complexity was created when a number of the independent Princely States, most notably Hyderabad and Kashmir, decided not to become part of either India or Pakistan. In the religious, political, cultural and inter-communal mayhem that occurred before, during and after Partition, millions were displaced and millions more lost their lives [125]. The British withdrawal from India produced the bitterest of consequences and scars, which would take generations to heal.

Since its creation in 1947, life for the newly independent Pakistan had certainly not been easy. At times the country seemed to just lurch from crisis to crisis. The first Prime Minister had been assassinated in 1951, and an Islamic Republic declared in 1956. Two years later President Mirza had repealed the constitution and imposed Martial Law, only to be deposed in a coup d'etat led by General Ayub Khan, who then in turn proclaimed himself President. There had been a short disastrous war with India in 1965, and although still in power President Khan's once iron grip was now slipping.

The Pakistan that greeted Cowdrey and his team when they flew into Karachi was a country again on the edge. There had been a temporary lull in the riots and disturbances that had been taking place in many cities, but nobody really knew what would happen next. To try and appease the opposition the Government had lifted the curfew that had been in place in Karachi and Dacca (now Dhaka), although the army presence was still evident on the streets.

The following day, the British High Commissioner in Pakistan, Sir Cyril Pickard wrote a letter to the Foreign and Commonwealth Office in London in which he tried to make sense of the current situation following the latest radio broadcast by President Ayub Khan [126]. Amendments to the Constitution, a handover of power to a fragmented opposition or even the reinstatement of Martial Law were all still possibilities. The Government though was in a belligerent mood, with reports that troops had been given orders to shoot on sight during the previous week when five major cities had been under curfew [127].

In addition to all of the local problems, the British High Commission also had the visit of the MCC to deal with. There was real concern about the safety of British High Commission offices in East Pakistan following cancellation of matches in that part of the country. The situation in West Pakistan was not a great deal better, and by 12 February, Pickard was communicating with London about contingency plans in the event 'of large scale disturbances in Pakistan which will effect our administration, staffing and safety in various ways' [128]. Even allowing for the use of normal diplomatic language, things did not look good.

By the time the MCC arrived in Pakistan, there had already been many conversations between Les Ames, Colin Cowdrey and representatives of the British High Commission. It is not clear how aware Ames and Cowdrey, or the MCC back at Lord's, really were of the deteriorating situation in the country. No record of any of the conversations between the MCC and the British High Commission at the time now remains in the Foreign and Commonwealth Office files stored in the National Archives.

The importance of the upcoming series to people in Pakistan was not to be underestimated. This was only the second time MCC had visited the country to play an official Test series (the previous visit had been led by Ted Dexter in 1961/62). Like much else in the country's short history, in comparison to its neighbour the path to Test status had not been easy.

India had become a Test playing country in 1926 following election as a Full-Member of what was then the Imperial Cricket Conference (ICC). Following Partition in 1947 there clearly needed to be some adjustment to the membership of the ICC to take account of political changes that had occurred. It might have seemed that the way forward was clear; the redefined India would remain a Full-Member of the ICC while the newly created Pakistan would be given equivalent status as quickly as possible. Little in this region was straightforward, and ICC membership was no exception.

The Annual Meeting of the ICC in July 1948 decided that the membership status of the 'new' India would be changed from Full to Provisional for two years. This would allow time for decisions on the country's membership of the Commonwealth of Nations to be made. During this period India continued to have Test status. Two years later, in 1950, the Conference agreed that since Partition 'had not materially affected the standard of play of representative teams selected by the Indian board ... there was no longer any reason for withholding the privilege of Full membership' [129].

For Pakistan, things were different. In 1948 the country had no governing structure for the sport, no Test match grounds, no recognised domestic first-class cricket competition and very few grass wickets. Matting wickets were widely used In Pakistan until the early 1960s, and their use hindered the ability of Pakistani players to adapt to pitches on overseas tours. As one observer of Pakistan cricket concluded, 'After Partition, Pakistan cricketers found themselves members of a third-class cricketing nation' [130].

The first years were indeed tough. The Board of Control for Cricket of Pakistan (BCCP) was formed on 1 May 1948 in the pavilion of Lahore Gymkhana Cricket Ground. The Board consisted of a President (Nawab Iftikhar Hussain Khan), three Vice Presidents chosen from the provinces to try and ensure broad representation, a treasurer and secretary. All worked on a honorary basis. They had little choice, the Board had no permanent home, few resources, and no money. The office was kept in a tin trunk, which was usually found at the home of the Board's Secretary [131]. The first task was quite simply to keep cricket in Pakistan alive. They needed to persuade Pakistani cricketers to keep playing, assemble a national team and achieve Test status as quickly as possible. This was quite a challenge for such a small group. Keeping morale high, when their Indian neighbours had just finished playing a Test series in Australia and would be beginning a home series against the West Indies at the end of the year, must have also been extremely difficult.

Difficult was also a word, which could be used to describe Pakistan's efforts to be admitted as a Member of the ICC. By mid 1950, with the knowledge that India would shortly revert back to being a Full Member, many in Pakistan were becoming increasingly frustrated as it seemed that their application for membership was going nowhere. Even the *Times,* a newspaper more usually considered a supporter of the establishment, published an article in its main news section that openly criticised the MCC. The newspaper's correspondent in Karachi suggested there 'had been few signs of willingness to help Pakistan to secure election' and that 'several reasons for delay have been advanced, on technical and procedural grounds, and these have often been couched in terms which could certainly have been more happily phrased' [132]. Such was the prominence of this article, the MCC found itself in the rare position of having to issue a statement to defend itself.

Things did not get any easier over the next two years with claim and counter claim over why the process was taking so long. Finally, by the beginning of 1952 it looked as though Pakistan would be formally proposed for membership at the ICC meeting in June. Passions were still running high though, as in February the captain of the Pakistan Cricket Team wrote a letter to the *Times* which confidently stated that the standard of Pakistan cricket was now such that its 'right to membership of the I.C.C. cannot be challenged'. The letter defiantly concluded that 'Some had birth right to the membership: we have won it' [133]. Finally on the 28 July 1952, Pakistan was admitted as a Full Member of the ICC. They began their life as a Test playing country at the beginning of October that year, when a national team led by Abdul Kardar arrived in Amritsar for a series of matches which included five Tests against India.

Since that first Test match in 1952, Pakistan had played 53 Tests by the time they met England in 1969. Like most international sides, their record when playing at home was better than when playing overseas. Of the 22 Test matches they had played at home, only 4 had been lost.

MCC had first visited Pakistan to play Test cricket in 1961/62. In a long and arduous tour of India, Pakistan and Ceylon lasting over four months, the tourists led by Ted Dexter had played 24 matches. A five Test series against India had been lost 2-0 and a three Test series against Pakistan won 1-0. Played in front of huge crowds, the Test matches had too often been disappointing. Resulting in attritional cricket with defensive bowling, containing field placings and batsman focused on occupying the crease. Leslie Smith writing in *The Cricketer* probably reflected the views of many in subtitling his review '*Reflections on a Dismal Tour*' [134].

Pakistan had been well beaten by England in a three Test series when they had last visited the country in 1967. England expected the forthcoming return series in Pakistan to be a lot tougher.

Talk of the Test series was still premature since Ames and Cowdrey in somewhat unreliable communication with MCC officials back at Lord's, had yet to decide whether the tour would even continue. On disembarking the aircraft at Karachi, Cowdrey and Ames spent four hours with the Secretary of the Board of Control for Cricket of Pakistan (BCCP), the Deputy British High Commissioner and the military adviser to the British High Commission trying to agree on a schedule of matches that could be played in locations considered safe. Both sides were under pressure. The Secretary of the BCCP would not have been keen on reporting failure to his superior, a personal adviser to President Ayub Khan. While from the MCC perspective Cowdrey and Ames were well aware how unsettled the players were becoming as negotiations struggled on.

Finally after around another ten hours of face-to-face talks, and numerous telephone conversations, agreement was reached on a revised itinerary for the rest of the tour. There were still unknowns about the quality of accommodation, travel options and pitch conditions at some of the venues, but it seemed this was the best that Ames and Cowdrey could hope for. The players might have been unhappy, but they were really not in a position to complain too loudly. After all they were being paid the fee they would have received for a four-month tour of South Africa for just seven weeks away. The correspondent of the *Daily Telegraph* suggested that in the end 'pressure put on them from a high level decided captain and manager ... that the proper course was to go' [135].

The plan now was for the MCC to play three warm up matches before the first Test, due to start in Lahore on 21 February. With the Test match in Dacca cancelled for security reasons, only two Test matches rather than three would now be played, with the second now scheduled for Karachi. Whether everything would hold together was of course open to question, there was not a great deal of optimism around.

The changes meant that the first two three-day matches would now be played back to back, Bahawalpur followed by Lyallpur (now

Faisalabad). Six days of continuous cricket, and some arduous travel might not have seemed the best way of preparing for a Test match. However, the thinking was that this would at least provide practice against top quality opposition and since the MCC now planned to make Lahore their base for the eleven days before the Test match (during which they would play a three day match in Sahiwal), there would be plenty of time to prepare for the Test.

It was not just the visitors that needed match practice. While most of the Pakistani players who would line up against England in the forthcoming series still played for domestic teams, it had already been two months since the local first-class competition the Qaid-I-Azam Trophy had ended, and nearly four years since Pakistan had played a Test match at home. The team would also have a new leader, the selectors having already announced that Saeed Ahmed would replace Hanif Mohammad as captain against England. A controversial decision which had already been hotly debated in the press.

The MCC party finally left Karachi on the afternoon of 4 February for Bahawalpur. Graveney and D'Oliveira stayed behind to practice, expecting to join their colleagues in Lyallpur later in the week. The reason was simply to provide seats on the aircraft, so that at least two of the British press could get to the match. Yet another indication of the somewhat surreal conditions that were beginning to define this tour.

The three warm-up matches that were now scheduled before the first Test were intended to give the players a chance to adapt to playing on cricket pitches so different to those they were used to back in England. Most Pakistani cricket wickets were devoid of grass, slow with little bounce and designed to last at least five days without breaking up. This meant that fast bowlers offered little threat once the first few overs had been bowled and the shine had disappeared from the ball. Medium pace bowlers were unable to get the ball to swing, and spin bowlers could rarely rely on footmarks or deteriorating pitch conditions for help. The challenge quite simply would be for England to bowl Pakistan out twice.

The first of the warm up matches was played at the Bahawal Stadium, 800 km from Karachi in south-eastern Punjab. The stadium has the honour of being the location where in January 1955 Hanif Mohammad scored the first century by any Pakistani in a Test match. Sadly the match against India was the only time the stadium had hosted a Test, and since 2003 even lost its first-class status.

The Board of Control XI was captained by Mushtaq Mohammad. He was well known to most of the MCC players having played county cricket for Northants since 1966. Cowdrey of course captained the MCC for this opening fixture. Since Graveney and D'Oliveira were still in Karachi, Alan Knott was promoted to open the batting with Prideaux, with Edrich dropping down to the middle order. The MCC line up was therefore Prideaux. Knott, Fletcher, Cowdrey, Edrich, Murray, Underwood, Pocock, Snow, Cottam and Hobbs. Of these only the reserve wicket keeper Murray (the one player in the squad to have toured Pakistan with MCC in 1961/62) would not be under consideration for the first Test match, unless of course Knott was injured.

On the first morning when both captains inspected the pitch, they found as expected a playing surface devoid of grass, one which would favour the batsmen on either side. Taking wickets was going to be a struggle on a surface offering little assistance to pace bowlers and spin bowlers alike. Artificial declarations were required from both sides in order to try and achieve a result. On the final day the Board of Control XI declared their second innings on 173 – 8, setting the MCC an unlikely target of 218 in 150 minutes to win the match. Going for the runs was never an option for the tourists; their sole objective was not to lose. Although with 15 overs left in the day's play, the MCC had struggled to 83 – 4, defeat would have required a dramatic collapse. This was never likely and the match ended in a tame draw. Knott, Fletcher and Edrich got some runs but all found it difficult to score quickly on such a slow pitch. As far as the bowling was concerned, the fast bowlers soon learnt how difficult it was going to be to take wickets, while Underwood's 6 – 40 in the Control XI's second innings showed he was not just a bowler for English pitches. Overall though, there were no great surprises. The MCC looked like a team who had not played competitive cricket for a while. There was room for improvement, particularly in their fast bowling, fielding and running between wickets.

While the players were trying to focus on cricket, away from the hinterland of Bahawalpur the political landscape was still far from certain. In Karachi, the President has tried to placate his opponents by offering to lift the general state of emergency, which had been in force since 1965. One of his most high profile opponents, Zulifikar Ali Bhutto, currently being held in a Lahore prison responded by threatening to go on hunger strike unless the general emergency was not lifted within a week. Another significant part of the disconnected opposition were the country's university students. These would soon become an important factor in deciding whether the Test matches would take place. For the moment their leaders were demanding that all their requests were met before they would take part in talks with the President, also threatening to turn against other sections of the opposition if any compromises were agreed. It seemed that things were beginning to heat up again [136].

With the match at Bahawalpur over, the players had no time to rest, analyse their performance or think about the implication of any injuries. Once changed they boarded a coach for a precarious, dusty 70 mile drive to Multan where they stayed overnight. They were up at 5.30 the following morning in order to take a two hour charter flight to Lyallpur to begin a three-day match against Central Zone. Arriving less than hour before play was due to start, this was not exactly ideal preparation for a Test match.

Central Zone was led by the new national captain Saeed Ahmed, and included at least four players who almost certainly would be in Pakistan's side for the first Test. For the MCC, Graveney, D'Oliveira and Brown came into the side in place of Edrich, Hobbs and Underwood. This ensured that all members of the squad would have played at least one match before the final warm up fixture.

The match did not start well. MCC arrived late, lost the toss and were asked to bowl first. Expecting a long day in the field, they would have been more than satisfied after half an hour when the scoreboard showed 16-2. Bowling with good pace and accuracy, Snow had removed Central Zone's two most experienced players Hanif and Saeed. At the end of a shortened day in which only 62 overs were possible, the hosts had struggled to 168 – 7. MCC had fielded well, taken four good catches and D'Oliveira who had been bought up playing on matting wickets, had taken 3 for 9.

The only cloud on the horizon was the persistent rumour that the itinerary would again be changed. The *Sunday Times* was reporting that Les Ames had received repeated requests from the BCCP to add a Test match in Dacca to the schedule, along with a telegram from Lord's saying that 'the decision was his, but it was hoped that he would co-operate with the Pakistan authorities if he felt able to do so' [137]. With no reliable information on how safe Dacca now was, this only added to the view among many of the players that this was neither the time nor place to be playing cricket.

The second day against Central Zone, clearly marked this out as D'Oliveira's match. After another 24 overs, the hosts declared at 198 – 7. In reply MCC, scoring more quickly than their opponents reached 198 – 6 before Cowdrey declared., leaving Central Zone on 17 – 0 at the end of the day. Cowdrey and Graveney both scored some runs with the later looking the more comfortable of the two, but the stand out performance of the day was a 102 by D'Oliveira. Growing in confidence as his innings progressed, his form with both bat and ball was a good omen for the forthcoming Test. This was the second century D'Oliveira had scored at Lyallpur. The previous had been as a member of a Commonwealth X1 in November 1963. At that time he had just finished the English season top of the batting averages in the Lancashire League, after a fourth year playing for Middleton. Since then it had been a truly amazing journey.

The day also produced another instalment in the ever changing tour schedule saga when Les Ames released a statement explaining why, despite the rumours, the team would not be going to East Pakistan. News of riots outside the British High Commission in Dacca because of MCC's alleged refusal to play there, had pushed Ames and Cowdrey into the unenviable position of having to make cricket decisions which had political consequences.

The match against Central Zone petered out to a predictable and tame draw on the final day. Central Zone batted slowly and for too long before Saeed declared their second innings closed at 170 – 8. Hanif had pleased his supporters in the crowd by scoring 50, but it had been taken far too long, 154 minutes. From MCC's point of view Cottam's 5 – 35 showed that the young Hampshire pace bowler was learning to bowl on slower unhelpful pitches. Set an improbable target of scoring 171 runs in 100 minutes, MCC never realistically considered going for it, and in the end dawdled to 61 – 0 by the close of play.

The most interesting event of a slow day was almost certainly the crowd trouble that erupted when the police escorted a young autograph hunter off the field. Angry spectators turned on the police, who caused play to be stopped when they had to take shelter in front of the bowler's sightscreen. Leaving for Lahore that night, Cowdrey and his team could now look forward to four days rest and recuperation before beginning their final warm-up game on 11 February.

The inland tour had been an arduous ten days. Travelling in coaches on dusty, and at times hazardous roads; staying in government or factory Rest Houses with limited resources which were often fully stretched; and eating food of variable quality. None the less, the players bravely accepted that this was part of the overseas tour experience; an attitude to be admired. At times they must have felt as though the administration at Lord's was detached from their everyday struggles and unable to resolve even the simplest problems. For most it was unlike anything they had ever experienced in their cricket career. Importantly in rural Punjab they had been safe. This was a relatively trouble free part of the country, where Ayub Khan still had some support.

Now in the regional capital Lahore, the tourists had the benefit of staying in an international hotel, the use of good quality practice facilities but were more conscious of the worsening political situation.

Two days after the MCC's arrival in the city the police had fought a four-hour battle with a crowd of about 5,000 students, and the following day anti-Government protesters had burnt down the showrooms of the Oxford University Press for no other reason than they were the publishers of the President's autobiography. On the 14 February, the day before their last warm up game, there was a national strike in both East and West Pakistan. The front windows of the team's hotel were boarded up, armed security guards posted outside, and the players kept in the hotel, in order to ensure they did not unwittingly get caught up in any of the street protests.

Uncertainty

The final warm-up game in Sahiwal, a 100 miles from Lahore started on 15 February. The West Pakistan Governor's XI was captained by Intikhab Alam. Remarkably for a player of such obvious talent he was still playing league cricket, having just completed another season for West of Scotland in the Western Union League. He had though agreed to join Surrey for the 1969 season and would quickly become a key player and crowd favourite, playing for them until 1981 (as an International he played in 47 Test matches for Pakistan, 17 of these as captain). Also in the opposition line-up was Asif Iqbal, a county colleague of Cowdrey, Knott and Underwood. Two others who would soon become familiar to spectators back in Britain were Safraz Nawaz a 20 year old medium-fast bowler from Punjab University who had made an immediate impression on Roger Prideaux during MCC's net practice and would soon join Northamptonshire; and Zaheer Abbas who would later join Gloucestershire and go on to be one of Pakistan's best batsmen of the 1970s and early 1980s.

The MCC fielded the eleven they expected to start in the first Test. The luxury coach that arrived in the morning to take the players on the two hour drive to Sahiwal looked as though it had been most recently used for transporting livestock rather than people. Ames had to do some fast negotiating to find cars to take the players to the ground instead. The coach/cattle truck was used to take the team's luggage.

The match itself turned out to be a wash out in both senses. For the third time in a row Cowdrey lost the toss and was asked to field first. Heavy rain then ended play after only one session with the Governor's XI having scored 87-1. The highlight in what little play was possible, was an attractive 39 not out by Asif. Hitting both Underwood and Pocock for three boundaries just before lunch whetted the appetite for what might come later. Sadly that was not only the end of play for the day, but for the entire match. Further rain overnight and again the following morning turned the ground into a quagmire and by mid afternoon with little hope of any play even on the final day, the match was abandoned.

Unfortunately, the question of playing a Test match in Dacca just would not go away. The politics between East and West Pakistan had escalated to the point where the East Pakistan Federation were threatening to call for the rest of the tour to be cancelled unless a Test match in Dacca was reinstated. Finally Les Ames received a formal request from the BCCP to switch the second Test match from Karachi to Dacca. Given the difficulty of talking with the different parties involved, it was decided that representatives of the BCCP, MCC and British High Commission would meet as quickly as possible to try and agree yet another itinerary. Ames insisted that the President of the BCCP be present this time, so that decisions would not need to be passed on for final approval.

The meeting took place on 17 February in Rawalpindi. Those present were Ames, Cowdrey and the team's vice-captain Tom Graveney representing the MCC, Fida Hassan, President of the BCCP, the President of the Karachi Cricket Association and the Deputy British High Commissioner. Graveney was still adamant that the players did not want to go to Dacca, but the decision had become a blatantly political one now [138]. After a 90 minute long meeting it was agreed that in the time the MCC had left in Pakistan that they would now play only three more matches, all four day Tests. The first beginning in Lahore on 21 February, the second in Dacca on the 28 and the final in Karachi on 6 March.

International Cricket Conference rules made it clear that the duration of a Test match was a matter for negotiation between the two countries concerned. The only limitation being that total playing hours should not exceed 30. Test matches normally took place over 5 days, with 6 hours play each day. This time each Test match was restricted to four days, at the insistence of the President. He was aware that the longer the match the more difficult it would be to maintain law and order. Although there was a curfew in place in Dacca, Ames had been assured that their players would have police protection, with the army within reach if needed [139].

Establishing any form of reliable communication between Pakistan and the United Kingdom was very difficult. A telegram from Griffith to Ames on 17 February in which he said 'Your message received via Foreign Office. Fully approve suggested amendments to itinerary. Please notify revised dates when known' [140] showed that those back at Lord's were essentially reduced to watching developments from the side-lines. Yet again, the players must have felt isolated with little or no control over everyday events.

Uncertainty

Returning to Lahore late on 17 February, Cowdrey had two issues in front of him. The first was to persuade the players that Dacca was in fact now a safe place to play cricket. The second and more immediate problem was to get the team into the right frame of mind to begin playing a Test match in just three days time.

7

Pakistan v England
First Test Match
Lahore Stadium
21 – 24 February 1969

It had been nearly four years since Pakistan last played a Test match in Lahore. Therefore speculation of who might be playing and how they might perform should have been intense. These were no ordinary times. The question for most was not who would be playing but whether the Test match would be played at all.

Whatever assurances about safety Cowdrey might have given the players on his return from Rawalpindi, the reality was that the political landscape was changing fast. It was unpredictable, and the Government's grip on power was failing. In an attempt to regain control, President Khan had released opposition leaders from jail. These included Zulfikar Ali Bhutto, then arguably the most popular politician in West Pakistan. The leader of the recently formed pro-Chinese Pakistan Peoples' Party had been greeted by hundreds of thousands of supporters as he made his way to Karachi following release from detention. In East Pakistan, Sheikh Mujibur Rahman the leader of the National Awami Party had also been released from jail. He was on trial for allegedly plotting the creation of an independent East Pakistan.

President Khan offered to hold talks with the different opposition factions but these had been refused by the most powerful leaders, including Bhutto and Rahman. Each seemed to have different objectives and personal agendas.

There was still a curfew in many cities, including Dacca, and rioters were still being shot for breaking it. On the 19 February, an increasingly desperate President who seemed to be having constant changes of mind, met with the leaders of the three armed forces and asked them to impose martial law in all cities in East and West Pakistan [141]. They refused, and the following day even the pro-Government *Pakistan Times* was calling for a new Government of national unity, which included moderate opposition leaders [142]. It seemed inevitable that fundamental change was not far away, but it was not clear whether such a change would be peaceful. The question for Ames was, would it still be possible or indeed wise to play cricket in such an environment.

The England players were living in a protected bubble, unable to keep up with political developments locally, and with little knowledge of how the tour was being received back home. Instant communication that is now taken for granted was still a thing of the future. English newspapers arrived in Pakistan at least a day after publication and international telephone calls were unreliable and expensive.

Cricket supporters in England had the same problem in reverse. Floods and snow were causing havoc in many parts of the country in late February, and so news of England's progress in Pakistan may not have been a matter of urgency for everybody. Those who were keen to know relied almost entirely on newspaper reports for match information. Live television broadcasts were not possible and for this series there were no plans to show the highlights of each Test. Radio did not provide much more, limiting its coverage to match updates in some news bulletins, and a longer review as part of a 15 minute cricket segment on the BBC Radio 3's Saturday Sports programme.

Newspaper coverage of MCC's progress in Pakistan was competing with another Test series on the other side of the world. As England were preparing for their first Test, Bill Lawry's young Australian side were completing a comprehensive series victory against the West Indies. While Colin Cowdrey was meeting with his players following the agreement to now play in Dacca, at the Sydney Cricket Ground Doug Walters was becoming the first Australian to score a double century and century in the same Test match. Time had finally caught up with a number of the West Indies who had been fixtures in the side for so long. For household names, such as Wes Hall and Charlie Griffith this series would be their last. By common agreement (there were no Test rankings at that time), the West Indies were no longer the best cricket side in the world. That honour would now reside with Australia, England or South Africa. This though was for the future, the immediate problem for England was to choose a side to beat Pakistan.

When the England selectors (Cowdrey, Graveney, Ames and Edrich) came to name the team for the first Test, they had little recent form to help them. None of the touring party had played more than 100 minutes of competitive cricket during the last 11 days [143]. With the schedule for a number of the pre-match net sessions also having to be rearranged because of disputes over which side could use them first, this was not exactly the best preparation for a Test match.

The selectors had fourteen players to choose from, but in reality this was only thirteen, as with Knott fit, Murray the reserve wicket keeper was no longer needed. The final twelve selected for the first Test were Colin Cowdrey (captain), Roger Prideaux, John Edrich, Keith Fletcher, Tom Graveney, Basil D'Oliveira, Alan Knott, Pat Pocock, Derek Underwood, Bob Cottam, David Brown and John Snow. The leg-spin bowler Robin Hobbs was left out. Although a leg-spinner would normally be the type of bowler most likely to cause problems on the batsman friendly wicket expected in Lahore, Hobbs had only played in the first warm up match, been harshly treated by some of the Pakistan batsmen and suffered an injury. The selectors probably decided that he was too big a risk, at least for the first Test. The press was also reporting that whether Snow played or not, would depend on overcoming an injury he had sustained [144]. This was not quite true, but Ames and Cowdrey probably felt that the wider world did not need to know the real reason at this stage. There had already been enough controversy on the tour.

The Pakistan selectors also had some challenges in naming a team for the first Test. It had been eighteen months since the hosts had last played

Test cricket, so there was little information on players' current form. Not surprisingly they relied on the core of the side that had played England at the Oval in August 1967.

Domestic cricket in Pakistan was not a great help in choosing players for the Test team. It did not yet have the depth of the County Championship in England and was focused around a knockout competition, the Quaid-E-Azam Trophy Tournament. In 1968 twelve teams had competed for the Trophy, with all matches played over 4 days except for the final, which was 5. The final of the Tournament which had been played at the beginning of December, was again contested by the two most powerful teams in the country; Karachi and Lahore. On this occasion the weather intervened and Lahore won on first innings performance [145].

Pakistan had a new captain Saeed Ahmed, but it would have been almost unthinkable in the current climate for the outgoing captain Hanif Mohammad not to be picked. Although he was now 34 the player nick named 'the little master' had been an almost automatic choice since his debut against India in 1952. As captain of Karachi it would have been a brave selection decision indeed to leave him out.

The eleven named for the first Test were Mohammad Ilyas, Aftab Gul, Saeed Ahmed, Mushtaq Mohammad, Asif Iqbal, Hanif Mohammad, Majid Khan, Shafqat Rana, Intikhab Alam, Wasim Bari and Asif Masood. All but two of those chosen had played for either Lahore or Karachi during the previous season. Three had also played in the county championship during the English summer (Mushtaq Mohammad, Asif Iqbal and Majid Khan) while Intikhab Alam was about to join Surrey.

On paper the team had a very strong batting line-up, with Majid batting at number 7. Above him there was a mixture of those with a reputation for attacking batting such as Iqbal and Mushtaq, and those with a more traditional style such as Hanif. One surprising name in the side was Aftab Gul. The 23 year old was captain of Lahore, but did not yet have a batting record, which would have automatically warranted selection for the national team. Aftab though, was also an influential student leader and Member of the powerful Student Action Committee. He was currently on bail for his activities as a student organiser for the Pakistan Peoples' Party. Reflecting the increasingly surreal environment in which the tour was taking place, it was rumoured that he had been chosen not just on cricket ability but also to ensure that local student activists did not disrupt the match. The truth was that his batting average the previous season had been better than all the others who were candidates to open the batting for Pakistan [146].

The bowling attack could have been summarised as weak in seam but strong in spin. The seam bowling duties would be shared between Asif Masood and Asif Iqbal or Majid Khan. This would be the 23 year old Masood's first Test, and although a promising right hand medium, rather than fast bowler, he was inexperienced at this level. Iqbal and Majid were both high quality cricketers, useful seam bowlers at first-class level but not at the standard normally required to open the bowling in a Test match.

The spin bowling options were more promising. In Intikhab they had one of the best leg-spin bowlers in international cricket at that time. He would be supported by the leg-spin of Mushtaq and off-spin of Saeed.

This was a strong team, which England would do well to bowl out twice in four days. A draw seemed to be the almost inevitable result. Michael Melford, reporting for the *Daily Telegraph* summed it up perfectly when he wrote 'Any suggestion that the match might be other than a draw, is met with hearty laughter from local cricketers' [147].

Day 1 – Friday 21 February

Constructed in 1959, the Lahore Stadium (renovated in 1996 it is now known as the Gaddafi Stadium) had a Jekyll and Hyde personality. Outside, the red brick facade with its multiple arches projected an air of colonial elegance, on the inside though, it was basic, bare and concrete. For the wealthier spectators there was a small amount of individual covered seating, but for the majority it was tiered concrete benches in uncovered sections. Viewed from the playing area these stands looked like unfinished terraced houses without a rear wall or roof. Disconcertingly for the players, there was little to stop spectators coming onto the field, just some rather frail looking low wire fencing.

The stadium had an official capacity of 60,000 but on the 21 February 1969 things were different. Only around 10,000 were present to see the start of the match, more worrying not all were there just to watch the cricket.

Government restrictions had for some time banned demonstrations, meetings and assemblies of more than four people. There was nothing to stop agitators attending a cricket match!

The day began with England deciding not to play three seam bowlers and relegating John Snow to twelfth man. The responsibility for opening the bowling would now be shared by David Brown and Bob Cottam. It could be argued that Cottam deserved his chance in recognition of the progress he had made in the warm up matches, but preferring Brown to Snow was far more debatable. A year before, Snow had been England's outstanding bowler in the Caribbean, and so far in Pakistan he had played in all three warm up matches taking 5 wickets while Brown had yet to claim his first.

In his autobiography Snow suggests that his omission may not have been for cricketing reasons, but have had more to do with ignoring a request from his captain to bowl off his long run in the final net practice. Snow argued that he did not believe he had anything to gain bowling flat out immediately after days of inactivity, and was only risking injury [148]. Neither Colin Cowdrey or Tom Graveney were impressed by the attitude of their temperamental fast bowler, and so he was left out of the Test side. This was not the first time that Snow had clashed with authority during his career, and it would not be the last. Even so, John Augustine Snow, the son of a vicar and a published poet, is considered to have been one of England's most potent post-war fast bowlers.

The two captains went through the pre-match preliminaries, most importantly the traditional toss of the coin. Cowdrey correctly called 'heads' and elected to bat first. Having packed their team with batsmen and all-rounders, Pakistan's chance of winning the match was severely dented when they lost the toss.

Finally, after all the uncertainty, accompanied by excited cheering and applause from the partisan crowd, the umpires walked onto the field. Shujauddin Siddiqi and Munawar Hussain were followed by the fielding side led out by Saeed Ahmed for the first time, and then England's two opening batsmen John Edrich and Roger Prideaux – the first Test between Pakistan and England was finally underway.

Edrich and Prideaux began by facing Asif Masood and Asif Iqbal. In his first Test, Masood was perhaps too keen to impress and bowled erratically, while at the other end Iqbal and then Majid Khan were tidy without being threatening. Neither were regular bowlers for their English counties, and so it was somewhat strange to be given the responsibility of sharing the new ball in a Test match.

Prideaux, playing in only his second Test, had started confidently but became increasingly uncomfortable before giving the erratic Masood his first Test wicket. He had scored just 9 runs in 75 minutes. Cowdrey playing his 101st Test match joined Edrich at the wicket.

When Intikhab Alam came on to bowl the complexion of the match changed. The high class leg-spinner created problems almost immediately for both batsmen. The scoring slowed, and the restless crowd began to show their disapproval with a slow handclap. It was a struggle, but by lunch England had reached 79 for 1. Edrich, although not in great form, had as usual proved tenacious, and fought his way with at times an unsettling mixture of aggression and defence to another Test 50.

At lunch, the first real signs of crowd trouble occurred when thousands ran onto the field, many across the wicket itself, without any intervention from the police. Some were aiming to find seats in the more expensive stands, while others seemed just intent on causing trouble. Aftab Gul, in his role as local student leader rather than Pakistan batsman, tried to pacify the crowd and persuade them to leave the field. Even so, the start of play after lunch was delayed, and when the England batsmen finally appeared they were accompanied to the wicket surrounded by several hundred spectators.

In the afternoon session the distractions increased, with the crowd becoming more unruly and spectators now fighting amongst themselves. Incredibly, Cowdrey continued on, apparently undisturbed by it all, seeming to keep his concentration against what was mainly a spin bowling attack, while his partners came and went. Edrich was first out playing an over ambitious shot at Intikhab and being caught at mid-on. Cowdrey was then lucky to survive two chances, both off Intikhab. First he edged the ball to slips and Majid just failed to hold a difficult chance, and then shortly afterwards he misjudged a delivery and again gave a chance to slip which Hanif failed to hold. Graveney's innings was brief, before he too fell to Intikhab. Keith Fletcher another in only his second Test, struggled but he and Cowdrey reached the tea interval with England at 171 for 3.

The crowd was becoming more boisterous, and Cowdrey and Fletcher had to force themselves through a throng of students in order to get to the wicket after tea. There seemed to be almost nobody controlling the behaviour of the crowd. Against this increasingly difficult background Fletcher continued to struggle before rather unluckily being given out caught at forward short-leg off the bowling of Saeed for 20. At that stage with the score on 182 for 4, England was in some trouble.

Cowdrey though continued serenely on, showing confidence against fast and slow bowling alike, before almost inevitably reaching his twenty second Test century with a majestic pull shot off Majid which raced to the boundary. While technically not one of his best hundreds, he surely could not have scored one in more challenging circumstances. One ball later he was out, caught behind off a rising delivery, which surprised him.

At this stage things really started to disintegrate. As Cowdrey walked off the field, students started breaking up chairs and throwing them at each other. On reaching the boundary, Cowdrey decided play was impossible in such conditions and gestured to Basil D'Oliveira to also leave the field. Aftab, again in the capacity of peacemaker raced across to plead with D'Oliveira to stay, while he calmed the crowd down. Eventually Alan Knott joined D'Oliveira and remarkably play continued; Knott busy and nimble footed and D'Oliveira confident and aggressive. The pair played on for a further twenty minutes, before to the relief of many in the England camp bad light brought the day to a close. England had reached a respectable but by no means match winning 226 for 5. The players left the field protected by a corridor of police reinforcements which had belatedly arrived, while the crowd had already swarmed onto the field. In an interview at the end of the day Cowdrey in something of an understatement admitted he had found it hard to apply himself but 'yet in a curious way I enjoyed it' [149].

He was to make a similar statement five years later when he unexpectedly found himself again batting at number three for England. This time he was playing against Australia on the fastest pitch in the world in Perth. Facing a barrage of bouncers from Dennis Lillee and Jeff Thomson, then two of the most hostile bowlers in international cricket, he showed that even at 41 he had the technique and temperament to deal with the situation. At one stage he walked down the pitch to his beleaguered batting partner David Lloyd and said 'This is rather fun, old chap, isn't it?' [150].

Les Ames was certainly not having fun. The MCC tour Manager was appalled by the lack of security at the ground, and the ability of the crowd to seemingly do whatever they pleased. Normally calm and dignified when trying to resolve even the most difficult situation, and there had been many on the tour so far, this time his patience had run out. Quite simply, Ames had warned the Lahore Commissioner 'Unless you bring the crowd under control, I shall instruct my team to withdraw from the match' [151].

As if that were not enough drama for one day, that afternoon President Ayub Khan had announced his decision not to run in the following year's Presidential elections, and to reintroduce a parliamentary system. Even though following the announcement, thousands came onto the streets claiming 'Revolution has won' [152], this was not really an end to trouble in the country. Ames and his players must have already been wondering how this would affect the weak assurances they had been given about their security during the next Test in Dacca.

Close of play – England 1st innings 226 – 5, (D'Oliveira 16*, Knott 5*)

Day 2 – Saturday 22 February

The Lahore Commissioner kept his word, providing the security that was so obviously missing on the first day. The playing area was ringed by police, while more heavily protected reinforcements waited out of sight behind the stands, ready to assist if required.

The attendance, which had been so poor the previous day, had been boosted on day 2 with a local public holiday being declared. Hopefully they would concentrate on the cricket, and the disturbances and pitch invasions, which had so marred the game so far, would be absent.

The start was slow, with no runs scored in the first 15 minutes. D'Oliveira and Knott were aware that they were the last batsmen with the ability to contribute in a major way. If one of them was out quickly 226 for 5 could quickly become 250 or so all out. A score of 300 was the minimum most observers thought was necessary on this pitch. D'Oliveira eventually broke the drought with first a run, and then to show he was not going to be kept quiet for long, a belligerent hooked six off of Masood.

Just like the previous day, when Intikhab came on to bowl, the game took on a different complexion. D'Oliveira was first out, mistiming a pull shot which was taken by Mohammad Ilyas at mid wicket, a difficult catch he made look easy. Saeed now bought himself on to bowl. With spin at both ends and an attacking field, he was hoping to remove the rest of the England batsmen cheaply. Underwood came and went without scoring. Knott realising that the remaining batsmen may not last long began to hit out, striking Saeed for three consecutive boundaries. Saeed though got his revenge, taking the wickets of Brown and then most importantly Knott in consecutive overs. The 22 year old, playing in only his tenth Test was showing that in addition to being the best wicket-keeper in England, he was becoming a more than useful batsman at the highest level. Finally just before lunch, Pocock took a huge swing at another clever Intikhab delivery, missed it and was comprehensively bowled. England was all out for 306. They had added 80 runs in the morning session, with 47 of these coming from Knott.

Saeed and Intikhab finished the innings with four wickets each, the later demonstrating again why in most eyes he was then considered the best leg spin bowler in world cricket. As they left the field for lunch, England would have been reasonably satisfied but well aware that without Cowdrey's innings the previous day they would have been in serious trouble.

The afternoon session began disastrously for Pakistan. Ilyas, was out first ball, plumb lbw to a fast wicked delivery from David Brown. This was certainly not the conditions under which the incoming batsman Saeed wanted to start his first innings as captain. He settled his nerves (and those of many in the crowd) by stroking the first delivery from Brown through the covers elegantly for three, followed by a confident stroke off the debutant Cottam. Saeed's partner Aftab was finding things more difficult, but after nearly an hour of tense combative cricket the pair had settled and Pakistan had reached 28 for 1.

Cowdrey then made his first bowling change bringing on D'Oliveira. Saeed dispatched his first delivery to the boundary, but was then caught by Knott. The wicketkeeper appeared to misjudge the catch, letting the ball bounce from his gloves before acrobatically reclaiming it inches from the ground. The next over, without adding to their total, the home side lost another wicket when Aftab edged a Brown delivery to slip where D'Oliveira made a fine one handed catch. A dismal 32 for 3 got worse when Mushtaq Mohammed who had struggled for 40 minutes, tried to hook a bouncer from Cottam and was confidently caught by Fletcher at square leg for just 4. This was Cottam's first Test wicket and Pakistan had been reduced to 52 for 4. This brought Hanif to the wicket to join Asif Iqbal who had been working hard to reign in his natural tendency for attacking play. Hanif was in a difficult position. He was not in the best of form, and it was no secret that he was beginning to struggle against fast, short pitched bowling. There were also those in the crowd that wanted him to fail, for no other reason than he was captain of Karachi. However, the pair hung on until the tea interval, with Iqbal on 28 and Hanif on 7.

It did not get any better after tea when Hanif edged a delivery from Brown onto his wicket, Pakistan were now 72 for 5. Majid Khan and Asif Iqbal, two of the English based players, then began a fight back. Majid had just completed his first season with Glamorgan, and scored over 1200 runs finishing second in the county's batting averages. This was no mean achievement given that Glamorgan's home ground at Sophia Gardens, Cardiff had a new pitch which was causing all batsmen more than its fair share of problems.

Today it was Asif Iqbal who was shining, in particular when playing expansive shots against Underwood and Pocock. He reached a well made 50, and just when the hopes of the crowd were beginning to rise, the recovery was suddenly halted. Majid played a poor shot against Underwood, which resulted in a straightforward catch to Pocock at extra cover. Asif continued to play one flamboyant stroke after another, seeming to find few of the difficulties in the pitch that had so unsettled his colleagues. Having reached 70, he made the first mistake of his innings when he tried to cut a good length ball from Cottam, and edged it to D'Oliveira at second slip. Although Pakistan were in a precarious situation at 145 for 7, Shafqat and Intikhab continued to play uninhibited (some would say reckless) shots. Surprisingly even in the final over of the day, rather than play for tomorrow, Intikhab tried to hit Pocock out of the ground. He mistimed his stroke, and skied a catch to who else but D'Oliveira. Pakistan ended the day on an undistinguished 176 for 8. Although a draw still seemed the most likely result, if there was to be a winner it now could surely only be England.

Close of play – England 1st innings 306 all out
Pakistan 1st innings 176 – 8, (Shafqat 22★)

Day 3 – Sunday 23 February

Starting the day 130 runs behind England with only two wickets left, the situation did not look promising for Pakistan. On a misty, hazy Sunday morning which had again been declared a public holiday in an effort to boost the attendance, Cowdrey opened the bowling with Cottam and Pocock. Shafqat the surviving overnight batsman was joined by the 20 year old wicket-keeper Wasim Bari. It was a difficult situation for the batsmen, the side needed runs but of course could not afford to lose wickets. Shafqat went for the attacking option. After briefly settling in, he swept and pulled Pocock for two successive boundaries, briefly raising the hopes, and noise level, of the crowd. Sadly it did not last long, as when he tried the same philosophy against Cottam he almost immediately edged a chance which Knott acrobatically took behind the stumps. Masood playing his first Test innings, proved to be no novice with the bat, and the final wicket added a breezy 22 runs before he missed a sharply moving delivery from Cottam and was bowled. Pakistan were all out for 209, 97 runs behind England. This was not how it was meant to have been, on a pitch, which was apparently so benign.

In contrast to the England innings, it was the seam bowlers rather than the spin bowlers who had taken the majority of the wickets. Cottam in his first Test finished the innings with a well deserved 4 for 50, while Brown who did not bowl on day 3 because of a sprained ankle) took 3 for 43.

There was 65 minutes for England to bat before lunch, and the plan was simple, to score as many runs as possible as quickly as possible. At lunch, with a score of 34 for 2 it was not quite working out that way. Masood had overcome the nerves he experienced in the first innings and was now showing the pace and control which had bought him to the attention of the selectors in the first place. At the other end, Majid was also bowling with hostility, and in only the second over of the innings struck the first blow. Prideaux played forward to a huge in-swinging delivery, missed it and was bowled for only 5. It had not been a great Test match for Prideaux. Ten minutes before lunch, Edrich was also out, caught trying to force Masood through the covers. With a lead of 131 at the break England surely had no need to panic.

By mid-afternoon, England had slumped to 68 for 5 and panic was definitely on the cards. The game that only England could win the previous evening was moving in Pakistan's favour. Cowdrey, Graveney and D'Oliveira had all been dismissed cheaply; the later handicapped by a pulled thigh muscle. With Brown struggling, the England bowling attack was also suddenly beginning to look a bit light.

In spite of the delicate stage of the match, Fletcher and Knott batted with skill, attacking the bowling whenever possible. Using fast footwork to negate any spin, they relied heavily on cut and sweep strokes to keep the score moving. By tea England had rallied to 97 for 5, a lead of 194. With eight hours play left in the match, England were beginning to drag themselves back again to a position where they could not lose.

After tea, aware that he needed to take another wicket quickly or else the game would slip away, Saeed went to an all spin attack of Intikhab and himself. The pitch no longer seemed to have the terrors of the first day, and Fletcher playing with confidence quickly reached his first 50 in Test cricket. Just when Saeed was beginning to run out of ideas of how to break the stubborn partnership, Knott was comprehensively bowled by Masood for a valuable 30. His partnership of 68 with Fletcher had turned the match in England's favour. The new batsman Underwood played a number of over ambitious shots, connecting with one, but was soon out for 6. With 25 minutes left of the day's play, and lots of close fielders trying to unsettle them, Brown and Fletcher then adopted a purely defensive approach, playing for tomorrow. When play ended 15 minutes early because of bad light, England had reached a solid 174 for 7.

With an overall lead of 271, England had regained the initiative and again put themselves in a position from which it seemed they could not lose. Fletcher on 69 not out, ably supported by Knott had ensured that England would sleep better of the two sides that night.

Close of play – Pakistan 1st inning 209 all out
England 2nd innings 174 – 7, (Fletcher 69★, Brown 12★)

Day 4 – Monday 24 February

For the England players about to continue their battle with Pakistan that day, the cancelled tour of South Africa must now have seemed a thing of the past. Over in England, individuals who had been connected with this event were still making the news. Overnight it had been announced that the Reverend David Sheppard had been appointed Bishop of Woolwich. This prominent anti-apartheid campaigner would now have an even more public platform from which speak in the battles ahead [153].

Back at the cricket, England started the final day with a lead of 271 and three wickets in hand. It was now up to Cowdrey to decide how much longer to bat and when to declare. There was a minimum of 90 overs left in the day's play and England probably already had enough runs to ensure they could not lose. The trick was to try and engineer a win; setting a target which was low enough to tempt the opposition to have a go but not so low that they actually reached it.

On this occasion the England captain also had a second factor to consider, he had a weakened bowling attack. D'Oliveira had declared himself unfit to bowl before play began for the day, and Brown had a sprained ankle which would hamper his ability to bowl. With only three fully fit front line bowlers, the worry was that if Pakistan got a good start, the middle order stroke players Asif, Mushtaq and Majid, could make severe hay.

The naturally cautious Cowdrey decided to bat on. Fletcher and Brown played with controlled aggression, while Saeed tried to restrict the scoring using defensive fields. Having added 27 runs to their overnight score with this game of cat and mouse, Fletcher tried once too often to hit across a delivery from Majid and was bowled. Although disappointed not to have reached his first Test century, his 83 had been invaluable, coming at a time when England were in danger of losing the game.

Brown, happier against the new ball when it was taken rather than the spin attack, grew in confidence. With some glorious straight drives, which batsmen higher up the order would have been proud of, he reached 44 before his partner Pocock was bowled by Saeed. The partnership had put on a breezy 21 in 18 minutes, with all but one coming from Brown. At this point Cowdrey declared England's innings closed on 225 for 9. Pakistan had been set a target of 323 runs to win, or more realistically needed to bat for the remaining five hours to draw the match.

Having set the target, Cowdrey went off to hospital to have an X-ray on a damaged arm, and so it was Graveney who led England on to the field for the beginning of Pakistan's second innings. The immediate objective for Ilyas and Aftab was to survive the 55 minutes to lunch. Unfortunately their start was almost as disastrous as in the first innings. This time it was the second over before a wicket fell, rather than first ball. With only six runs on the board, Ilyas tried to hook a bouncer from the seemingly tireless Brown, misjudged it and was brilliantly caught one handed at leg slip by Fletcher. Like Prideaux, it had not been a great match for the Pakistani opening batsman.

Brown who had needed massive strapping on his ankle to even get onto the field, bowled unchanged up until lunch and then for 40 minutes afterwards. It was feared that if he stopped, his ankle would stiffen up and that he would be unable to bowl for the rest of the match. At the break Saeed and Aftab had reached a steady but unspectacular 41 for 1. The equation to win was now 282 runs in 240 minutes, unlikely unless there was a significant acceleration in scoring rate in the afternoon session.

After lunch the scoring slowed rather than increased. Skilful bowling by Brown (who was unbelievably still going) and Underwood, combined with clever field placings, made runs increasingly difficult to come by. Four maiden overs in succession increased the frustration of the crowd and the pressure on the batsmen. When Cottam replaced Brown, Saeed trying to break the shackles dragged a delivery which came back into him onto his middle stump.

Asif the hero of the first innings strode confidently to the wicket. Maybe he was a little too confident this time. After facing just two deliveries, he jumped down the wicket to drive Cottam, only to misjudge the shot and present the bowler with a left landed catch which he held with confidence. In the next over Aftab who had been patiently trying to build an innings, pulled a delivery from Underwood in the air to mid-wicket where Pocock took another good catch. In seven minutes Pakistan had lost 3 wickets and slumped to 71 for 4. The outside chance of winning had disappeared. With three hours of play left, they now had to concentrate on not losing.

Graveney tried to unsettled the new batsmen Mushtaq and Majid, by placing lots of close in fielders. He knew that if he could take one more wicket quickly the remaining batsmen might panic, especially in front of such an unpredictable crowd. However there really were no demons in the pitch, and once the batsmen realised this they began to move from defence to attack and by tea Pakistan had reached the comparative safety of 131 for 4.

After tea Majid hit the first two deliveries to the boundary, to bring up a sparkling, 50. This was the signal for hundreds of spectator to run onto the field, followed quickly by police. Fortunately the invaders were relatively good natured, and the ground was cleared and play restarted after 5 minutes. Majid was eventually out for 68, driving at Brown who remarkably had come onto bowl yet again. With the score on 156 for 5 Hanif joined Mushtaq and this was a catalyst for trouble. The ex-captain laboured for over half an hour to score four runs. The crowd became restless and agitated.

Sections of the crowd soon began chanting anti-Hanif slogans. The unrest spread as spectators and police started to clash, throwing first fruit and then parts of chairs at each other. Troops began to intervene and at this point Graveney decided enough was enough and led the England team from the field. They returned 10 minutes later when some semblance of order had been achieved. The final 50 minutes of the Test match were played out in surreal conditions. The mood of the crowd was of greater concern to those on the field than the match itself, which was now certainly destined for a draw.

When the day's play was bought to a close, Pakistan had reached 203 for 5. The players did not hang around but sprinted straight for the safety of the dressing room to avoid being swamped by the spectators already swarming onto the field.

Close of play – England 2nd innings 225 – 9 dec.
Pakistan 2nd innings 203 – 5, (Mushtaq 34★, Hanif 23★)
Match Drawn

A match which was predicted to be a dull draw, had in fact been more exciting than it had deserved to be given the crowd disturbances that marred the first and last day's play. Sadly, headlines such as 'Armed Troops on Patrol as England Draw' [154] would dominate the newspapers back in Britain the next day. As for the England team, many must have been thinking if this was meant to be a well managed crowd, what on earth are we going to face in Dacca.

8

Pakistan v England
Second Test Match
Dacca Stadium
28 February – 3 March 1969

A day after finishing the match in Lahore, the MCC tourists made the long flight across India to Dacca, the regional capital of East Pakistan. Unrest continued across the country with people being killed or injured in clashes with the police or army in at least seven towns and cities. Of biggest concern to the MCC was the fact that most of these had occurred in East Pakistan, a region they had been assured was safe [155]. Although the players would not have necessarily been aware of Pakistan's history, conflict between the East and West of the country was nothing new.

The birth of Pakistan following the Partition of British India in 1947 was always likely to be problematic. Creating a country with two geographical regions sixteen hundred kilometres apart was always likely to fail. Almost right from the start East Pakistan felt too often like a poor relative of West Pakistan rather than an equal.

The first capital of the country, the majority of the government and military elite and most of the private sector were located in the West, while the East with its larger and poorer population was dominated by agriculture. This feeling of East Pakistan being treated almost like a colony governed from the West was not helped by the decision less than a year after Independence, that Urdu would become the official language of the country. Most of those living in East Pakistan were Bengalis with their own language. Such a decision made them feel even more like second class citizens. The issue of language was resolved in 1956 by giving Bengali (or Bangla) joint status with Urdu as the official languages of the country. In most other respects though there had been little improvement for those living in East Pakistan, and by 1969 the disparity between West and East had actually widened [156]. It is not surprising that there were now calls not just for change, but for East Pakistan to become an independent country.

After the disruptions during the first Test match, there can have been little doubt that security rather than cricket would have been uppermost in the minds of management and players alike. What they did not know was that students who had been a factor in the crowd trouble in the first Test would now become responsible for ensuring their security in the match ahead.

Students had played an important part in driving forward the national uprising, ever since the first minor disturbances at Gordon College in Rawalpindi the previous November. At that time the President had completely underestimated the significance of these protests believing that they could be stopped whenever he wanted by closing all the education institutions, bribing the leaders and using force if necessary. Over the next five months student protests had spread, and also encouraged other groups to join. By the time Cowdrey and his colleagues arrived in Dacca, Government authority in the city had completely collapsed and responsibility for maintaining law and order had been taken over by the local Student Action Committee [157].

When Cowdrey, Ames and Graveney had met with the Board of Control for Cricket in Pakistan (BCCP) in Rawalpindi ten days earlier, they had agreed to play a Test match in East Pakistan on the understanding that the players would receive police protection with army backup if necessary. After arriving at Dacca airport the team travelled by coach to their hotel. During the journey Graveney noticed that while the roads were quiet, there also seemed to be no police around. Asking where the promised protection was, he was told 'the Army are camped ten miles out, and the only police in the city are traffic police. The city is being run by the local students' [158]. Later that day, a reception hosted by the Deputy British High Commissioner had been organised to give the local expatriate community a chance to meet the MCC tourists. Such events were a normal part of the tour programme which the players were expected to endure. On this occasion, after a relatively short time, the players were diplomatically ushered back to their hotel, while local guests remained behind. The community had been gathered not just to meet the players, but to discuss evacuation plans should the situation deteriorate [159]. The mood of those players wanting to cancel the tour and go home would not have been improved by these first hours in Dacca.

While privately Les Ames may have wondered whether it was worth continuing with the tour, under pressure from the British High Commission he was at least prepared to see what plans were being proposed for ensuring the safety of the players during the upcoming Test match.

The initial omens were not encouraging. The student leaders had insisted that no police were to be present on the streets or at the stadium. If this was the case they would guarantee control of the crowd during the match, if not student demonstrators would ensure the match did not take place. Ames and Cowdrey, and members of the British High Commission found themselves discussing whether a Test match between Pakistan and England would go ahead, not with high ranking cricket and police officials but with four representatives of the Student Action Committee, led by a 26 year old law student Tofail Ahmed.

The afternoon before the Test match was due to start, the pragmatic Ames announced that arrangements for running the match had been agreed. He and the captain, if not necessarily all the players, were happy that the plans put forward for controlling the crowd were realistic and that the match could go ahead [160]. Against this somewhat surreal background, there was still the small matter of deciding who would actually be playing the following day.

The sombre spirit of the tourists had received a huge boost of optimism the previous day, when the ever-positive Colin Milburn had flown into Dacca to reinforce their batting. Known almost universally around the cricket world as Ollie, many had considered Milburn's failure to gain selection for the South African tour as unjust as D'Oliveira's omission.

Never one to dwell on disappointments, after completing a moderate season for Northamptonshire, Milburn had taken up an offer to return to Western Australia for another season down under. The State side was now captained by England exile Tony Lock. Under his astute leadership Milburn flourished, often playing an uninhibited 'crash' batting role at the top of the order. In one match against Queensland he had hit a commanding 243 runs (181 being scored in a devastating spell between lunch and tea). Although Western Australia ended runners up to South Australia in the Sheffield Shield, Milburn scored more runs than anybody else in the competition that season (811 in 13 innings). The disappointments of the previous English summer were now well in the past.

After a gruelling 38 hour journey from Perth, the irrepressible Milburn arrived tanned and still smiling at Dacca to be met by all his team mates and a press corp. Almost immediately he 'restored the morale of a party which had increasingly talked in terms of mutiny' [161].

Milburn was keen to play, but with both Cowdrey and D'Oliveira now considered fit enough to start, the selectors decided to name the same 12 players they had used in Lahore. The choice on the day would probably be whether to include Snow at the expense of one of the spin bowlers. While the weather was likely to be hotter than for the first Test, the same problem remained – how to bowl Pakistan out twice in four days on what would what was again bound to be a slow pitch. Ames was certainly not optimistic after seeing the pitch, suggesting that you would not get Bradman out for under 300 on it.

Pakistan has gone for more of a change, naming the eleven who had played in Lahore plus the left arm spin bowler Pervez Sajjad, the opening batsman Salahuddin, and a young fast bowler from Dacca, Niaz Ahmed.

Day 1 – Friday 28 February

The second Test match was being played in a special place in the history of Pakistan cricket. Dacca stadium had been the venue for the first Test match to be played in Pakistan, which started on New Year's Day 1955. Amazingly, six weeks before, the location had been little more than a makeshift cricket ground with rather improvised seating which had been used for occasional local matches. From October 1954, thousands of labourers had worked night and day to construct a stadium fit for such an important occasion. Not only the first Test match to be played on Pakistan soil but against non other than their fierce rivals India. Since then, the Dacca Stadium had been the venue for 4 more Test matches. The most recent against Ted Dexter's England side in January 1961 had ended in a tame draw. The pitch and weather conditions did not suggest that outcome of the upcoming match would be any different.

The day began with the two sides needing to name their final teams for the match ahead. As usual for this time of year, it was hot and humid in Dacca; an atmosphere likely to help pace bowlers swing the ball, but not for long. The pitch itself was bare and shiny and unlikely to give much help to any bowler, fast or slow. The England selectors opted for a predominately pace bowling attack with Pocock making way for Snow. The final eleven chosen were Edrich, Prideaux, Graveney, Fletcher, Cowdrey, D'Oliveira, Knott, Brown, Snow, Underwood and Cottam.

The home selectors were more adventurous, making three changes from the team which had started in Lahore. Aftab Gul, perhaps as he later dryly remarked having served his purpose as a student mediator [162], was replaced by Salahuddin. Shafqat Rana was declared unfit and replaced by Pervez Sajjad. Most contentious of all Asif Masood who had showed promise in his first Test match was replaced by Niaz Ahmed, playing in only his second Test match. His only other Test had been against England at Trent Bridge in 1967. There was a perception that, as with Gul in Lahore, his selection may have been based on more than cricketing factors. Niaz was after all the only player from East Pakistan in the side (although he was born in India). The final eleven were Mohammad Ilyas, Salahuddin, Saeed Ahmed, Asif Iqbal, Mushtaq Mohammed, Majid Khan, Hanif Mohammed, Intikab Alam, Wasim Bari, Niaz Ahmed and Pervez Sajjad. The selectors had opted for four front line spin bowlers and one seam bowler, while England had done exactly the opposite. Surely only one of these strategies could be right.

Saeed won the toss and decided to bat first. So began what Peter Smith writing in *Playfair Cricket Monthly* described as 'one of the most extraordinary Test matches on record' [163]. 'Extraordinary' though almost certainly refers to the conditions under which the match was played, rather than the cricket itself.

As they had promised the Student Action Committee took total responsibility for controlling the crowd of around 15,000, and ensuring the safety of players during the match. There was not a policeman or soldier in sight. Spectators were separated from the field of play by an eight-foot high barbed wire fence. The boundary marking the field of play had then been set a further fifteen yards from this fence. Thirty student leaders with megaphones were stationed around the ground in the space between the fence and boundary edge, with each responsible for watching a section of the crowd. Students had also been assigned to accompany the players to and from the field of play [164]. Remarkably, in a country on the edge of martial law, the system worked. The match was relatively trouble free with the players again able to concentrate on their cricket rather than worry about their well being.

Sadly the day's cricket was largely uneventful with little that would stay in the memory for long. Snow opened the bowling for England, but it was immediately obvious that this was a pitch, which was almost lifeless, of help to neither bowler nor batsman. Snow and Brown bowled with accuracy and as much hostility as the flat pitch would allow, but the opening batsmen were not prepared to take any risks, maybe for good reasons. After a poor match at Lahore, Ilyas was probably playing for his future, while his partner Salahuddin had not played a Test match since 1965 and was opening the batting for the first time. Not surprisingly only 39 runs were scored in the first hour's play, with the only wicket to fall being that of Salahuddin. He tried to play an unconvincing hook against a rare Snow bouncer and was caught by Brown at long leg.

Saeed strode to the wicket with the air of a captain wanting to stamp his authority on the innings. Playing in cavalier fashion, and with a huge amount of luck, after just two overs he had already scored 19 runs. This could not last on a pitch totally unsuited to such adventure, and after just 20 minutes he played across a full toss from Brown, missed it and was comprehensively bowled. Ilyas and a far from fit Asif then struggled to add runs. It took almost 90 minutes for Pakistan's score to reach 50.

Ilyas though was looking less convincing the longer he stayed at the wicket. It was no great surprise that just before lunch he was out when he also tried to hook Snow and was caught behind by the ever industrious Knott. A lunch score of 63 for 3 was far from what Pakistan would have expected, while England would have been content.

The situation did not improve for Pakistan when play resumed, after one session they were already on the defensive. Asif and Mushtaq, two of the most attacking batsmen in the side set about trying to rebuild the innings, but of course without getting out. Neither was comfortable with being tied down for long, and Asif was also suffering a high temperature following a bout of influenza. No matter how they tried, runs came at a snails pace. Accurate England bowling and lively fielding meant that the score moved forward mostly in singles. Boundaries were a rarity, with the occasional lofted drive when Underwood tried flighting the ball. Asif was next out 20 minutes before tea when he played a loose off drive and was bowled by Brown. His 44 runs had taken 2 hours 40 minutes, and at tea Pakistan had laboured to 130 for 4.

After tea, the game almost ground to a standstill, with the batsmen unable to score runs while the bowlers looked unlikely to take wickets. Not surprisingly the patience of the crowd finally began to wear out. With the usual slow hand clapping and bugle calls failing to accelerate the scoring, some in the stands lit small bonfires to amuse themselves. Mushtaq who had now been joined by Majid, continued to struggle. Like so many of his colleagues his natural fluency was being totally stifled by a slow pitch and accurate English bowling. Finally with the score at 168 for 5, and after an innings of nearly 4 hours Mushtaq tried an ambitious back foot shot at a delivery from Snow and was caught for 52. His innings only contained 4 fours showing how difficult it had been.

At the close of play, the Mohammed brothers, Majid and Hanif had dragged the score to 175 for 5. Only 46 runs had been scored in the final session of 32 overs. It was attritional cricket played in oven like heat. England had not helped by bowling a barely adequate 87 overs in the day, but there had also been 6 drink breaks. One of these had rather bizarrely been extended to 8 minutes to enable a local television commentator to conduct an interview with Cowdrey and Mushtaq. Snow and Brown had shared the wickets, but in truth all the England bowlers had played their part in never allowing the Pakistan batsmen to break free. Most importantly of all there had been no major pitch invasions. It had been England's day in more ways than one.

Close of play – Pakistan 1st innings 176 – 5, (Majid 24*, Hanif 1*)

Day 2 – Saturday 1 March

During the night Dacca was hit by a wild storm, with high winds causing destruction and devastation to infrastructure in the area. At the cricket ground anything not tied down was blown around, but most of the damage was superficial and the ground staff were sure that this could be made good before play was due to begin again. Of more serious concern was the building housing the cricket scoreboard, both the building and the scoreboard were badly damaged. Local carpenters were called from their beds, and worked through the night in difficult conditions to ensure the scoreboard was repaired and working again before the players walked onto the field for the start of day two. As far as the most important part of the ground was concerned, it seemed that the solid but uncovered pitch had fortunately escaped undamaged.

When play began, Cowdrey immediately took the new ball. The overnight batsmen, Majid and Hanif, were aware that they needed to accelerate the scoring if Pakistan were to have a chance of winning. Unfortunately they perhaps tried to attack too soon and within 4 overs the side had slumped to 186 for 7. Majid after being beaten twice by Brown, managed to snick a delivery to the wicketkeeper, while Hanif playing back to Snow and missing, was palpably lbw.

The end of the innings should not have been far away, but rather strangely Cowdrey gave the remaining batsmen a lifeline. Setting a defensive rather than attacking field, with at times seven men on the boundary, Intikhab first with Wasim as a partner, and then Niaz managed to move the score along in singles and twos without taking too many risks. The bowlers became frustrated, fielding occasionally erratic, and the last three wickets added another 60 runs to the total. When Cottam finally ended the innings 5 minutes before the interval by bowling Pervez, the total had reached

246. As they left the field at lunch, the England players would have been disappointed. They had reduced the hosts to 186 for 7, and then let them off the hook. England now had a target that was larger than it should have been, and they would now be batting on a pitch that was beginning to show signs of deteriorating in the steaming heat.

Prideaux and Edrich began the England innings after lunch. Under grey, cloudy skies it was a nervous start, with Prideaux in particular a cause for concern. So far it had been a poor tour of Pakistan for the new opening batsman; 71 runs in 6 innings. It now seemed that the longer he was at the wicket the more his confidence was evaporating. It took him 35 minutes to score his first run against the relatively benign pace bowling of Majid and Niaz. After just 11 exploratory overs Saeed switched to an all spin attack with plenty of fielders around the bat. It was no great surprise that almost immediately Prideaux was out. He was deemed to have edged a turning delivery from Pervez to Hanif in the slips. Prideaux later suggested that the ball had turned so viscously that both he and the wicketkeeper missed it [165]. As is often the case when you are struggling for form luck goes against you. At the other end Edrich had more luck. He played and missed regularly, at times batting unconvincingly but gradually he settled.

Edrich was joined by Graveney who had been promoted to number three because Cowdrey was still troubled by his hand injury. The two batsmen had totally contrasting styles; Edrich poking and prodding but tenacious as always while Graveney all elegance played sweeps and drives. They managed to add 44 runs for the second wicket before Edrich was well caught by Mushtaq at short leg off Intikhab. Fletcher, also promoted, came to the wicket and by tea they had battled their way to 64 for 2.

The final session of the day was a disaster for England. Saeed continued with an all spin attack. Fletcher tried to move the close in fielders by hitting boundaries when the rare loose ball was bowled. He hit two textbook back foot cover drives off Intikhab but when the score had reached 96 he misjudged a delivery from Saeed, hitting the ball to mid-off where Hanif took his second catch of the innings.

Graveney was then joined by his captain. Cowdrey's walk to the wicket was accompanied by a great ovation from the crowd. They were acknowledging both his major achievements as a cricketer and the role he had played to ensuring this Test match was actually taking place. Sadly England's two most senior batsmen were not together for long. After bringing up the England 100, Graveney tried to sweep a short straight delivery from Pervez and was bowled. His 44 runs had been entertaining but at 100 for four, England were wobbling. Thirteen runs later it got even worse when Cowdrey was lbw to the same bowler for just 7. D'Oliveira and Knott were now at the wicket, and surely represented the last chance of getting a competitive score.

This time there was to be no rescue mission by the ever-busy Knott. Having scored just 2, he was deceived into hitting a return catch to Pervez. Brown then provided Hanif with his third catch of the innings, this time off Saeed. England had collapsed losing five wickets for 66 runs since tea. D'Oliveira and Snow hung on, although not without luck. D'Oliveira should have been out shortly before the close when a simple catch, which either the bowler or short leg should have taken, was caught by neither. When bad light ended play five minutes early England were 139 for 7. It had been Pakistan's day in all respects. Their spin bowlers had taken all the England wickets to fall so far, and on a deteriorating pitch defeat for visitors was suddenly a real possibility.

Close of play – Pakistan 1st innings 246 all out
England 1st innings 139 – 7, (D'Oliveira 16★, Snow 7★)

Day 3 – Sunday 2 March

England began day three 107 runs behind with only three wickets left. D'Oliveira and Snow's challenge was as much about using up time as scoring runs. As a batting all-rounder D'Oliveira was more than capable of adapting to the situation. He had played on many similar pitches during his formative years in South Africa. For Snow it was a different matter. While he had a Test 50 to his name, in his last ten innings he had had only reached doubled figures three times. Like many fast bowlers he could only play a patient blocking game for so long, before deciding that the ball needed to be dispatched over the boundary.

D'Oliveira 16 not out at the start then played what he later described as 'the greatest innings of my life' [166]. Like Cowdrey's contribution at Lahore, it almost certainly saved England from defeat. Sadly his innings did not receive all the recognition it deserved in the following day's newspapers. That day there was really only one story in town, the maiden flight of the Anglo-French supersonic airliner *Concorde*.

Under blue skies with a hint of summer in the air, D'Oliveira and Snow began batting against an all spin attack. Snow in particular made use of his pad as much as his bat to defend and it was 6 overs before the first run of the day was scored. D'Oliveira then had another piece of luck when Hanif, who up until then had been so good in the field, was unable to take a difficult catch in the slips off of Intikab's bowling. Runs came at a trickle, and so just after an hour Saeed decided he had to try and make something happen. He therefore took the second new ball. This is a decision which is often notoriously difficult for captains. A new ball is harder and comes off the bat quicker making runs easier to score but it also has the potential to move in the air and off the pitch at least for the first few overs, and therefore increase the possibility of taking a wicket.

This time Saeed's gamble paid off. In his second over with the new ball Snow drove a delivery from Niaz elegantly to the boundary for 4. Deciding that he was now a batsman, Snow attempted the same shot off the next delivery and was caught in the slips. England was now 170 for 8. Getting closer, but the hosts still had a useful first inning lead of 76. The new batsman Underwood started confidently and in the period until lunch helped D'Oliveira add another 35 runs. In one over to the dismay of Saeed he drove the captain for three 4s. At lunch England had advanced to 204 for 8. They were pulling themselves back into the match.

After lunch, D'Oliveira and Underwood continued to frustrate Pakistan, until Underwood eventually mistimed a shot against Mushtaq and was caught at deep mid-on for a very valuable 22. England were now 236 for 9, only 10 runs behind. Any hope of a result in the match was receding fast. The main point of interest was whether the new batsman Cottam could survive long enough for D'Oliveira to reach a century. The tension increased, but finally after 265 minutes at the wicket, D'Oliveira pulled a delivery from Pervez to the boundary for 4 to reach his third Test century (but his first overseas). A small number of enthusiastic supporters were allowed onto the field to congratulate D'Oliveira but unlike in Lahore, it was all good natured and play quickly resumed. Having reached his century D'Oliveira played with increasing freedom, but it was Cottam who was eventually out giving Hanif his fourth catch of the innings. England were all out for 274 a lead of 28, with D'Oliveira a match saving 114 not out. As the players left the field for an early tea, Pakistan would have been the more disappointed of the two teams. England had been 130 for 7 but they were unable to finish them off.

When Pakistan began their second innings after tea, Cowdrey realised that the only way he could fashion a win from a match which was heading inevitably for a draw was by attack. After only five overs he dispensed with the seam bowling option put six close in fielders around the bat, and bought Underwood on to bowl. As he had shown the previous summer against Australia, in the right conditions Underwood could run through a side in a short time. With his third delivery he had Salahuddin lbw, and three balls later almost got the prize wicket of Asif with a delivery that kept low. Realising that continuing to play with fields close to the bat could spell disaster, both Ilyas and Asif went for the risky option of attacking the bowler. Both played a number of attractive drives to the boundary, and just when it looked as though the strategy was working Asif tried to cut a delivery from Underwood, missed it and was bowled. Two runs later Ilyas tried an ambitious drive against Cottam and was easily caught at mid-on (this would be Ilyas's last stroke in Test cricket). Pakistan was 50 for 3, only 26 runs in the lead with 7 wickets left. Saeed and Mushtaq them batted for the remainder of the session, and with a mixture of good batting and some luck took their side's score at the close of play to 77 for 3. They were 49 ahead. The door was open for England, but only just.

Close of play – England 1st innings 274 all out
Pakistan 2nd innings 77 – 3, (Mushtaq 18★, Saeed 10★)

Day 4 – Monday 3 March
At the start of the final day's play, all three results were still possible. Pakistan was only 49 runs ahead with seven wickets left. If they wanted to win the match they needed to score quickly in order to set England a tempting target, which they might be bowled out chasing. This would involve Pakistan taking chances, maybe losing wickets and giving England

an opportunity to win. In the end neither side was willing to risk losing the match and the day was perfectly summarised by the *Guardian* headline 'Dismal end to the second Test' [167].

The overnight batsmen Saeed and Mushtaq quickly made their intentions clear. To stay in as long as possible with defence the main objective. Scoring runs was almost an afterthought. Underwood was England's main hope, but the pitch was just too slow for his style of bowling. Although there was the occasional half chance, the truth was that even with seven fielders around the bat survival was possible, if not always straightforward. Cottam bowled much of the morning in tandem with Underwood, and while he was accurate, he never looked likely to take a big batch of wickets. When in desperation D'Oliveira even experimented with a few off spin deliveries it was clear that England badly missed a second specialist spin bowler.

Only 11 runs were scored in the first hour. Mushtaq was not always comfortable against Underwood and his was the first wicket to fall when he edged a catch to D'Oliveira in the slips, 35 minutes before lunch. Majid now joined Saeed and the pair reached lunch with Pakistan 111 for 4. It was not exactly riveting cricket, only 34 runs had been scored in two hours. The game was now all but dead and destined for a draw.

The cricket did not any better after lunch with only 16 runs being scored in the first hour. After three and a half hours at the wicket, Saeed again played forward to Underwood but this time the ball gripped the pitch, turned and caught the edge of his bat giving Knott a simple catch behind the stumps (c Knott b Underwood had already become a very regular entry on Kent County Cricket Club scorecards). Hanif joined Majid but did not last long before giving Underwood his sixth wicket. Pakistan were now 147 for 6, a lead of 119, but still Saeed did not declare. The crowd was becoming lively, the noise levels increasing and fights beginning to break out. The Student Security Officers who had been so effective during the first three days, were now finding it increasingly difficult to keep order.

After tea, Saeed finally decided that Pakistan could not lose and declared on 195 for 6, a lead of 167. To the frustration of sections of the crowd Majid was left on 49 not out. England needed to score 168 runs in 70 minutes to win. This was of course more or less impossible, and Edrich and Prideaux dispensed the last rites, scoring only 33 runs in 20 overs. The 'dismal draw' beckoned [168].

Off the field sections of the crowd near the VIP enclosure were becoming increasingly troublesome. Fighting battles among themselves, individuals used whatever they could lay their hands on for ammunition. Fearing the worst, the local television company decided it was time pack up their expensive equipment in order to make a quick getaway if necessary [169].

The record books will show that the second Test match between Pakistan and England ended in a tame draw. In truth both sides had an opportunity to win, but neither were prepared to risk losing. As they flew to Karachi that evening, unlikely as it may have seemed at that moment, Colin Cowdrey had just captained England in a Test match for the last time.

Close of play – Pakistan 2nd innings 195 – 6 dec.
England 2nd innings 33 – 0, (Edrich 12★, Prideaux 18★)
Match Drawn

The game had been played in conditions, which although an improvement on those of the previous Test, were still well below those normally associated with international cricket. The players again accepted all this without much complaint, but their patience and tolerance must surely have been wearing thin.

9

Pakistan v England
Third Test Match
The National Stadium, Karachi
6 – 8 March 1969

The second Test match over, the MCC tour party left Dacca almost immediately, arriving back in Karachi late on the evening of the 3 March. The Student Action Committee had kept their word during the match and a lull in hostilities had been observed. The following day was a different matter. East Pakistan was paralysed by a strike co-ordinated by the students and other opposition groups. They were beginning a campaign to force changes to the system used by the Government to administer and control the population.

The English cricketers had been previously assured by the student leaders that their grievances were not with them or the English people as a whole. This was also now changing. Extracts from the memoirs of the newspaper magnate Cecil King had just been published in the *Sunday Times* in Britain [170]. These included remarks about the founder of Pakistan Mohammad Ali Jinnah, which many in the country found deeply offensive. This had already led to official protests at Government level and would have only added fuel to those demonstrating across the country.

Ayub Khan's decision not to stand for re-election did little to calm the explosive political situation in the country. Up until that point the different opposition factions had at least one thing in common; the desire to replace the President and his regime. Now with the prospect of the Government disintegrating, each opposition group had to think about life after the President.

In West Pakistan, the charismatic Zulfikar Ali Bhutto was by far the most popular political leader. The agenda of his Pakistan People's Party worried America, Britain and their allies. One moment Bhutto described it as socialism akin to a Scandinavian model and the next there was talk of closer links with China.

In East Pakistan it was not Bhutto but Shaikh Mujibur Rahman, who was the dominant voice. Leader of the Awami League his demand for autonomy for the eastern province, with perhaps independence on the horizon was popular with many of the population who had felt ignored by those in West Pakistan for so long. Here Bhutto and the Pakistan People's Party were under attack from both Rahman and religious leaders in the mosques, who considered their brand of socialism as something that was incompatible with Islamic law.

As for the radical student movement who had been the catalyst of the uprising, their agenda was a mixture of parochial demands and idealistic aspirations. Bhutto was not a natural ally for students of the right, some who had described him as the 'revolutionary who has missed his first revolution' [171]. For the students on the left it was the Islamic ideology of Rahman which was the problem.

While these disparate groups jostled for the support of the population, the real power in the country, the military were watching and waiting. Also observing from the side-lines was the British High Commission. In the best understated traditions of diplomatic language they were 'giving renewed consideration to the security of British staff and British subjects, taking the present circumstances into account' and evacuation plans were being 're-examined' [172]. One assumes this also included the MCC tourists.

After the relative calm, rather surreal atmosphere of Dacca, the team found themselves back in the claustrophobic and excitable cauldron of Karachi. Ames realised that using students for security would no longer be adequate, and that a serious police presence would be needed this time.

Even the more seasoned travellers in the party were now beginning to feel the strain of the situation, and in many cases becoming genuinely concerned for their safety. Experience of the tour so far, provided little confidence in the ability of the authorities to provide adequate security. Vice-Captain Graveney, who had gradually become a spokesman for the team concluded that there was 'a genuine feeling that they had been kicked around long enough in one guise or another for ends other than cricket' [173]. The mood to abandon the series and return home was growing. Keith Fletcher, on his first tour of Pakistan, expressed the thoughts of many when he later wrote 'the cricket was meaningless, and we were by this stage concerned with little more than a safe passage home' [174]. This was certainly not the best atmosphere in which to prepare a team for a deciding Test match.

The first two Tests had been scheduled for four days, rather than the usual five. Although officially, this condition came from the Board of Control for Cricket in Pakistan, unofficially it most probably came from the President himself. It was also agreed that if the series was drawn after the first two Tests, that the Third would be extended to five days in order to try and produce a result.

Locals expected the pitch to be slow with some assistance for spin bowlers. Even so, Hanif for who Karachi was his home ground, still expected the pitch to last eight days [175]. It was surprising to say the least when the England selectors announced that, as in Dacca, the team would contain three fast bowlers at the expense of a spin bowler. Watching the pitch drying out, they fortunately quickly realized their error, and added Pocock and Hobbs to the eleven who who had played in Dacca. The other change was to drop Prideaux in favour of Milburn. Prideaux had struggled in Pakistan managing a total of only 36 runs in four Test innings. Having played in three Tests so far, it was reasonable to assume that he was still finding his way in international cricket. Sadly, the man whose withdrawal from the previous summer's final Test match against the Australians had given D'Oliveira the opportunity to force his way into the squad for South Africa, would never play for England again.

119

Pakistan made four changes to the side that had come close to winning in Dacca. The opening batsmen Ilyas was as expected dropped, along with the bowlers Niaz Ahmad and Pervez Saijad. Salahuddin was also omitted because of an injury to his bowling finger. They were replaced by Aftab Gul, Shafquat Rana and Asif Masood who were all back having been dropped after the first Test in Lahore. Also added to the squad was the 20 year old fast bowler Safraz Nawaz, who ironically Prideaux had just provisionally signed for his county side Northamptonshire.

Day 1 – Thursday 6 March

In 1969 Karachi was experiencing rapid growth, and already had a population approaching 3 million. Like many other cities in the same circumstances it had significant numbers of poorly planned, cheaply constructed, ugly buildings.

In many ways, the National Stadium reflected the city. It had been built in a hurry, and had none of the architectural elegance of the Gaddafi Stadium in Lahore. A functional concrete structure, it provided cover from the scorching sun for those in the VIP enclosure. For the rest, there was somewhere to sit but little else. Of greater concern to the England players was the frail, low level fencing that was used to notionally separate the spectators from the field of play. It was not much of an obstacle for those determined to disrupt play.

When the final teams were announced before the start of play; England had had decided to play an extra spin bowler. The Essex leg-spin bowler Robin Hobbs therefore replaced Bob Cottam in the side. Hobbs had only played one match on tour so far, but the selectors decided it was worth the risk, as it would give Cowdrey added variety in his bowling options. Cottam could have considered himself unlucky, as he had down little wrong in the tour. Also as already announced Milburn would now open the innings with Edrich instead of Prideaux. The final eleven chosen were John Edrich, Colin Milburn, Tom Graveney, Colin Cowdrey, Keith Fletcher, Basil D'Oliveira, Alan Knott, John Snow, David Brown, Derek Underwood and Robin Hobbs.

Having already named their final eleven the day before, the Pakistan selectors only had to decide whether Hanif or Wasim would open the innings with Aftab. In the end they decided to choose the experienced Hanif, who would be playing on home soil. The final eleven for Pakistan were Aftab Gul, Hanif Mohammad, Mushtaq Mohammed, Asif Iqbal, Saeed Ahmed, Majid Khan, Shafqat Rana, Intikab Alam, Wasim Bari, Asif Masood and Safraz Nawaz.

The addition of Hobbs to the England team looked to be a risk worth taking when Cowdrey won the toss, and of course decided to bat first. With a 10.00 am start there was still dew on the outfield, but almost no help in the pitch for the opening bowlers Masood and Majid. Milburn started full of confidence and after half an hour England had already made 33 with Milburn having scored 24. He was then pinned down by Masood and the debutante Sarfaz, but showed his increased maturity by patiently playing through this period. Edrich was not as confident as Milburn but still appeared relatively untroubled until Intikhab came on to bowl. With the score at 75, Edrich misjudged a sweep shot and was caught at forward short leg for 32. This was the third time in five innings that Edrich had lost his wicket to his future county colleague. Milburn then began to expand his range of attacking shots reaching his 50 before lunch. This was the excuse for the first pitch invasion of the day. Although play was quickly resumed this did not bode well for the rest of the day. Shortly afterwards, the players left the field for lunch with England comfortable at 89 for 1.

After lunch, Saeed used a mixed pace attack, with Intikhab at one end and one of his fast bowlers at the other. With a defensive field in place, Graveney found it difficult to score but Milburn had no such problems. He imperiously hoisted Intikhab over square leg for six, and raced through what are meant to be the nervous nineties hitting the other leg spin bowler Mushtaq for two fours in an over. A large man of over 17 stone (107 kg) Milburn was non the less extremely quick on his feet. He was quickly in position to execute a range of savage square cuts, perfectly timed hook shots or fierce pull shots. Thirty five minutes after lunch Milburn reached his second Test century. It had taken 163 deliveries with 13 fours and a six and England were 153 for 1.

Unfortunately the landmark was the signal for a prolonged period of crowd trouble. First a group of spectators came running onto the field to 'congratulate' him on reaching a hundred. With Milburn besieged, Graveney used bat to try and clear the youths away and allegedly struck one in doing so. The police were unusually efficient is clearing this disturbance, but almost immediately a much bigger pre-planned demonstration started from in front of the players' dressing room. A procession of local Karachi cricketers started walking around the boundary carrying banners. Some slogans called for the resignation of the selectors and others for the return of the local hero Hanif as Captain instead of Saeed. Hanif was from Karachi while Saeed was from Lahore. The Lahore versus Karachi rivalry had undertones of the North verses South debate so often played out in Britain. Cowdrey himself had been at the centre of such a row when he had replaced Yorkshire's Brian Close as England Captain for the tour of the Caribbean the previous winter.

At the same time other spectators were running across the pitch to the players' dressing rooms to complain about Graveney's assault of one of the demonstrators. The police seemed to be unable, or unwilling, to take charge of the situation and clear the playing area, and so the Pakistan fielders along with Milburn and Graveney left the field.

Tea was taken early, but even so 50 minutes playing time were lost. When play finally resumed the England batsmen continued serenely on as though nothing had happened, with Graveney now beginning to dominate. When he reached his fifty just before the close, there was yet another pitch invasion which this time was cleared quickly.

When play finished for the day England had reached a commanding 226 for 1. The Pakistan bowlers had stuck to their task, but on an unresponsive pitch chances had been few. This had overwhelmingly been England's day but cricket had been the loser. As the players left the field, again with spectators seemingly free to go wherever they wanted, many would have been wondering just how much longer the match would continue. Back at Lord's the MCC were also becoming increasingly worried. Secretary Billy Griffith sent a telegram to Ames. As had been the case for so much of the tour, the message 'All here concerned about riots' again left the decisions squarely with Ames and Cowdrey [176].

Close of play
England 1st innings 226 – 1, (Milburn 137★, Graveney 51★)

Day 2 – Friday 7 March

The record book shows that during the second day England moved their score on to 412 for 6 in 75 overs, with Graveney duly completing another Test century. In reality though the day was one of increasing chaos where cricket often took second place.

At the start of play, Saeed immediately took the new ball and Milburn did not last long. He had only added 2 to his overnight score when he tried to cut a good delivery from Masood and was well caught by Wasim behind the stumps. This had been a commanding innings by Milburn and as he walked from the field, the selectors would have been satisfied that the 27 year old could now become a regular member of the England team. Sadly, neither they nor Milburn knew that he had just played his last innings for England.

Cowdrey joined the increasingly confident Graveney, and in just over an hour the pair had competed a 50 run partnership. Just after that however, Cowdrey edged a turning delivery from Intikhab which was well caught by Hanif in the slips. Graveney seemed unaffected by the increased disturbances in the crowd, playing both spin and fast bowling serenely with equal confidence. Twenty minutes before lunch, he reached the eleventh Test century of his career by straight driving a delivery from Intikhab to the boundary. This was effectively the end of the serious cricket for the day. Graveney's century was the trigger for a pitch invasion which forced the players off the field during which they took an early lunch.

The crowd who appeared to have taken complete control then demanded that all police were removed from the ground if the match were to continue. Remarkably the cricket authorities agreed and not surprisingly there were a further five major pitch invasions, and countless other disturbances over the remaining day's play.

Following the tea break, the locally popular Majid had to force a way through the crowd and in effect clear a path for his captain to get onto the field. The local protests against Saeed continued to rumble on, and concern was now growing as to what might happen when he eventually came out to bat.

In the final session, England had moved their score onto 412 for 6, when a fight amongst a group of spectators spilled onto the playing area, and the players again walked off. With only five minutes left until the scheduled close, the umpires wisely declared an end of play for the day. As the correspondent of the *Guardian* noted 'By then the players on both sides were just going through the motions of providing a cricket match. It will be impossible to play this ill-fated final Test properly now' [177].

That evening the two captains and Les Ames met with officials of the Karachi Cricket Association and it was agreed that if there were any further disturbances then the match would be abandoned. Even the tolerant Ames had to finally admit defeat. Commenting after the meeting he said 'We have done our best. Now it is a question of getting through the remaining three days as best as possible' [178].

For the England captain though the series was over. The previous evening his wife had telephoned to tell him that his father-in-law Stuart Chiesman (a previous President of Kent County Cricket Club) had died. Cowdrey flew back to Britain that night making it clear he would not speak to the Press until the rest of the MCC party was back home. It had been a tough tour for Cowdrey. Even so it was somewhat surprising that, unlike for his vice – captain, a tour so full of incident did not get a single mention in his autobiography [179].

Close of play – England 1st innings 412 – 6, (Knott 38★, Snow 6★)

Day 3 – Saturday 8 March
Fifteen minutes before lunch on day three the inevitable happened and MCC's troubled tour of Pakistan finally came to an end. Following the numerous pitch invasions and disturbances the previous day, barbed

wire had been used to reinforce the fencing separating the stands used by the general public from the playing area. Even so it was with some apprehension that the overnight batsmen Knott and Snow walked onto the field at the start of play. As the result of a general strike in the city which had paralysed the public transport system, there was a smaller crowd than for the previous days ready to watch the action. Also present in the VIP enclosure for the first time in the series was the President of the Board of Control for Cricket in Pakistan, Syed Fida Hassan.

In the somewhat surreal atmosphere the cricket over the first hour was almost normal. Knott batted steadily, reaching his 50 with a single off of Masood. The next delivery Snow was bowled for 9. He had only added 3 to his overnight score but provided good support for Knott. Sensing that a declaration may be due, the England wicketkeeper accelerated the scoring, but in doing so took more risks. There was perhaps an opportunity to reach his first Test century. David Brown played his part, with fast running between the wickets and as lunch approached with Knott on 96 it looked as though a Test century would be achieved.

Suddenly, a group of banner carrying demonstrators who had assembled outside of the ground broke down the gates and swarmed onto the field demanding that the match be stopped. The demonstrators were soon joined by others from the crowd as the players ran for the safety of the pavilion. The pitch was trampled on, stumps ripped up and broken, and benches hurled into the VIP area. The match was clearly over. The concern now was solely for the safety of the players. It was important to get them away from the ground as quickly as possible. The England players were smuggled from the ground still in their cricket gear, the crowd being told that lunch was being taken. When it was announced that the match had in fact been abandoned, the mayhem increased with the mob setting fire to the awnings surrounding the ground.

Close of play – England 1st innings 502 – 7, (Knott 96★, Brown 25★)
Match Abandoned as a Draw

After five weeks during which he had overcome so many problems, even the phlegmatic Ames had to admit defeat, and it was no doubt with some relief that the team flew out of Karachi Airport later that evening. Before leaving a clearly sad and tired Ames said 'I have done everything possible to keep the tour alive though I think it should have been called off by the Pakistan Board when we arrived' adding that 'though it is no decision of mine, there will have to be a radical change before another tour takes place here' [180].

A tour in which cricket increasingly became irrelevant was finally over. What Michael Melford later called 'the futile tour' [181] had sadly come to a predictable end. Seventeen days later President Ayub Khan himself was also gone, having resigned and handed the running of the country over to the military. Martial law was once again imposed in Pakistan.

With the tour party now safely home a Leader article in the *Times* concluded that 'the planning of overseas tours will have to take far more account of the political climate than could have been imagined even a year ago'. Of more concern to those at Lord's, the paper also questioned 'whether the South African visit in 1970 can escape political interference, any more than did the selection of D'Oliveira for the M.C.C. team for South Africa' [182]. The next conflict was already on the horizon.

Part 3

April 1969 – May 1970

From One Crisis to Another

10

It Might All Just Go Away
April 1969 – September 1969

Both the MCC and the England captain Colin Cowdrey must have been greatly relieved to see the spring of 1969 approaching. They could only hope that the turmoil of the D'Oliveira Affair and chaos of the winter tour would soon be a thing of the past.

On paper at least, the cricket season ahead looked like an opportunity to return to normal. England was scheduled to play two touring teams. First the West Indies for three Tests and then later in the summer New Zealand. Although it was dangerous to take anything for granted, Cowdrey would have been quietly confident of winning both series. The once dominant West Indies were a side in transition, while New Zealand though capable of the occasional upset at home, had never won a Test match, let alone a series, against England.

The first Test match of the summer was not until mid-June and so there were plenty of other things for players to worry about before selection for the England side became a consideration.

Once a winter tour was over it was usual for both the tour manager and captain to write a report for consideration by the MCC Committee. On this occasion it is not clear if these reports were ever written. There is copy of either in the MCC archives at Lord's.

For the press, there were still newspaper columns to fill. Cricket correspondents usually reflected on the winter tour, at least for a few days after the party had returned. There would be opinions on which players had made progress and so could be judged successes. Often more prominently, as bad news sells, there would be speculation on who had been disappointing, and whether they would get another chance.

This time because of the chaotic environment in which the tour has taken place, it was dangerous to draw too many career changing conclusions. As far as the specialist batsmen were concerned most agreed Prideaux had struggled, but the itinerary gave almost no chance to find form if you started badly. Milburn on the other hand had been a great success in his one innings, which begged the question why he was not in the tour party from the start. Of the other less experienced players Fletcher and Knott had confirmed their potential.

Among the bowlers there had been few surprises. Snow and Brown were as hostile as the slow pitches would allow, with D'Oliveira offering some support. Cottam playing in his first series had been a success, quickly learning how to adapt his technique to slower pitches. As for the spin bowlers, Underwood already such a danger on English pitches, was now showing that he was learning how to become a similar threat on batsmen friendly pitches overseas. Pocock, the youngest player on tour was the biggest disappointment, playing in only one Test and taking only one wicket.

The standout figure of the tour for most observers had not been a player but the Tour Manager. As Cowdrey increasingly struggled to make decisions and agree with his vice-captain Graveney, the burden of keeping the tour going fell more and more on to Les Ames. The tour report in *Wisden* concluded that 'English cricket owes much to Ames for the dignified and sensible part he played amid so much incompetence and worse' [183]. While this had not been one of Cowdrey's better tours as captain, there was no suggestion that he would not be leading England against the West Indies in three months time.

Colin Cowdrey had been reappointed England captain in 1967 following the controversial sacking of Brian Close (a story worth a book in itself [184]). At the time he had imagined his future based around a five-tour plan. The key steps in this plan were to:-

i) Win the 1968 winter series in the West Indies; ii) Regain the Ashes against Australia at home in 1968; iii) Win the 1968/9 winter series in South Africa; iv) Win the 1970 home series against South Africa and then to finish his international career with perhaps the biggest prize of all v) Retain the Ashes in Australia in the winter tour of 1970/71.

Cowdrey himself wrote 'I hoped to return to Australia for a fifth time, this time as England captain, and win the Ashes with a team I had built, nurtured and encouraged' [185].

The first step had been achieved; the second step had been thwarted by the weather; step three defeated by politics but the final two steps in the plan were still feasible. There were not many obvious obstacles in the coming season to upset the dream finish he yearned for. By the end of May, with the new season only just starting to gain momentum, these hopes would lay in tatters.

As players prepared for the 1969 cricket season, South Africa's tour of England was still a year away. However, the visit was already beginning to exercise the minds of some in the British Government and the MCC. In mid-March Denis Howell, the Minister of Sport met with Billy Griffith to discuss sanctions imposed on Rhodesia by the United Nations in 1965. Holders of Rhodesian passports were now barred from entering Britain. There was the possibility that one or two of the South African tourists might be Rhodesians. After the furore over D'Oliveira, the British Embassy in Cape Town were very aware that any attempt to place conditions on who the South African selectors could choose for the next tour of England would cause major problems [186]. With the D'Oliveira Affair long gone from the front pages of the British newspapers, it was hoped that the cricket press could now start looking to the season ahead. By the first week of April this was already a forlorn hope.

On 4 April the respected sports journalist James Manning wrote a newspaper article revisiting the lucrative contract that D'Oliveira had been offered to coach in South Africa over the winter of 1968/69 [187]. The following day the *Times* reopened the debate over the non-selection of D'Oliveira by publishing an article suggesting that officials at Lord's had 'withheld from the public an important piece of evidence' related to the selection of the original team for the winter tour of South Africa and that 'they should consider putting all their cards on the table' as 'the matter is not yet closed' [188]. Two days later the D'Oliveira Affair was back on the front pages. Lord Cobham had made public details of his meeting with John Vorster and the message he had subsequently passed onto the MCC [189].

Aware that D'Oliveira was about to publish a book telling his side of the story, the MCC had little option but to prepare a very detailed statement on the events surrounding the selection of the side for South Africa, the part information obtained from Sir Alec Douglas-Home and Lord Cobham had played in the process and who knew what when [190]. Speculation that something was not quite right only increased when the press statement due to be released following the meeting of the MCC Committee on 9 April was delayed until the following day. Peter Wilson, one of the journalists waiting for the press release was clearly not impressed, calling those at Lord's 'the Muddled Cricket Czars' [191]. The next day the headline on the front page of the *Daily Telegraph* revealed 'MCC Admits Warning on D'Oliveira' [192] while the back page of the *Daily Mirror* was dominated by the message 'MCC: We Kept Quiet on Dolly' [193]. That evening the Reverend David Sheppard and Denis Howell, the Minister of Sport were guests on BBC television's flagship sports news programme *Sportsnight with Coleman*. Howell was facing questions in the House of Commons on the latest revelations and whether the 1970 South African tour should still go ahead. At this stage he was sticking to the Government line that any decision to cancel rested with those at Lord's. The D'Oliveira Affair, and more importantly the coming South African tour were well and truly back in the mainstream news.

Over in South Africa, Prime Minister Vorster and his Nationalist Government were not happy. The insinuation that the offer of a coaching contract to D'Oliveira had been an attempt to bribe him into withdrawing as a candidate for the winter tour was resented.

At his first opportunity to speak in the House of Assembly following the MCC press statement, Vorster confirmed that he had met Lord Cobham and Sir Alec Douglas-Home. He refused to disclose details of their conversations and whether he has asked these to be passed onto the MCC. The Government were also concerned that cancelling the forthcoming tour to England was even being mentioned in the English press, but they were also in no mood to allow a visiting South African cricket team to be caught up in anti-apartheid demonstrations [194].

On 1 May the MCC Cricket Council met, and after lengthy consideration 'the Council confirmed that the invitation to the South African Cricket Association to send a team in 1970 still stands' [195]. The South Africa cricket team had last played a Test match in February 1967 and the prospect of playing a five Test series against England was mouth watering. This would certainly help answer the frequently asked question of who was the best Test side in the world. However this was still a year away and before that there was the 1969 English cricket season, which was about to stir.

The start of the 1969 English cricket season came closer with the arrival of the West Indies touring team in London on 21 April. The tourists were greeted by a dismal, cold, wet morning, a world away from the hot tropical evening they had left behind in Barbados. Their captain was Garry Sobers, by common consent the outstanding all round cricketer of his generation – perhaps one of the best of all time. He had been a member of arguably the strongest Test side in the world for the last fifteen years, since 1964 as captain. When he had first been appointed the West Indies had won series in Australia, England and India; all notoriously difficult places for visiting sides to win.

Since then things had been less straightforward with a drawn home series against England, and disappointing away series in Australia and New Zealand. The truth was that age had caught up with many of the players who had been the backbone of the team for so long. The fast bowling partnership of Wes Hall and Charlie Griffith who had struck fear into so many opposition opening batsmen were gone. Also now missing were Seymour Nurse who had retired from international cricket and Rohan Kanhai who was not available for this tour. Both had been long serving members in the middle order of an at times destructive batting line-up. The West Indies were a team in transition. As the new players struggled to establish themselves, responsibility increasingly fell on Sobers to make up for the deficiencies by contributing even more with both bat and ball.

In the last calendar year he had played a full English season as captain of Nottinghamshire, during which he had topped the county's batting averages and been second in the bowling averages. He had then captained the West Indies in a five Test series against Australia followed by a three Test series in New Zealand. Not surprisingly by the end of the New Zealand tour in late March, Sobers was exhausted.

A month's recuperation playing golf in Barbados had helped, but nobody was expecting miracles from the tourists this time. Seven of the sixteen man party were new to Test cricket, and ten new to English conditions. Even Sobers had not seen all of his new team mates play yet! England would surely be favourites to win the first of the summer's international series.

Five days after stepping off the aircraft at Heathrow, the West Indies had their first taste of playing in English conditions. A match against the Duke of Norfolk's XI had become the traditional opener for many touring sides. Played at the picturesque Arundel Castle Cricket Ground, the one-day fixture was part social event, a relaxed affair more like an International Cavaliers match and a chance for players to blow away the cobwebs after in some cases months without cricket. The Duke of Norfolk's side was a mixture of current Test players, rising stars and a few ex-England players nearer the end of their career. This time the line-up also included Barry Richards, a player England would expect to have to deal with the following season. He could play against the West Indies in this type of match but not as a member of a South African Test side.

As usual, proceedings were carefully managed by both captains to ensure a close finish. On this occasion, chasing 191 for 5 declared the tourists reached the target with Clive Lloyd, one of the West Indies hopes for the future, hitting four powerful boundaries off successive deliveries to win the match. Emphasising the newness of everything, during the Duke of Norfolk's innings, Sobers had been watching his two opening bowlers Philbert Blair and Grayson Shillingford actually bowl for the first time. The weather was cloudy but better than predicted. Even so spectator numbers were not large. On this particular Saturday there were other things to distract the sports enthusiast.

While the West Indies were batting at Arundel, across in North London the FA Cup Final was taking place. 100,000 people were crammed into

Wembley Stadium to watch Manchester City play Leicester City. Millions more were watching on television, what for many was the showpiece event of the football season.

With their England international trio of Francis Lee, Mike Summerbee and Colin Bell, Manchester City were pre-match favourites. Playing with spirit and flair Leicester were certainly not overawed by the quality and experience of their opponents, and for the first half the match was described by one reporter 'as a credit to British football' [196]. Unfortunately Leicester's challenged petered out, and in the end although they only lost 1-0, in the last half hour they never looked like achieving a win.

Monday's sports headlines were dominated, not by a report of the FA Cup final, but the new one-day cricket competition, which had started the previous afternoon. The Player's County League was the first weekly one-day competition for first-class counties to be introduced in England. The Gillette Cup had been running since 1963, but of course some spectators would only see one match a year if their side was beaten in the first round of the competition. The Player's County League was designed to encourage spectators back to watching cricket at the weekend by providing the opportunity to see a complete match on a Sunday afternoon every week of the season. Starting at 2 pm, a match consisted of one innings per side. Each innings was limited to 40 overs. In order to ensure a variety of bowlers were used and that proceedings moved at a reasonable rate, no bowler was permitted to bowl more than 8 overs, with a bowler's run-up limited to 15 yards (13.7 metres). All seventeen first-class counties were scheduled to play each other once, either home or away. Sponsored by John Player & Sons there was prize money for the eventual winners and runners up of the league, the winner of each match, and financial incentives for bowlers to take 4 wickets in a match or batsmen to hit sixes.

The response of both the public and media to this new type of cricket was positive. For instance, in spite a bitterly cold day, over 2000 had turned up to watch Somerset play Leicestershire at Weston-Super-Mare. The *Daily Express* was in no doubt that this was a part of the future of cricket. The back page of the newspaper, their leading sports page, was dominated by the headline 'Smashing' [197]. Crawford White had been at the match between Middlesex and Yorkshire at Lord's, which was attended by

5000. Reflecting the views of many who had watched one of first round of matches, either live or on BBC2, he concluded that 'If this all-action standard is maintained the new League is a winner' [198].

There were though losers, in this case it was the International Cavaliers. Since 1965, Rothmans had financially backed the Cavaliers and working with the BBC delivered four hours of cricket every Sunday during the summer. Given their history in supporting cricket, Rothmans were hopeful of being the sponsor of the new competition. There was though significant competition with at least '20 potential sponsors interested' [199]. There was also a great deal of lobbying in the press from those keen to keep the Cavaliers alongside or incorporate them into the new competition.

In the end the contract was not awarded to Rothmans but to one of their competitors in the tobacco business, John Player and Sons. Not only that, but the future of the International Cavaliers was now also in doubt. One of the conditions of the sponsorship agreement was that counties would not permit their players to take part in any televised matches other than the Sunday League [200]. Without television coverage the International Cavaliers were no longer such an attractive commercial proposition to Rothmans, and after struggling for another two seasons, in 1970 they were disbanded.

Some traditional cricket supporters saw one-day (or limited over) cricket as little more than a novelty. It is unlikely though that even the most enthusiastic supporters of the new competition could have foreseen the massive influence this type of cricket would have on the future development and financial health of the game both domestically and internationally. Indeed, a credible case could be made for suggesting that without one-day cricket, and developments such as the ICC Cricket World Cup, the Big Bash League in Australia and the Indian Premier League the game of cricket would not have survived. Although it may not have seemed so at the time, the Gillette Cup and Player's Sunday League were the quiet beginning of a cricket revolution.

After the excitement of the new Sunday League, a week later on 3 May the County Championship got underway. Based around three-day matches, the County Championship was much maligned. There were those who believed the three-day format with the frequent use of declarations needed to achieve a result, did not prepare players for the intensity of five day Test cricket. Others felt that the three-day format did not fit the needs of spectators, most of who had to work during the week, and so at best could only watch the first day of a match. Even so, this was still the competition that most professional cricketers wanted to win. Being crowned County Champions, and therefore the best week in, week out over a whole season was still seen as the pinnacle of achievement in English domestic first-class cricket.

In 1968 a powerful Yorkshire side had been crowned County Champions for the third year in a row. They began the defence of their title against Glamorgan on a grey Saturday at Swansea. Most observers anticipated, that while not exactly struggling, Yorkshire would at least not have things all their own way in 1969.

After three days of rain interrupted cricket, the match between Glamorgan and Yorkshire ended in an exciting draw. The home side needing to score 167 in their second innings, were hanging on at 109 for 9 when play ended. Few would have predicted that by mid-September, Glamorgan would be crowned County Champions for only the second time in their history, while Yorkshire would end the season in the lowest position they had ever finished.

1968 had been the first season in which the Counties had been able to recruit overseas cricketers without the need for them to satisfy a qualification period. Not all counties had taken this opportunity, perhaps Garry Sobers joining Nottinghamshire being the biggest box office signing. For 1969 though, most counties had decided that an 'overseas star' was now an essential part of their offer if they wanted to attract more spectators. The only two counties who decided not to do this were Derbyshire and Yorkshire. The first was probably due to financial constraints, while in Yorkshire's case it was tradition (some would say arrogance). They still insisted that players had to have been born in Yorkshire to play for the county. The prospect of an overseas player seemed some way off.

For some cricketers, May was the month in which they hoped to demonstrate to the national selectors that they should be in the England side for the first Test match of the summer. In this case against the West Indies at Old Trafford on 12 June.

One player who certainly started the season with real hope was the flamboyant 27 year old Northamptonshire batsman, Colin Milburn. The disappointment of missing out on the tour of South Africa the previous year, was now well and truly in the past. He had returned from a successful winter playing State cricket for West Australia and scored 139 as a late replacement for England against Pakistan in Karachi on the way home. His confidence was high and his chances of securing an England batting spot for the first Test would have been boosted by scoring 83 for the MCC against Yorkshire, and then a blistering 158 in is his first County Championship match of the season against Leicestershire. The bowling he demolished that day was no average county attack. It included an Australian Test bowler (Graham McKenzie) and three England Test bowlers (Raymond Illingworth, Barry Knight and Jack Birkenshaw).

Things got even better on the afternoon of 23 May, when following Northamptonshire's defeat of the West Indies in a three-day match, the Secretary Ken Turner offered Milburn a contract to secure his long term future with the club. Setting off that Friday evening to attend a birthday party at the nearby Sywell Airport Hotel he must have felt that life was pretty good.

After, by his standards, a quiet evening, Milburn and two team mates left the party to return home. Ten minutes before midnight Colin Milburn's life and career were changed forever. The car he was driving collided with an oncoming lorry. Not wearing a seat belt Milburn was thrown through the car's windscreen. He was taken to Northampton General Hospital with facial injuries and glass splinters in both eyes. The consultant ophthalmologist called in to perform an emergency operation 'decided there was no hope of saving his left eye. The best he could do was remove slivers of glass from Milburn's forehead and his right eye' [201] and remove the left eye altogether. Two days later the ever optimistic, and now one eyed Milburn, was already confidently predicting that 'I will play on' [202]. John Arlott writing in the *Guardian* while for one moment not doubting Milburn's determination was well aware that the loss of the left eye to a right handed batsman would mean

It Might All Just Go Away

that 'his problems of adjustment will be profound', and something that had only rarely been overcome at Test level [203]. Sadly Arlott was right. Colin Milburn never played Test cricket again, and after a number of attempts to play first-class cricket, retired from the game altogether. England and Northamptonshire had lost a player who could have gone on to achieve so much more in the game.

The loss of Milburn was not the only problem for English cricket that May weekend. Colin Cowdrey playing in a Player's County League match for Kent against Glamorgan slipped while running a quick single, and snapped an Achilles tendon in his left leg. Following an operation the next day, it was considered doubtful whether the 37 year old would be back playing cricket again that season [204]. Although Cowdrey had not yet been named as captain for the upcoming series against the West Indies, this was considered to be just a formality. The selectors now faced the problem of who to appoint, to what most assumed would be a care-taker role until Cowdrey was fit again.

It seemed probable that Tom Graveney, who had been Cowdrey's vice-captain in the last three Test series would be given the role. So when it was announced that Roger Prideaux, captain of Northamptonshire, would lead the MCC for the three-day match against the West Indies beginning on 31 May, few eyebrows were raised. After all the selectors knew all about Graveney both as a captain and player. Prideaux on the other hand had managed little of note after a promising debut against Australia the previous summer, and now needed as much practice as he could get to retain his place in the England side.

Since their arrival, only five of the 38 days cricket the West Indians should have played had not been interrupted by the weather. The match against the MCC was no exception, with much of the third day being lost to rain. The play that was possible allowed each side to complete their first innings and MCC to start its second. The selectors learned little. With Barrington, Dexter, Milburn and Cowdrey now not available, potential middle order replacements did nothing to support their case for inclusion in the Test team. Prideaux, Fletcher, Hampshire, D'Oliveira and Birkenshaw managed a total of 18 runs between them in MCC's first innings of 200. Edrich on the other hand, found little difficulty in scoring 125 with a freedom he did not always show when shouldering the responsibility of opening the batting for England.

After the torrent of unwelcome publicity that the D'Oliveira affair had created, the England selectors must have hoped that they would slip quietly once again into the background as far as decisions for the 1969 season were concerned. If this was their intention, then they did not get off to a good start.

On the evening of 4 June the front page of the *Guardian* boldly reported 'Illingworth, the exile, to captain England' [205]. The captain of England for the first Test match against the West Indies would not be Tom Graveney but Ray Illingworth. On paper at least, the appointment seemed odd. The 36 year old had almost no experience of captaincy at first-class let alone Test level. He had only been captain of Leicestershire since the beginning of the season following his move from Yorkshire. At international level, his case was not particularly strong either. He had played 30 Test matches, but was by no means an automatic selection. However, among fellow professionals the important role Illingworth had played as tactical advisor to the captain Brian Close in the all conquering Yorkshire team in recent years was well known [206]. Some were in no doubt about Illingworth's suitability for the role of England captain. For instance, Alan Knott, who played under six different captains during a fifteen year Test career, considered Illingworth to be 'the best captain I ever played under' [207].

As usual with selection decisions, the reasons for overlooking Graveney were nor divulged not even to the man himself. In an autobiography published the following year [208], clearly disappointed, he speculates on why he was overlooked. He suggests that his readiness to voice the players complaints during the winter tour of Pakistan may have counted against him. Graveney also anticipated that the series against the West Indies would be the last of his Test career. In this he proved to be correct but not for the reasons he expected.

The twelve England players selected for the first Test against the West Indies, had a familiarity about it but also showed the influence of the new captain. Phil Sharpe an ex-Yorkshire colleague was chosen for his first Test in five years presumably to replace Milburn, while Barry Knight one of Illingworth's new team mates at Leicestershire was added as a seam bowler. John Hampshire, another Yorkshireman, was also in the squad of twelve, but left out on the first morning of the match in favour of an extra bowler. The eleven of Ray Illingworth (captain) Geoffrey Boycott, John Edrich, Phil Sharpe, Tom Graveney, Basil D'Oliveira, Alan Knott, Barry Knight, David Brown, Derek Underwood and John Snow showed an attacking intent with five front line bowlers and an all-rounder.

In contrast to the experience in the England side, the West Indies eleven was full of uncertainty. In the team of Garry Sobers (captain) Roy Fredericks, Joey Carew, Basil Butcher, Charlie Davis, Clive Lloyd, Maurice Foster, John Shepherd, Jackie Hendriks, Vanburn Holder and Lance Gibbs; Foster, Shepherd and Holder were playing their first Test match and there were only three front line bowlers. It seemed that a huge amount would rest on the shoulders of Butcher, Gibbs and Sobers while the newer players found their feet. That was a lot to ask as Sobers in particular looked tired, and was showing the signs of having played just too much cricket over the last year.

On the morning of the 12 June the sun was finally shining on Old Trafford, Manchester. After such a poor May, it was the start of a heat wave which would last well into autumn. The pitch and outfield looked immaculate and the crowd was buzzing. Looking onto this iconic example of summer in England, was a new member of the BBC television commentary team. Colin Milburn must have been wishing he could be batting on a day like this.

The expectation of a good day's cricket rose even higher in the crowd of nearly 11,000 when Illingworth won the toss and naturally chose to bat first. By the end of two days England had already put themselves into an almost unassailable position. Having scored 413 in their first innings with Boycott contributing a measured 128, and Edrich, Graveney and D'Oliveira 50s, the West Indies had been reduced to 104 for 6 in reply. On a glorious Saturday in front of a crowd of 21,000 the West Indies managed to limp to 147 all out, with Snow and Brown taking four wickets each, Illingworth, showing attacking intent, asked the West Indies to follow on. They batted with more discipline in their second innings but still only managed 275 with just Fredericks getting past 50 and the seam bowlers again doing the damage. Boycott and Edrich were left a simple task of scoring just twelve runs to win. Ten minutes after midday on the fifth day England convincingly won the match by ten wickets. When they had last played the West Indies at Old Trafford in 1966, the visitors had crushed England, winning by an innings and 40 runs. This time things had been very different. Ilingworth's debut as captain had been impressive in all respects.

The weekend of the Test match was one of contrasting fortunes for the two Worcestershire players in the England team. The man from Cape Town, who had overcome so many obstacles to play cricket in England, was now Basil D'Oliveira OBE. He received the award for services to cricket in the Queen's Birthday Honours.

For D'Oliveira's county captain, the news was not so good. Tom Graveney was reported to the Test and County Cricket Board, for playing in a match on the Sunday, which had been arranged as part of his benefit year. He had requested permission to play, but as was normal for England players contracted to play in a Test match this had been refused. Gravening ignored the decision, and played in the match but was aware that there might be consequences.

There were consequences, which again made the front pages of the national newspapers. The Disciplinary Sub-Committee of the Test and County Cricket Board was hastily convened on 19 June, and found Graveney guilty of 'a serious breach of discipline' [209]. He was severely reprimanded and barred from selection for the next three Test matches. The Old Trafford Test match had been his seventy ninth and would be his last. The name 'Graveney T. W. ', would not appear in an England line-up again.

The England side for second Test at Lord's obviously now needed a replacement for Graveney. The selectors chose Peter Parfitt the Middlesex captain. Playing his first Test for three years, he would have the advantage of playing on his home ground. They also added the young Derbyshire fast bowler Alan Ward to the squad although the expectation was that he was unlikely to play. The final eleven chosen on the first morning of the match as expected included Parfitt but John Hampshire was now in the side. He was making his debut in Test cricket, and had been selected instead of Underwood. This time the selectors decided to play only four front line bowlers.

The tourists made three changes including giving debuts to the young pace bowler Grayson Shillingford and wicketkeeper Michael Findlay, the first Windward Islanders to represent the West Indies (the monopoly of Barbados, Guyana, Jamaica and Trinidad as the source for the Test team was gradually beginning to be broken).

The Lord's Test match is one of the showpiece occasions of the English summer. This time it did not disappoint. Good crowds enjoyed warm and sunny weather for the whole five days. On Saturday the gates were closed with 27,000 spectators already inside before the start time of 11 am.

The West Indies won the toss, and naturally chose to bat first. It was clear almost from the start that the pitch was true and hard, and that this would be a match in which the bowlers would struggle to take wickets. By the end of the first day the West Indies had reached 246 – 4. Nothing special, but not a disaster either. The England bowling had been workman like. The visitors eventually finished their first innings on 380 but it took until nearly tea on the second day to get there.

England stumbled a little at the start of their first innings, but eventually reached 344. Again though it took time and it was not until mid-morning on the fourth day that the visitors began their second innings. While a draw looked almost inevitable, three players would remember this match as the one in which they scored their first Test century. For the visitors Davis, and for England Hampshire and Illingworth.

In order to try and force a result, Sobers declared on the final day, setting England a target of 332 to win in five hours. A century by Boycott gave the innings a strong foundation, and Sharpe tried valiantly to lead a charge for victory. However the task was beyond him alone, and England ultimately batted out the remaining overs of the match for a draw.

It had been a much better performance by the West Indies, but Butcher and crucially Sobers still seemed short of their best. As far as the West Indies captain was concerned, one experienced cricket journalist warned that 'At Lord's he seemed to be a great player effortlessly warming up' [210]. People had written Sobers off at their peril before,

On the other hand, Illingworth again showed skilful tactical ability, scored a century in England's first innings and took three wickets in the

West Indies second innings. His impressive start as the England captain continued.

Just when things seemed to be going well again, the morning copy of the *Times* on 10 July would have set the alarm bells ringing at Lord's. The only photograph on the front page showed demonstrators interrupting play in a match between Oxford University and a Wilfred Isaacs XI [211]. Cricket and South Africa were back in the news.

The match was part of a tour of Britain by a group of young South African cricketers, privately organised and funded by the Johannesburg businessman Wilfred Isaacs. As far as the Young Liberals and other groups opposed to apartheid were concerned, this was still a team, which had been chosen on racial lines. Peter Hain took on the responsibility for organising direct-action demonstrations to disrupt as many of the matches as possible during the rest of the two-month tour [212]. Ominously, leaflets handed out at the Oxford match warned that this and other disruptions planned, were 'a trial run for next year's official tour of this country' [213].

Perhaps with an eye to the future, the England selectors recalled Keith Fletcher, the 25-year-old Essex batsman, in place of Parfitt for the third Test match at Headingley, Leeds. As usual they left themselves the option of playing the extra batsman or bowler. On the morning of the match they decided on five bowlers and so the England eleven were Ray Illingworth (captain), Geoffrey Boycott, John Edrich, Phil Sharpe, John Hampshire, Basil D'Oliveira, Alan Knott, Barry Knight, Derek Underwood, David Brown and John Snow. The West Indies were unchanged from the eleven that had started at Lord's.

England won the toss, and in grey but dry conditions Illingworth chose to bat first. By the close of the first day England had struggled to 194 for 7, with only Edrich, D'Oliveira and Knott making worthwhile contributions to the score. The partisan Headingley crowd would have been particularly disappointed to see the Yorkshiremen in the side manage only 20 runs between all four of them (although some of the less generous may have no longer considered Illingworth to be a true Yorkshireman).

Bowling England out for 223 an hour into the second day, the West Indies would have been reasonably satisfied, especially as the weather was predicted to become warmer and the pitch easier. The seam bowlers Shepherd, Holder and Sobers had taken most of the wickets. The visitors would have been less pleased at the end of the day, having been bowled out for 167 in just 65 overs. The fact that Boycott had been dismissed for 0, would have not been much compensation. They had handed the advantage somewhat meekly to England.

On what John Arlott called 'the annual feast of Yorkshire cricket' [214], Headingley Test Saturday the crowd saw the West Indies captain show why he should never be written off. In what, even by his exceptional standards, was a remarkable spell of fast-medium pace bowling, Sobers aided by Holder pulled the West Indies back into the match. The visitors were severely handicapped by the loss of Shepherd (being treated in hospital for a back injury), but even so restricting England to 214 for 9, a lead of 276 they would have fancied their chances of winning.

An hour into the fourth day, England were finally all out, and the visitors had the target of scoring 303 to win the match and draw the series. Time was not an issue, with eleven hours play still possible.

A few overs before the close of the day's play, the West Indies were 219 for 3 with Butcher and Lloyd playing well. Victory seemed a possibility, maybe even a probability. Illingworth then demonstrated imaginative captaincy by implementing continuous changes in bowling, with each bowler having only a one over spell. This disturbed the batsmen and the visitors lost 4 wickets for 9 runs in 15 minutes. At the close of play the West Indies were 240 for 7 still 63 runs behind, and the chance of victory seemingly gone.

On the last morning the tail end batsmen caused some concern as they inched towards victory, but ultimately the task was too great and they were bowled out for 272. England won the match by 30 runs, and the series 2-0.

Illingworth was rewarded by being appointed captain for the three Test series against New Zealand. England was the better side, but there were still some problems. Most importantly, the hole in the middle order batting left by the absence of Milburn, Cowdrey, Barrington and Graveney had yet to be satisfactorily filled.

Sobers and his team would have been disappointed. There had been a number of opportunities to at least draw the series, but they had failed to take them. For Basil Butcher, another West Indian great, this was also the end of his Test career.

No matter what else happened that day, Sunday 16 July 1969 will be remembered by most people around the world as the day Apollo 11 lifted off from Cape Kennedy. On board were Neil Armstrong, Edwin 'Buzz' Aldrin and Michael Collins. Four days later, watched by an estimated television audience of 600 million, Armstrong and Aldrin would be the first humans to set foot on the moon. For once even cricket took second place.

Back on earth, the New Zealand tourists, England's opponents for the second half of a twin tour summer had been in Britain since the 10 June. Led by Graham Dowling they were confident of improving on the 3-0 series loss they had suffered when they last visited in 1965. Their confidence had been buoyed by having just drawn a series against the West Indies at home. Dowling with the optimism you would probably expect from the captain at the beginning of a tour cautioned 'We are a fitter, more determined side now. I give you due warning not to take the Kiwis lightly' [215]. The more optimistic in the party may even have had hopes of finally winning a Test match against England.

As the first Test approached at the end of July, the optimism was still there. They had played eight matches on tour, drawing most but beating Scotland. The one loss had been a narrow one against Essex, when New Zealand had been caught on a turning pitch in the fourth innings.

The optimism would have still been there on the second day of the first Test at Lord's. Illingworth had won the toss, batted first but England had been bowled out for 190 with only the captain scoring more than 50. In reply New Zealand were 70 for 1 by lunch on the second day. Then it all went wrong as the New Zealand batsmen disintegrated against the highly effective spin bowling of Underwood and Illingworth. They were bowled out for 169. Moral high, England's batting improved in their second innings and they managed 340 with Edrich scoring a century and Sharpe and Knight getting near 50. Set an unlikely 361 to win, New Zealand never got near. Turner batted throughout the innings for 43 runs, but New Zealand were bowled out for 131, on the fourth day. Underwood was almost unplayable, taking 7 for 32, and 12 wickets in the match.

The second Test match at Tent Bridge, Nottingham was badly affected by the weather, with nearly two full days being lost to rain. New Zealand batted with more authority, but England had the better of a match that was always going to be drawn.

In the third Test match at the Kennington Oval. London, New Zealand were again unable to cope with the bowling of Underwood. Winning the toss, the tourists batted first and were bowled out for 150 with Underwood and Illingworth taking 8 wickets between them. Although England only managed 242 in their first innings, New Zealand were bowled out for 229 when batting a second time, with Underwood taking 6 wickets. England scored the 138 runs they needed to win relatively easily and won the match by 8 wickets, and the series 2-0. The tale of the series was that the New Zealand batsmen simply were unable to cope with the England bowling. None of the top five New Zealand batsmen managed to score consistently, with only four reaching 50 on any occasion. Underwood took 24 wickets at an average of 9.16, Illingworth 10 wickets at 15.4. and Ward 10 at 21.0

The selectors would have learned little new over the summer. England had won two series they had been expected to win. The hole in the middle order batting left by the absence of Milburn, Cowdrey, Barrington and Graveney had yet to be filled. None of those tried so far had played with the authority to suggest that they might become an automatic selection. Illingworth had done all that could be expected of him as the stand-in captain.

With the international matches for the summer over, attention turned to the domestic competitions which were all drawing to a close. On the 5 September at Sophia Gardens, Cardiff, Glamorgan won the County Championship for only the second time in their history. They were also the first side to go though a whole season unbeaten since Lancashire in 1930. While the county had few Test stars, it showed what a tightly knit team who enjoyed their cricket could achieve.

For the previous year's county champions Yorkshire, 1969 was a nothing less than a shock. The county which had won the championship for the previous three years suddenly became mortal. They finished in thirteenth place, the lowest position in their history. There were of course mitigating circumstances. Trueman and Taylor had retired, Illingworth had moved to Leicestershire and Close and Nicholson were absent injured for much of the season. Despite the compensation of winning the Gillette Cup at Lord's on 6 September, it would have been hard for the normally proud Yorkshire club to accept such a fall from grace.

Probably the most pleasing outcome of the season was the success of the new Player's County League. Won by Lancashire, the Sunday afternoon competition had had proved popular attracting a total of 280,000 spectators by the end of the season. This was only 47,000 less than the aggregate attendance for all County Championship matches played the rest of the week.

As the season drifted to a close, a rain affected match between Kent and Essex at Dover on 13 September which would normally have not have attracted much attention, suddenly became a game to watch for many in the media. Batting at number six for Kent, Colin Cowdrey was playing his first County Championship match in nearly four months. He only scored two but most importantly for him, he was back playing cricket, and the following season he would be ready to take back his role as England captain.

With no winter tour scheduled, the England players would have to find other things to occupy them. Over in the Southern hemisphere there was the Test series between South Africa and Australia to look forward to at the beginning of 1970. This would give some idea of the opposition that England could expect during the summer of 1970 when South Africa visited Britain. Not everybody was looking forward to the visit of the South African cricket team. The Stop the Seventy Tour campaign was about to be born.

11

Stop the Seventy Tour
October 1969 – May 1970

Those reading the 'In Brief' section of the *Times* on 21 January 1969 could have been forgiven for not noticing a paragraph headed 'Threat to cricket'. The 40 word news item was the sort of information that readers would often skip or read and quickly forget. In this case the Southern African Commission of the National League of Young Liberals had warned that they would 'disrupt cricket matches between England and South Africa if the proposed tour by South Africa in 1970 is not cancelled' [216]. It was no surprise that this piece of news had little effect on the Cricket Council, and those at Lord's responsible for organising the forthcoming cricket tour.

During the 1960s calls for action from political pressure groups such as this were common. Most rarely went much beyond press releases, leaflets, posters and perhaps a few banner carrying demonstrators.

In its early days, the Anti-Apartheid Movement (AAM) was typical of this type of organisation. It had started life as the Boycott Movement, formed in 1959 to encourage the British public to stop buying goods from South Africa. However, following the Sharpeville massacre in 1960, the Boycott Movement was renamed the Anti-Apartheid Movement and broadened its aims to include supporting economic sanctions and encouraging the complete isolation of apartheid South Africa.

One of the areas targeted for isolation was sport, particularly the white dominated games of cricket and rugby union. In 1965, the AAM planned a campaign to persuade people to boycott any cricket match played by the South African touring team during their summer visit to Britain. The team was considered an example of the country's apartheid policy, having been selected from only white cricketers. Illustrating the passive nature of the planned protests, David Ennals MP the Movement's President made it clear that although it was intended to protest outside all grounds where the tourists were playing, there were no plans to interfere with the matches themselves [217].

Although no doubt well intentioned, most demonstrations were rather ad-hoc and rarely made the national press. An exception was the tourists' first match against Derbyshire at Chesterfield, although it was not the type of publicity that the AAM would have wanted. Noting that only 30 protesters had turned up, and that these had left at lunchtime. A picture on the front page of the *Sunday Telegraph* of a protester blowing up a balloon was accompanied by a rather mocking headline 'Inflated Opposition for S. African Cricketers' [218]. The campaign did manage one success of note, dissuading the Queen and Prime Minister from continuing the tradition of attending the first day of the Test Match at Lord's. However this was not mentioned in most press reports of the match at the time.

Four years later another anti-apartheid group announced its intention to disrupt the tour of the South African cricket team planned for 1970. However, the tools protesters were now prepared to use to achieve their objective had changed significantly. This time the cricket establishment and the British Government would ignore these threats at their peril.

On 10 September 1969 at a Fleet Street public house *The White Swan* a press conference was held to announce the launch of the '*Stop the Seventy Tour*' campaign [219]. The meeting was chaired by a 19-year-old engineering student, unknown to most in the cricket world. This would soon change. Within weeks, Peter Hain would become the public face of what for many was one of the most successful pressure-group actions in post-war British political history.

A first year engineering student may seem an unlikely person to lead a high profile campaign targeting the emotive and complicated world of sport and politics in South Africa. However, Hain and his family had first hand experience of living under an apartheid Government, and the consequences of opposing their policies.

Peter Hain was born in Nairobi, Kenya in 1950 but within two years his parents had moved the family back to South Africa so that his father could take up a new job as an architect. As a white boy growing up first in Natal and then later in Pretoria, Hain experienced the privileges of being white in an apartheid system. Though not particularly wealthy the family lived in a comfortable house with spacious grounds, and as was normal a black servant.

As he grew up, and went to school, he soon learnt the way in which the Government's apartheid policies controlled nearly every part of your life. Living in a whites-only area, attending a whites-only school, travelling each day on a whites-only bus and playing cricket against whites-only teams was only the start.

While many whites in South Africa, either supported or turned a blind eye to the National Party's apartheid policies, Hain's parents did not. The regime's brutal discrimination laws did not rest easily with them, and they soon became members of the non-racial Liberal Party, ultimately becoming Chairman and Secretary of the Pretoria branch. Their political activity bought them into contact with others looking for change in South Africa like Nelson Mandela and Walter Sisulu but also made them targets for the State Security Police. Their telephone was tapped, mail intercepted and the house often under surveillance. It was not only the Government that disapproved of Walter and Adelaine Hain's activities, there was also problems within their community. As Peter later wrote 'Many whites in Pretoria remained bitterly opposed to the very existence of the Liberal Party' [220].

The African National Congress had long been a banned organisation, and its leader Nelson Mandela was eventually caught and jailed for life in 1964. John Vorster, the hard line Minister of Justice (later to become Prime Minister) now began to target all anti-apartheid activists including members of the Liberal Party. Thousands were detained or banned from any political activity. Some segments of the opposition were becoming more militant, arguing that this was the only way left to achieve change. John Harris, a white school teacher and friend of the Hain family was hung in 1965 for his part in a bomb attack carried out by the African

Resistance Movement on Johannesburg railway station. Harris was the only white person executed in South Africa for a crime committed during the struggle against apartheid.

Hain's parents both had banning orders imposed on them, and Peter's father soon found it impossible to get work as an architect. He could not travel outside Pretoria without permission and it was made known that any company offering him work would no longer receive government contracts. With no other alternative open if he wanted to continue to support his family, Walter Hain made the difficult decision to accept a offer of employment in Britain. In the spring of 1966 the Hain family left South Africa. The Security Police ensured they would not be coming back by cancelling Walter and Adelaine Hain's South African citizenship and issuing them with one-way exit permits.

A General Election was held in the United Kingdom on the 31 March 1966. The incumbent Labour Government led by Harold Wilson had only been in office just over 16 months, but was finding working with a majority of only 4 MPs difficult. With the government doing well in the opinion polls Wilson called a snap election, which the Labour Party won convincingly, increasing their majority in Parliament to 97 seats. A day later a Union Castle liner on route from Cape Town docked at Southampton with the Hain family among those on board.

One of the first things that needed to be resolved by Walter and Adelaine Hain was the education of their children. Peter and his brother were enrolled at Emanuel School, Battersea. Through intense study, Peter caught up the education he had missed and went on to obtain three good A levels, sufficient to be offered a place on a degree course in mechanical engineering at the prestigious Imperial College, London. The academic study was preceded by a year long apprenticeship with the diesel fuel injection specialists CAV, which he began in September 1968.

Along with his commitments at school and then CAV, Hain revived his interest in politics. Within a year of arriving in Britain he had joined the Anti-Apartheid Movement (AAM) but not surprisingly the addition of a 17-year-old schoolboy to the membership list went unnoticed. It was the

Young Liberals, which he joined around the same time that gave him a home from which he could develop politically.

In the 1960s the Young Liberals were seen as being radicals, pro-active in many areas including opposing apartheid. This did not always sit comfortably with the Liberal mainstream that was more moderate. However from 1967 the Liberal Party had in Jeremy Thorpe a new young leader who was receptive to change.

As an exiled South African, Hain very quickly became a Member of the Young Liberals 'Southern African Commission', giving him the opportunity to meet leading anti-apartheid activists such as Dennis Brutus (South African Non-Racial Olympic Committee) and Thabo Mbeki (African National Congress). By the autumn of 1968 Hain had been elected onto the Young Liberals National Executive Committee, and within 6 months he was advocating direct action at sports events; disrupting the events themselves in order to draw attention to an issue [221]. Direct Action was first used by a group of Young Liberals led by Hain during Wilfred Isaacs' cricket tour in the summer of 1969. Protests at the Isaacs' XI matches drew little comment from the media. However, the manager of the tour E. R. (Ronnie) Eriksen was so concerned by the effect protests had on the tour's matches, he wrote to the MCC Cricket Council with a raft of suggestions for additional security procedures that he thought would be required to protect the proposed South African tour. These included significant numbers of police to deal with demonstrators, use of plain clothes police officers at the team's hotel and reducing the proposed schedule of matches, with none being played in Scotland or Ireland [222].

The potential for direct action to achieve results was such that by August 1969 a disparate collection of organisations had joined together to form the Stop the Seventy Tour (STST) Committee. As well as the Young Liberals and Anti-Apartheid Movement there were groups with political affiliations across the whole spectrum. These included the Young Communist League, the International Socialists, the United National Youth and the Movement for Colonial Freedom. All had the same objective, to stop the proposed South African cricket tour in 1970.

On the 10 September 1969 STST held a press conference to announce itself to the wider world. As Press Officer and Convenor of the

Committee, Peter Hain soon found himself acting as the commentator at this event. The next day the press had promoted him to Chair of the STST [223]. At the press conference he had promised 'mass demonstrations and disruption throughout the 1970 cricket tour' [224].

Illustrating the rather ad-hoc organisation of the Committee at that time, when it was realised that the Springbok rugby tour of Britain and Ireland was due to start on 5 November, STST's objectives were quickly expanded to include disruption of matches on this tour as well.

As opposition to the proposed 1970 South African cricket tour built up, the official line from the MCC remained that it should go ahead as planned. The British Government though were beginning to have doubts. As early as April 1969, the Sports Minister, Denis Howell had met with the President (R. Aird) and Secretary (S. C. Griffith) of the MCC to discuss the forthcoming tour. Howell had information that SAN-ROC was planning to disrupt matches during the tour in order to gain publicity for their anti-apartheid cause. While maintaining the line that in no circumstances could the Government be seen to be advising the MCC to cancel the tour, Howell emphasised the significant advantages that would come from such a move [225].

By early October, Billy Griffith's view that the tour should go ahead was beginning to waiver. The Manager of the Wilfred Isaacs XI had told Griffith that even though the number of demonstrators was small, play had been interrupted in all fixtures but one during their recent tour. He thought with the numbers likely from the Stop the Seventy Committee, it would be nearly impossible to protect a Test match ground from disruption over a full five days. Equally worrying to Griffith was the fact that hard liners like G.O. C. (Gubby) Allen and Wilfred Isaacs himself were now beginning to question the wisdom of continuing with the tour [226].

Given the large hole in the finances of county cricket that cancellation of the tour would create, Griffith had already been thinking of alternatives should such a catastrophe occur (although as far as the wider world was concerned the South African tour was going ahead). In a meeting with a Home Office official he mentioned a fall-back option of a Rest of the World XI, captained by Garry Sobers or the Mansoor Ali Khan Pataudi (later Nawab of Pataudi) playing England in a five Test match series. Ironically the Rest of the World XI might include a number of players who would have almost certainly been members of the South African touring party, which this new series would be replacing [227].

The confidence of the MCC would not have been increased when on 19 October, Denis Howell appeared on the London Weekend Television Programme '*Sports Arena*' and said that he did not think the South African cricket team should tour Britain in 1970. While he made it clear that this was a personal view there was little doubt that many would consider this to be an indicator of the views of the British Government.

Such was the concern that statements like this could have on UK – South African relations and trade, Lord Chalfont, the Minister of State for Foreign and Commonwealth Affairs met with Howell and essentially rebuked him. He was advised that given the potential fallout should the South African cricket tour be cancelled, it would be 'wiser if Ministers said as little as possible publicly on the subject' [228]. Howell also agreed to consult the Foreign Office before making any further remarks, publicly or privately, about the forthcoming South African cricket tour.

Early on the 30 October, another South African side the Springboks rugby team arrived at Heathrow Airport for a three month tour of Britain and Ireland. The threats of disruption during the tour from anti-apartheid activists were not taken too seriously. When only 20 student protestors were present to shout slogans at the arriving players, the *Daily Telegraph* rather sarcastically observed that 'it was much too early in the morning for students to get worked up about anything' [229]. The reporter, like many in the press cohort, was of the view that with no protestors at the team's hotel or first press conference, the threat of militancy and disruption had been greatly exaggerated.

Corrie Bornman the manager of the Springboks had a similar view. That evening in a telephone interview with the *Cape Times* back home, be described the demonstrators he had encountered so far as 'just a bunch of kids' [230].

The 'kids' had already achieved a small victory with the tourists' opening fixture against Oxford University still in doubt. The threat of disruption from yet another group, the Oxford Fireworks Day Committee, had already been sufficient for the Thames Valley police to insist that the match planned for the University's quaint playing field styled Iffley Road Ground be cancelled. The replacement venue was kept secret until the day of the match, and then details prominently displayed in most national newspapers. For instance *The Times* front page had a headline 'Coach trips to Springbok protest' [231], the demonstrators were getting their cause promoted in prime media for free.

The fixture itself was switched to the home of English rugby, Twickenham, London. With a capacity of 62,000 the ground was ten times bigger than needed for the expected attendance, but it was easy to defend. On the day there was a significant police presence, with a total of 540 uniformed, plain clothes and mounted police more than adequate to deal with the 500 or so demonstrators. While there were chants and scuffles in the crowd though out the game, only two demonstrators managed to break through the police cauldron and run onto the field. The game ended with Oxford University winning a famous victory over the Springboks. The next day much of the reporting seemed more interested in the antics of the protestors rather than the game of rugby. Both sides in the anti-apartheid debate were claiming victory, and in a way both were right. The Rugby Football Union emphasised that the fixture had not been cancelled, disrupted or abandoned because of protests, while STST pointed to the wide press coverage their cause had achieved. Peter Hain expressed disappointment that more disruption had not been possible, but given that there had been just 24 hours notice of the venue he was pleased STST had managed to get 500 protestors to the ground. He promised better organised and increased numbers of protests for every one of the Springboks remaining fixtures [232].

Three matches later the confrontation between anti-apartheid protestors and the rugby world had become serious and violent. On the 15 November, Swansea played the Springboks. The rugby club employed a 100 or so stewards, in addition to the 637 police present, to keep increasingly disruptive protestors under control. Unfortunately, many of the stewards lacked discipline, and descriptions and pictures of violent clashes were prominent in the following day's newspapers. Such were the injuries sustained by both police and protestors that the Home Secretary, James Callaghan called for an urgent report from the Inspector of Constabulary. Questions were raised in the House of Commons and a week later the use of rugby stewards to remove demonstrators from the pitch in future games was banned.

In trying to reduce the effect of future protests the police and rugby authorities faced the problem that STST did not have a conventional structure or headquarters. Peter Hain was by agreement its public spokesman. More or less by default the telephone number of the Hain family home became the organisation's contact number, but that was all.

Decisions on the types of protests and the mobilization of people needed to implement them for each game rested with a local action group, all of which were independent. This meant that each game was the responsibility of a different group of people. As a result STST quickly evolved into a group of activists developing its own direct action projects, rather than a committee of representatives of organizations [233]. Remarkably the protest group with little central organisation worked. It prospered and grew. By 26 November in the match between the Springboks and Northern Counties in Manchester, 2,000 police were required to stop 7,000 demonstrators disrupting the match, with 150 being arrested. Front page coverage in national newspapers, with pictures of confrontations between police and protesters was becoming the norm. In addition other groups such as the Anti-Apartheid Movement and Young Liberals also joined in protests on an independent ad-hoc basis,

Peter Hain, as the voice of STST, then raised the stakes still further by announcing that disruptions would no longer just be just confined to the game but that 'the Springboks can expect direct action protests to follow their every movement [234]. The tour manager Corrie Bornman who two months previously had dismissed the anti-apartheid protestors as kids was now having to deal with discontent in his own camp. Morale had fallen 'to the extent that players voted to go home, and were compelled to stay only by management' [235].

The Springboks decided to continue and true to their word the anti-apartheid protestors hounded them as they 'trudged sourly through Britain, outwitted by demonstrators and largely outplayed by their international opponents' [236]. The tourists drew against Wales and Ireland, and lost to England and Scotland. Following the last game of tour, as the Springboks prepared to go home, reporters on television, radio and print media began to summarise the tour. As had been the case so often both sides claimed victory. John Tallent, the chairman of the Home Union Tours Committee declared ' We faced a challenge – and rugby football won the day' while Peter Hain concluded that 'We would have settled for a tenth of the impact' [237]. Ultimately the Springboks 1969/70 tour of Britain and Ireland would be remembered for things other than rugby.

MCC Secretary, Billy Griffith had watched the problems that the rugby administrators were having in dealing with STST protestors with increasing alarm. In late November, Griffith had again met with staff of the Home Office. One concluded that 'it was clear that the events surrounding the Springbok rugby matches had made an impression' [238]. Griffith was particularly concerned about the large number of police and significant amounts of money that would be needed to protect cricket grounds. There was also a concern that even then, success was not guaranteed. After all if despite a huge police presence it was proving difficult to prevent disruption to a rugby match lasting 80 minutes, what chance was there for a five day Test match.

It wasn't just Griffith who was beginning to have doubts. Having seen the problems at a recent Springbok rugby match the Secretary of one county cricket club had already told Griffith that a match against the South Africans which they were scheduled to play in 1970 would almost certainly not be possible.

The Test and County Cricket Board (TCCB) had a two day meeting scheduled beginning 10 December. With representatives from all 17 first class counties, one of the most important decisions they had to make this time was whether to recommend to the Cricket Council (MCC had been quietly dropped from the original title of this committee) that the following summer's South African tour should still go ahead. Normally this would have been an automatic decision but this time things were different.

The problems that the STST movement had caused the Springboks rugby tourists had clearly unsettled a number of county secretaries. It was not just the unprecedented number of police that might be needed at each match between the South Africans and the counties, but where the money was going to come from to pay for this. When the South Africans had last played a Test match at Lord's in 1965, the manpower needed to police the event had consisted of a police sergeant and five constables. Things were likely to be very different this time for both games against the counties and Test matches.

The cost of hiring a regular police constable was typically £10 a day (equivalent to a £175 in 2020). It was being suggested that maybe as much as £10,000 (equivalent to approximately £175,000 in 2020) would be required to police a three day match, while for a five day Test match even more would be needed. Such expenditure was beyond the capacity of many counties who were already struggling financially. This was just the cost of covering the days of the match itself. There was also the security costs needed to protect the pitch in the weeks leading up to the match. The problem was that nobody really knew how big the opposition would be by the time the South African cricketers arrived, and therefore exactly how many police would be required to keep order.

Comments from the normally publicity shy county secretaries were beginning to appear in the press in the days leading up to the TCCB meeting. Les Ames, manager of the previous winter's MCC tour of Ceylon and Pakistan had shown that he was certainly not someone who was easily defeated. Now Secretary of Kent County Cricket Club, even he commented that 'Although I am loathe to give in to a small minority. I feel it is in the best interests for the tour to be cancelled' [239]. The Secretary of the Sussex County Cricket Club was more forthright saying there was not 'a hope in hell' [240] of the tour going ahead in its present form.

As usual a press conference was held following the TCCB meeting. Billy Griffith, the Board's Secretary (and Secretary of the MCC and Cricket Council), read a statement confirming the TCCB's recommendation that the South African tour would still take place. The decision still had to be ratified by the Cricket Council in February but this was expected to be a formality. While the decision itself was not surprising, the fact that it was unanimous showed that the cricket establishment was closing ranks.

In view of the difficulties the Springboks rugby team had experienced, the TCCB reluctantly concluded that threats to disrupt the cricket tour could no longer be ignored. They formed an Emergency Executive Sub-committee to consider the feasibility of the original tour schedule, security precautions that would now be necessary, and the cost of providing them. Reflecting the unusual times the game was now finding itself in, the names of those serving on this committee were kept secret. The Chair of the Committee was in fact Maurice Allom [241].

Griffith also acknowledged that 'the counties are prepared to dip very deep into their pockets and the board will have to dig very deep into its pocket over this' [242]. In neither case were the pockets very deep, and those opposing the tour were only just getting into their stride.

A few days later Griffith had a meeting with Sir John Waldron, the Commissioner of Police at New Scotland Yard. With the decision made for the tour to go ahead, Griffith was keen to try and get estimates of how much policing would cost. As with the Government the Police were steering a careful line. In a note of the meeting, Waldron commented 'you will have seen from the press that it is the present intention of the MCC not to cancel the tour. It is not part of our duty to influence them one way or the other' [243].

On 1 January 1970 the world welcomed in not just a new year but also a new decade. As usual political and religious leaders reflected on the year ahead and considered what was to come.

In the multi-racial cricket debate the main protagonists would have no doubt been doing the same. The MCC and South African Cricket Association with their using sport to build bridges philosophy would have been hoping that the worst of the protests were over and that the South African cricket tour would now go ahead.

Peter Hain and other anti-apartheid campaigners on the other hand would have seen the turn of the year as just the beginning. They expected opposition to the tour to grow to such at extent that in the end the cricket authorities would have no alternative but to cancel it.

South Africa's Prime Minister John Vorster did not hope, his New Year message was characteristically blunt – do not expect any change. He was adamant that, whatever aspirational statements sports bodies in his country had made about multiracial sport, the Republic would not deviate from its policy of apartheid in sport. Hinting at the pressure cricket authorities were coming under from the rest of the world he was also defiant, stating 'it is preferable, rather to break off relations openly if differences cannot be bridged, rather than yield to Leftist and Communist pressures' [244].

As for the South African players, in many respects the pawns in the game, they were preparing themselves for a home Test series against Australia. On 2 January the Australians led by Bill Lawry landed in Johannesburg to start a twelve week tour, including four Test matches. This was the second half of a tour which on paper looked arduous and in practice turned out to be even worse.

The Australians had left Sydney on 15 October, spending twelve days in Ceylon (now Sri Lanka) where they played four matches, before moving onto India. The tour of India was taxing on the players. In addition to the usual heat, humidity and large distances to be covered between some matches, this time there was crowd problems. Huge numbers turned up to watch each day of every Test (typically 40,000 per day). Unfortunately not all were content to just watch the cricket. During the first Test there was a riot on the evening of the fourth day with other matches being marred by incidents from a pitch invasion, to bottles being thrown onto the field.

In a series dominated by spin bowlers, the Australians won 3-1, although it could have been closer if India had taken their chances. The Australians had put a lot into the tour and it was a tired team that left Bombay (now Mumbai) on 1 January. The cricket commentator Alan McGilvray was one of the press to meet the Australians when they landed at Jan Smuts Airport a day later. He wrote that the players 'looked haggard. Their eyes seemed to be standing out of their heads and some of them looked positively yellow' [245].

In comparison, the South Africans were fully charged and raring to go. Tour cancellations and the refusal of their Government to allow them to play non-white teams meant they had not played a Test match since February 1967. The side was now captained by Ali Bacher and contained world-class players such as Graeme Pollock and those who were on their way to be being world class such as Barry Richards and Mike Procter. The last two had already made an impression playing in English county cricket. The previous summer Richards had finished fourth in the first-class batting averages and Procter second in the bowling averages.

Right from day one of the first Test, the Australians were on the back foot, and no match for a powerful, motivated South African side playing in front of large partisan crowds. One of the Australian team Ashley Mallett later admitted that they were totally outplayed. 'Mike Procter and Peter Pollock steamrollered through our early batsmen in nearly every innings' while 'Barry Richards, playing in his first Test series … and the brilliant Graeme Pollock thrashed our bowlers into virtual submission' [246]. It was not just the Pollock brothers, Procter and Richards. Wherever you looked in the South African line-up there seemed to be a cricketer wanting to prove something, with Eddie Barlow being perhaps the best example. In the first Test the Australian captain tried to unsettle Barlow before he had faced a delivery with a few verbal taunts. Unfortunately this may have not been the wisest of decisions as it only raised Barlow's desire to succeed even further. A player who had so far had a poor season with the bat in domestic cricket went on to top score in the innings with 127.

The statistics for the series emphasised the problems the tourists were having. The normally reliable opening bowler Graham McKenzie who was clearly not well, took only one wicket for 333 in three Tests. Mike Procter, his opposite number in the South African side took 26 wickets at 13.57. Batting was little better, with only Ian Redpath managing an average above 40, and no Australian batsman scoring a Test century. In comparison Richards and Graeme Pollock ended the series with a batting average over 70. It was no surprise that South Africa won the series 4-0. Oozing confidence, they were clearly more than ready to take on England in a few months time.

While the South Africans were warming up for their tour of Britain, over in the country itself any illusion that opposition to the visit might be dwindling was quickly dispelled on the morning of 19 January. Most of the national newspaper front pages reported details of vandalism that had occurred at twelve county cricket grounds the previous night. In some cases slogans such as *'No Race In Sport'* and *'No 70's Tour'* had been painted on walls, fences or scoreboards, while in others a hole had been dug in the pitch at Cardiff and weed killer poured onto the pitch at Bristol.

Newspapers as politically diverse as the *Guardian* and *Daily Express* agreed that such incidents would not help the anti-apartheid cause. The Liberal supporting *Guardian,* a strong opponent of apartheid, thought the attacks 'self defeating and wrong'. They concluded that 'they are wrong because the right to protest does not encompass the right to shove one's views, however sound, down the throats of others' [247].

There was no rush to claim responsibility for this series of attacks. Maybe because this could make the organisation liable for prosecution. There was though a rush to claim no involvement. David Steele was adamant that the Anti-Apartheid Movement had played no part, stating that 'vandalism at cricket grounds will do nothing to end racialism in sport' [248]. Similarly, Peter Hain was quick to distance STST saying 'that his committee did not hold exclusive rights of protest against the coming racialist cricket tour' [249]. Surprisingly it was Louis Eaks, the Chairman of the Young Liberals who appeared in the newspapers and on radio suggesting that members had been participants in many of the major incidents. This was not seen as credible by many long time reporters of the anti-apartheid campaign in Britain. Forty two years later in his autobiography, Hain admitted that the attacks had in fact been 'a covert operation by key STST activists executed from the centre' [250]. The national committee had no knowledge of this, and similarly though young liberals may have been involved, Eaks had no prior knowledge of the action.

The attacks on the cricket grounds, while relatively minor, demonstrated that some in the groups opposing the tour were capable of organising direct action at more than one venue at once. On 29 January, the Home Secretary, James Callaghan met a delegation from the Cricket Council [251] to discuss the logistics of the tour, and in particular the problems of policing cricket grounds. Although it was not disputed that the decision to cancel the tour still rested with the Cricket Council, the Government was beginning to worry about the adverse effect that continuous coverage of confrontations between police and protestors might have on public opinion, in what after all could be an election year. The pressure on the cricket authorities to cancel the tour was slowly being increased.

On the 12 February the Cricket Council met at Lord's to decide whether the South African tour should go ahead. Leading up to the meeting both sides in the debate had increased the pressure, using every opportunity to make their case.

Almost inevitably, the decision was a compromise. The tour would go ahead but the number of matches to be played would be reduced from 28 to 12, and the length of the tour reduced from four months to 11 weeks [252]. Again both sides claimed victory, and again both were to some extent correct. The tour had not been cancelled but it had been severely altered.

In mid March with the tour still on, the South African players chosen to make the trip were named. As expected the team was captained by Ali Bacher, and built around the players who had just demolished Australia 4-0. Of the 14 players chosen, only 6 had been members of the tour led by Peter van der Merve in 1965. All were young then with little experience at the very top level. Now players such as Graeme Pollock, Peter Pollock and Eddie Barlow were experienced hardened cricketers reaching the peak of their career.

Although two of those in the team were touring for the first time, Barry Richards and Mike Procter were already well known to English spectators as the overseas players for Hampshire and Gloucestershire. On the day the team was announced the Australian tourists were playing Western Province. Mike Procter who normally batted at number eight for South Africa, came in at number five for his state side. Illustrating the strength of the side that England would soon be facing, Procter scored a 155, taking only 12 minutes to take his score from 100 to 155. High on confidence, the South Africans were likely to provide a very stern challenge to England.

The decision by the Cricket Council on 12 February that the tour should go ahead was certainly not the end of the matter as far as the main protagonists were concerned.

The pro-tour group was working to ensure that the grounds being used were as secure as possible. They were also working to build public opinion. For instance the Cricket Council produced a leaflet *'Why the '70 Tour'* which was sent to all MCC Members along with the Club's Annual

Report. The leaflet repeated the often used 'bridge building' argument and suggested how this had led to changes in South African sport. The leaflet also illustrated the bitterness that existed between the two groups, noting that 'yielding to pressure from a militant minority would subscribe to a victory for mob-rule'. Not the language of compromise. [253]

The STST were equally busy increasing the number of action groups and building links with the ever growing number of anti-apartheid groups being formed. These included David Sheppard's Fair Cricket Campaign and Jeff Crawford's the West Indian Campaign against Apartheid Cricket. Peter Hain not surprisingly lost interest in studying mechanical engineering. Realising the direction his career was now likely to go, he changed courses, registering to study economics and political science at Queen Mary College, London.

As the two main protagonists fought each other in the media, away from the public eye another interested party was at work. The Labour Government had now been in office since 1 April 1966 (the day the Hain family arrived in Britain). At that time the maximum length of the parliamentary term was five years with the Prime Minister having the authority to set the next election date. Harold Wilson had until 31 March 1971 to call a General Election. With the unpopular decimal currency due to be introduced in spring 1971, there were good reasons for Wilson to want the election over as soon as possible. First though he had to resolve the South African cricket tour problem.

There was increasing press coverage being given to methods anti-apartheid protesters were going to use to disrupt matches during the South African tour. Special Branch had been compiling fortnightly reports since the 7 April, trying to gain as much information as possible on STST [254]. Hain was now claiming that the organisation had 50,000 supporters and that 4,000 to 5,000 protestors at each match during the tour was realistic. A wide range of activities were being proposed to disrupt play. Ranging from using mirrors to shine light into batsmen's eyes to releasing swarms of locusts, continuous disruption during every match on the tour was now a real possibility. Wilson knew that such scenes would not be a good background against which to hold an election campaign.

Nonetheless, confident that the Cricket Council could be persuaded to cancel the tour, Harold Wilson visited Buckingham Palace on 18 May and advised the Queen to dissolve Parliament on 29 May.

Opposition to the tour was growing and BBC television crews were now threatening to black out coverage. The Cricket Council remained adamant that the tour would still go ahead. However, they held a meeting on 18 May to check that support for the tour among the committee members was still strong.

The Council 'decided by a substantial majority, that this Tour should proceed as arranged' but also stated 'that they have informed the South African Cricket Association that no further Test tours between South Africa and this country will take place until South African cricket is played and teams are selected on a multi-racial basis in South Africa [255].

With the arrival of South African tourists quickly approaching, and the Cricket Council still unwillingly to change its position, the Prime Minister himself became involved. He and the Home Secretary, James Callaghan had a number of conversations over the following days to discuss the strategy that should be used to persuade the Cricket Council to cancel the tour. It was also agreed that 'the Prime Minister should not be specifically referred to in any communication' [256].

Two days later on the morning of 21 May, the Home Secretary, James Callaghan had a meeting with the Chairman (Maurice Allom) and Secretary (Billy Griffith) of the Cricket Council. The pressure was now really on them to cancel the tour. While the Home Secretary accepted that the Council's responsibility was in relation to cricketing aspects of the tour he was concerned about broader public issues. He had in mind 'the implications of the tour for race relations, for the Commonwealth Games and for the police'. All these it was agreed were outside the competence of the Cricket Council [257]. Allom and his colleagues were in a corner from which it was impossible to escape.

It was therefore decided that the Home Secretary would write immediately to Maurice Allom requesting that they withdraw their invitation to the South African Cricket Association. This request was to be considered at an emergency meeting of the Council that afternoon. Action was being forced at a pace never experienced by the organisation before.

The following day the Home Secretary received a letter from Allom informing him that the Cricket Council had met to consider his formal request to cancel the tour. The terse letter rather begrudgingly concluded that 'they had no alternative but accede to the request and are informing the South African Cricket Association accordingly' [258]. On 22 May 1970, nine days before the South African tourists were due to land in London, the tour was officially called off.

Part 4

June 1970 – August 1970

England v Rest of the World

12

So What Now?
May 1970 – June 1970

The cancellation of the South African cricket tour when it came was quick and decisive. The Government had blinked first. Despite continuously saying that this was a matter for the cricket authorities alone, the Cricket Council were forced into a corner with the only option open to them to cancel.

This should not have come as too much of a shock. The Springbok rugby team had completed their scheduled tour in February. With anti-apartheid demonstrators making their presence felt at nearly every match, the press coverage was often more concerned with the tactics of the protestors rather than the rugby players. The disruption of the rugby tour was just a trial run, with much worse promised for the forthcoming cricket tour.

With a General Election due Harold Wilson and his Government wer just not prepared to risk pitched battles between police and protestors at Lord's, Edgbaston or Headingley Test matches being broadcast around the world.

On the 19 May in the Long Room at Lord's, Billy Griffith had read a press statement making it absolutely clear that the Cricket Council had no intention of cancelling the South Africa cricket tour. The Council was adamant that the tour was a lawful event and conscious of 'the dangers of a minority group being allowed to take the law into their own hands by direct action' [259]. It was clearly not going to be pressurised by the Government or bullied by protest groups into making a decision it did not believe represented the best interests of cricket.

Five days later the mood was very different. In an atmosphere described by one journalist as 'funereal' [260] Griffith announced a complete reversal with the news that the Cricket Council was now withdrawing its invitation to the South African Cricket Association. He read a terse press statement, which made it clear that cancellation of the tour was not something they had agreed with willingly. Phrases such as 'the Cricket Council had considered the formal request from Her Majesty's Government' [261] and 'with deep regret the Council were of the opinion that they had no alternative but accede to this request' [262] showed that the Council felt it had been forced into a corner.

As was normally the case Griffith would not divulge details of the conversations that had taken place during the Council meeting. He only revealed that although the decision had been by no means unanimous, no vote had been taken [263]. Again suggesting that those present believed they really had no alternative.

When the tour was cancelled there was passion and anger on both sides about the justice of that decision. The storm that had erupted after the D'Oliveira affair made the Cricket Council well aware that managing news of the tour cancellation and finding a replacement would be no easy matter.

The next morning the cancellation made the front pages of all of the major national newspapers in Britain. Many of the headlines highlighted the view that the Cricket Council's decision had not been taken willingly. The *Times* led with *Cricket Council call off tour 'with deep regret'* [264] while the Daily Mirror, a paper at the other end of the political spectrum expressed a similar sentiment with *It's Off, 'Regret' as Springbok cricket is cancelled* [265]. The Liberal leaning *Guardian* emphasised the passion behind the decision with *Delight and Fury as Tour is Cancelled* [266].

The editorial comments of many newspapers reflected the passion that this issue had generated. The Conservative leaning *Daily Telegraph* thought that it had been unnecessary for the Cricket Council to make the decision to cancel and that 'yesterday was a glorious red-letter day for intimidation, civil violence and disruption by a noisy and determined minority of peaceful pursuits wanted by a majority' [267]. The *Daily Express* was very clear who it thought should take the responsibility for the cancellation, saying 'Reluctant to come out openly and cancel the tour as an act of Government. Ministers have forced the Cricket Council to do their dirty work for them' [268].

On the other side of the argument the *Guardian* thought that 'the Cricket Council had taken the right decision, albeit under pressure' [269]. It also believed however that 'if Mr Callaghan had not intervened the Council would have allowed the South African tour to continue' [270].

Opinion in the cricketing world on whether or not the South African tour should be cancelled was polarised, much like it had been less than two years previously over the D'Oliveira affair. This time though more of the English cricket establishment were directly affected, and the rift between the two camps was wider and more acrimonious. The activities of various protest groups, in particular the Stop the Seventy Tour campaign, had raised the general public's awareness of apartheid and increased the numbers willing to join the activities to stop the tour.

On the other side of the debate, many county cricket administrators saw the actions of Peter Hain and other anti-apartheid leaders as literally a threat to their livelihood. With many counties struggling to make a profit, no South African tour would mean no lucrative game for their county against the touring side. There would also be uncertainty in what would now replace the share of Test series income each county would normally receive.

Professional cricketers were in general wary of speaking publicly on any issue, particularly one with such complicated political undertones. Most county cricket contracts prevented players from speaking publicly on cricketing matters without permission of their employer. Even if a player had wanted to air their views in a speech or newspaper article it is highly unlikely they would have been given permission to do so. With most playing contracts still being renewed annually, professional cricketers were understandably wary of putting their head above the parapet.

County cricketers who for so long had nobody to speak for them did now have a voice, although still a quiet one. The Cricketers' Association (now the Professional Cricketers' Association) was formed in September 1967 to represent the interests of the players as a whole. Not surprisingly a number of county chairmen were opposed to the idea of a 'player's union'. By 1970 the membership had grown to 250. Experienced county cricketers had been elected to the key positions; Mike Edwards (Chairman), John Murray (Treasurer) and Jack Bannister (Secretary). Perhaps most interestingly of all, the cricket writer and broadcaster John Arlott became the Cricket Association's Inaugural President. He remained an active champion of the organisation in this role until 1991.

In January 1970 the Cricketers' Association organised a well publicised referendum on the question of whether the forthcoming South African tour should be cancelled. With a turnout of 60%, 82% of the Members voted in favour of the tour going ahead [271]. It seemed that the average county cricketer either believed in the philosophy of using sport to build bridges or thought that politics had no place on the sports field.

The Association's President, John Arlott, was clearly at odds with most the members he represented. He was a passionate and outspoken, long-time opponent of apartheid. Although he believed that actions such as a trade embargo would have been more effective, none the less in April 1970 he announced that he would not broadcast any match played by the South African cricket team should the tour still go ahead. He also expected that as chief cricket correspondent of the *Guardian* 'he would be free to write and comment as he wishes' [272].

One of the first reactions to Arlott's decision was a larger number of letters than usual in the newspaper's post bag. 'Most were in favour but some were against with the most unpleasant letter coming from Peter May' [273]. Regarded by many as one of England's finest post-war batsmen, May was a former captain of England. He was also a Member of the Cricket Council, and a future Chairman of Test Selectors. He strongly believed that those calling for the isolation of South African cricket were 'harming the very people who they profess to help' [274].

Arlott and May held equally sincere views but on opposite sides of the argument. Yet there is no doubt that both were also passionate about cricket and preserving its future. Such disagreements were repeated in many cricket communities across the country. Not surprisingly, in this increasingly bitter dispute, some long time cricketing friendships were broken and never mended.

The question of whether the apartheid policy practised by the South African Government was purely an internal domestic issue or one in which the broader international community should get involved was a matter of opinion. This time though, apartheid could have became a factor in British politics, as it was clear that the Prime Minister would call a General Election sometime during the second half of 1970. The Conservative Party were in favour of the tour going ahead and were suggesting that a cancellation would show the Government incapable of preserving freedom in Britain or maintaining law and order. At a special Sunday meeting of the Cabinet on 17 May, Harold Wilson announced that he had decided that a General Election would be held on 18 June [275]. This had an element of risk as at that stage the Cricket Council were still adamant that the tour was going ahead.

Opinion polls suggested that the Labour Party has a 2.7% lead when the election was called, and that if this was sustained until election day that the Government would increase its overall majority to possibly as much as 60 seats. It was also the view of most political commentators that this election would be decided mainly on economic issues. Even so Wilson had wanted the problem of the South African tour solved and forgotten by voters by the time polling day came around.

Although most opinion polls the weekend before the election predicted a win for Labour, they proved to be wrong. On 18 June the Conservative Party had a surprise victory winning a majority of 31 seats. Edward Heath replaced Harold Wilson as Prime Minister.

It was not only the United Kingdom that was facing a General Election in the Spring of 1970. The South African Parliament had been dissolved on 2 March, and on 22 April white voters were being asked whether they wanted to continue to be governed by the National Party (NP) led by Dr John Vorster.

When the election was called, the National Party was almost untouchable with 126 seats in the 166 seat parliament. In theory the official opposition was the United Party (UP) led Sir de Villiers Graaff.

However in practice with only 39 seats there was little they could do to block legislation.

Under a manifesto with the title 'Separate Development', Vorster and his National Party proposed completing the implementation of his government's apartheid policy so as to totally separate the lives of whites and non-whites. Of most interest to the MCC and the Cricket Council was the intention to keep the playing and administration of white and non-white sport separate. The United Party also supported the apartheid policy but with a more flexible implementation. Although the National Party lost eight seats, they still convincingly won the election with 118 seats, a massive mandate to continue with their policy.

The reaction of the press in South Africa to the cancellation of the cricket tour of the United Kingdom was one of bitter disappointment. Both Afrikaans and English speakers 'seem to believe that the Labour Government have bowed to Communist inspired pressures exerted by an irresponsible minority' [276].

Fresh from election success, John Vorster's response was typically blunt, defiant and uncompromising. Speaking at a press conference during a two day visit to Rhodesia (now Zimbabwe), Vorster was scathing of what he considered a weak approach to law and order. In a speech to an audience who were on side, he said 'for a Government to submit so easily and so willingly to open blackmail is to me unbelievable. It is not cricket, or sport, that lost, but it is the forces of law and order' [277]. A few weeks later, the South African Minister of Sport, Frank Waring in a longer statement made it clear that 'the Government is in no way whatsoever going to be intimidated by the demands made for integrated multiracial sport in South Africa' [278].

Whatever the outside world may of thought, the apartheid policy would continue and selection of an international South African cricket team with white and non-white players was still a long way off.

On the 22 May, with the cricket season well under way there was the frightening possibility of an English summer without Test cricket. The visit of the South African team had been cancelled and at that point there was nothing scheduled to replace it.

So What Now?

A summer without an international cricket team touring would be a financial disaster. If the money from Test match receipts, matches between the touring side and the counties, and television rights was not replaced, many county clubs would find themselves in a very difficult position. The reality was that now a replacement for the cancelled tour had not only to be found but actually up and running in a matter of weeks. Although the official line right up to the end was that the South African tour was going ahead, in the background the Cricket Council Secretary Billy Griffith (he was also Secretary of the MCC and Test and County Cricket Board) had been thinking about alternatives should the unthinkable happen.

Arranging a five match Test series was not something to be taken lightly. For instance, planning for the 1968 visit of the Australians had started in 1966. By the end of May, the Australian tourists had already been playing cricket in England over a month.

Scheduling a series against another Test playing country at such short notice would be all but impossible. England had played Test series against New Zealand and the West Indies during the previous 18 months, and were due to play Australia, India and Pakistan in the near future.

Griffith was well aware that finding a replacement would not be easy. As long ago as October 1969 he had discussed the problem with R A James at the Home Office in Britain. The possibility of a tour by a Rest of the World XI was already one of the options under consideration [279]. Now, with so little time available, it looked to be the only realistic solution.

The idea of a Rest of the World XI was something that the average cricket supporter usually associated with an ad-hoc group of players that had been assembled for a one off charity or benefit match. Such matches were not classified as first-class, and not taken too seriously by the players since their main objective was to raise money for a specific charity or player.

In 1966 the concept was taken to a new level by the introduction of the World Cup Cricket tournament. Sponsored by the tobacco company Rothmans, a Rest of the World XI played a three-day match against an England XI during the end of season Scarborough Cricket Festival. They then took part in a triangular tournament of one day matches with England and the West Indies which was played at Lord's. The match at Scarborough was classified as first class and watched by 32,000 over the three days, as well as being broadcast by the BBC.

The two main questions that Griffith had to consider was whether a Rest of the World XI which had proved popular for a one-off game in front of a holiday crowd, would prove equally popular when playing a five match Test series. In addition would there be the same competitive edge between the two teams as experienced in a traditional Test match when it was country against country. Whatever the risks in reality there was little choice, it was this or nothing.

On 27 May, less than a week after the Test series against South Africa had been cancelled, the Test and County Cricket Board (TCCB) announced a replacement five Test series between England and the Rest of the World. In order to minimise disruption to the summer's first class cricket schedule, it was also decided that the matches would take place on the same dates as the cancelled Tests. Consequently, the first Test was due to start at Lord's in just three weeks!

On paper this looked an almost impossible deadline. A sponsor had to be found and a contract agreed, the captain and England team selected, the captain and a Rest of the World team selected, the matches advertised and tickets sold. As if that was not enough, calling these games Test matches, and deciding to award England caps had an element of risk attached. The meeting of the International Cricket Conference at which the status of these matches would be formally decided was not due to be held until 15 July, by which time three of the 'Tests' would have already been completed.

Having announced a replacement Test series, the TCCB passed this unenviable task with its three week deadline to a nine man Sub-Committee headed by C G A (Cecil) Paris. Based at Lord's they had to work at a pace and style totally unfamiliar to that normally used for organising a Test series. From their first meeting on 27 May the Sub-Committee began making decisions at an almost bewildering rate. Issues that would normally be reflected on between meetings, maybe by a working group now had to be resolved on the spot. They were also well aware that not everybody was in favour of this replacement series. For instance Cedric Rhoades, the plain speaking Chairman of Lancashire County Cricket Club described the proposed series as 'pantomime matches' [279]. He believed that no amount of money would compensate for their star overseas players Clive Lloyd and Farokh Engineer, who would almost certainly be in the Rest of the World XI, being missing for a large part of the summer. Especially as Lancashire were top of the County Championship at that time.

In 1970 financing Test matches was still a very conservative process, very different from the spectator focused, market driven methods used today. The main source of income was spectator receipts from the Test matches themselves. Most of this would be used to cover the costs of the MCC, pay the players, umpires and scorers, and provide much needed income to both the first-class and minor counties. The visiting side would usually have their tour costs covered by a combination of sponsorship from back home, and a percentage of Test match receipts. The other major source of income was the fees received from radio and television broadcasters.

This was kept for home use only, and divided between the counties and MCC. This time things were different. The visiting team had no home, and therefore no sponsorship. In addition, given the nature of the series it was not predicted how easy it would be to attract spectators to what many would consider not 'real' Test matches. The MCC was looking for a major sponsor for a home Test series for the first time in its history. Although a sponsor would not have long to promote and make the most of their role in the series, a surprising number of companies expressed an interest in taking this on.

After a rapid evaluation of the options, the contract was awarded to Arthur Guinness Son & Company, who were offering £20,000 (equivalent to £350,000) in 2020 to sponsor the event. £7,000 would be given to the TCCB for distribution to county clubs, £2,000 to the winner of each Test, with £3000 and a trophy being awarded to the winners of the series. In return it was agreed that the series would be advertised as 'England v the Rest of the World for the Guinness Trophy'.

While the offer from Guinness was indeed generous, the financial problems were by no means over. For televising the South African Test series the BBC had agreed to pay £75,000 (Equivalent to £.1,300,0000 in 2020). Now they were offering only £16,000 (equivalent to £280,000 in 2020) to televise maybe only three of the matches [279]. The anticipated income from ticket sales and merchandising associated with the South

African tour had been around £100,000 (equivalent to £ 1,750,000 in 2020). It was unlikely that the Rest of the World series would generate the same interest, and ticket sales were an unknown. There were so many questions, few answers and almost no time in which to find them. English cricket was between a rock and a very hard place.

13

England v Rest of the World
First Test Match
Lord's Cricket Ground, London
17 – 22 June 1970

With a Test series against the Rest of the World confirmed, the England selectors sat down to consider who should be appointed England captain. The real issue was not who would be captain this time but who would lead the team in Australia during the coming winter. Jim Swanton described the captaincy of the MCC in Australia as 'the greatest honour that is in any committee's gift to bestow' [280]. One of those who certainly shared that view was Colin Cowdrey. He had dreamed for so long of ending his international career captaining England to a series win 'down under'.

Just over eighteen months ago when he had led England to a thrilling Test match win against Australia at the Oval, following on from an equally tense series win in the Caribbean, it looked odds on that he would finally achieve his goal. Damaging an Achilles tendon in his left heel the previous May had kept him out of cricket for a year. His replacement Ray Illingworth had led England with skill and no little imagination to two series wins. Even so the view among many was that Illingworth was only holding the fort until Cowdrey had regained full fitness, and had a few more innings under his belt.

This provided the selectors with a dilemma. They could not now overlook Illingworth who had done everything asked of him. However if they named him as captain for the whole series and he was successful, it would be very difficult to justify replacing him as captain for the trip to Australia. On the other hand Cowdrey's significant international record surely also earned him a chance, having only lost his place because of injury.

There were also those who questioned whether both were not too old to lead the MCC on a long and arduous tour. Rumours were already coming out of Australia that Bill Lawry's days as captain of the national side were numbered, and that it was now only a matter of time before his young, combative vice-captain Ian Chappell, took over. In the end the England selectors compromised and named Illingworth as captain, but only the first Test match. In effect they were kicking the can down the road [281].

In choosing the team for the Lord's Test, the selectors had two options. Pick a team to win this Test using experienced cricketers or try out new players against very tough opposition who were expected to beat them. Surely better to find out now whether a player can cope rather than under a baking sun in front of a partisan ground at the Sydney Cricket Ground. There were now only a few opportunities to assess new players before the touring party for Australia had to be named.

Again the selectors compromised leaving out players such as Boycott, who was almost certain to tour in the winter but was currently right out of form. Similarly Cowdrey had been left out, as he himself admitted that he needed more time in order to become sharp and match fit [282]. With Tom Graveney now retired from Test cricket there were two or three batting positions on offer. Mike Denness was therefore given another chance to prove himself after a terrible first match against New Zealand the previous summer. His Kent colleague Brian Luckhurst and Alan Jones of Glamorgan had both been consistent run scorers in the County Championship in recent years, had topped their respective counties' batting averages the previous season and so deserved their opportunity at Test level.

The bowling needed less new blood apart from a fast bowler to support Snow and Ward or Brown. Ken Shuttleworth of Lancashire who had been spoken of as a potential England fast bowler for a while was given his chance. The final twelve selected for the first Test were Ray Illingworth (captain), John Edrich, Alan Jones, Brian Luckhurst, Mike

Denness, Basil D'Oliveira, Phil Sharpe, Alan Knott, Ken Shuttleworth, John Snow, Derek Underwood and Alan Ward. This was a side which many considered competitive when bowling but with suspect batting.

The MCC asked F. R. (Freddie) Brown the former England captain and future MCC President to be Manager of the Rest of the World team. He was to be joined by Les Ames and the captain to form a selection committee. Given the very short deadlines a captain for the Rest of the World had already been approached and agreed to take on the role in principle. Few would have argued with the choice of Garry Sobers, perhaps one the greatest all-rounders of all. Selected to play for the West Indies when was only 17, he had now been playing cricket for 16 years, increasingly all year round. There were therefore some who believed that Sobers would have little appetite for the proposed series, and would go through the motions in order to collect his fee. They were to be proved very wrong indeed.

While Brown had said that the ambition 'was to pick what we consider to be the best and most exciting team in the world today' [283], in reality the speed at which decisions had to be made meant that all but two chosen for the first Test were currently playing in county cricket. The two from overseas were the South Africans, Eddie Barlow and Graeme Pollock. Both had been selected as part of the squad for the tour which had been cancelled.

The final eleven named for the first Test were Garry Sobers (West Indies – captain), Barry Richards (South Africa), Eddie Barlow (South Africa), Rohan Kanhai (West Indies), Graeme Pollock (South Africa), Clive Lloyd (West Indies), Farokh Engineer (India), Intikhab Alam (Pakistan), Mike Procter (South Africa), Graham McKenzie (Australia) Lance Gibbs (West Indies). John Arlott considered the team to be 'as an exciting an eleven as has been brought together in our time' [284]. One example of the strength of the side was that the young, explosive South African all-rounder Mike Procter was batting at number nine! The day the team was announced he had hit 115 runs in a 139 minutes playing for his county side Gloucestershire against the current County Championship leaders Lancashire [285]. This was against a bowling attack led by Peter Lever and Ken Shuttleworth, both of who would play for England in the forthcoming series. Not an encouraging omen.

Normally before the first Test match of the summer, the sports pages of the weekend newspapers would lead with articles previewing the forthcoming match. There would be speculation on the shape of the touring side, and who in the England side were likely to do well. With bad news being such a strong characteristic in many British Sunday tabloid newspapers, readers were often more interested in who was playing for their place.

This time though cricket did not lead the sport pages – football did. In Mexico, the FIFA football world cup was now taking place. England as defending champions were news, though not just on the back pages. The England captain Bobby Moore had been arrested and charged with stealing a gold bracelet from a jewellers in Colombo on his way to Mexico. He was later released with no charges being made.

Not surprisingly, some of the England players had been distracted by these off field incidents. While not being convincing so far, England had at least reached the knock out stage of the competition. Their opponent, was almost inevitably West Germany. The beaten finalists four years ago would be looking for revenge. On the 14 June, BBC television had seven hours devoted to this must win game. Cricket was a long way from most sports enthusiasts thoughts.

Unlike in the World Cup final four years before, this time things did not go England's way. In the heat of a Mexican afternoon, England were leading 0 – 2 at half time, and looked well placed to go through to the semi-final. Sadly in the second half, the West German team fought back, winning 3-2 in extra time [286].

Day 1 – Wednesday 17 June

The Lord's Test match has always been considered to be one of the highlights of the English sporting calendar. The home of cricket would normally expect a full house for England's match against whoever was touring that summer. The previous year 100,000 had attended over the five days to watch England play the West Indies.

This year though, things were different in so many respects. The match was starting on a Wednesday with Thursday now being the day of a

General Election. If the match went the distance there would be play on Wednesday, Friday, Saturday, Monday and Tuesday. A very stop-start programme.

Illingworth did not need to worry about which of the original twelve to leave out, as on the morning of the match Edrich was declared unfit, still troubled by an injury to his left hand. England's top order now looked very inexperienced, There was only one Test cap between the top three batsmen. With D'Oliveira batting at number four, a position usually occupied by a specialist batsman rather than an all-rounder, the batting also looked vulnerable.

Illingworth won the toss, and although the cloudy and humid conditions would most likely favour seam and swing bowling early on, he decided to bat first. Most observers would have done the same, a captain would need a very good reason to put the opposition in first in a Test match.

Luckhurst and Jones, both in their first Test match walked out to bat in front of a ground less than half full. Even so, it would have been unusual if they had not been nervous. The 31 year old Alan Jones had been a consistent performer for Glamorgan and was regularly mentioned as being a candidate for England without ever quite being able to make a final XI. He had topped his counties batting averages the previous season, and this season he had already scored 165 not out against Hampshire. Finally he had his chance. Unfortunately, he was facing world class bowling. He nicked the first ball of the match from McKenzie unconvincingly over the slips for 4 runs. He survived a few fast in swinging deliveries from the other opening bowler Procter, before edging behind where Engineer threw himself to his left to take a athletic one handed catch. Jones out for 5. His partner Luckhurst lasted longer, but was no more convincing. Although he was certainly not lacking in concentration or determination, it seemed it needed all his skill just to survive. When he was finally out for 1 off Sobers, the *Times* correspondent said Luckhurst 'had spent 45 minutes vainly searching for the middle of his bat' [287]. None of the specialist batsmen that followed found it any easier. At lunch, against only part of this world class bowling attack, England were 44 for 7 with Illingworth and Underwood the not out batsmen. Sobers, whose motivation some had foolishly questioned had taken 5 wickets for 8 runs. While Procter had only taken one wicket, he had not allowed any batsman to build up confidence bowling an opening spell of seven overs off which only two scoring shots were possible. At lunch, those who had suggested that the Rest of the World team would just be going through the motions would be eating their words.

After the interval, just when it was expected that the Rest of the World would soon be batting, England finally showed some resistance. Illingworth with a mixture of solid decisive defence and attacking drives showed how it could be done. With his partner Underwood playing forward with confidence, the pair added 50 runs in 40 minutes. Underwood was then somewhat unluckily out. Smashing a poor delivery from Barlow through the covers for what he expected to be a certain 4, Lloyd made an outstanding catch, diving forward. After that Illingworth reached a well deserved 50 added another 31 runs with Ward for the ninth wicket. When Illingworth was finally out for a defiant 63, England had been bowled out for 127 in just 55 overs.

Sobers had been the chief destroyer, taking 6 for 21 in 20 overs. While Procter taking 1 for 20 in 13 overs had sapped the spirit out of England's top order, most of who were fully occupied just to keep him out. At the close of play Sobers admitted 'I honestly don't think I've ever bowled better. Everything just clicked' [288].

England was already in a position from which they almost certainly could not win, unless they were also able to bowl their opponents out for a low total. When the openers Barlow and Richards walked to the wicket this had to be their hope. Barlow had only been in the country for just four days, and had not played competitively for three months. Richards of course had been playing for Hampshire since the start of the season.

Although Snow and Ward were fast, hostile and accurate, they could not achieve the swing of Sobers, conditions had changed. The Rest of the World openers made 69 in 17 overs with few alarms, before Richards edged Ward to Sharpe at slip. A low catch he took with his usual ease. The new batsman Kanhai, not at his fluent best managed 21 before he edged D'Oliveira behind to Knott. There was then just time for Barlow to reach his 50 and Pollock to show what might be coming after the rest day. The Rest of the World at the close of play was 115 for 2, just 12 runs behind England, with 8 wickets in hand. It had been their day in all respects.

The teams had a day off on Thursday because in the United Kingdom it was Polling Day. After six years in power, Harold Wilson was asking for another five years for his Labour Government. The principal opposition, the Conservative and Unionist Party led by Edward Heath were behind in the opinion polls, and predictions were that Wilson would win with a comfortable majority. On election day, even the conservative leaning *Daily Telegraph,* was gently preparing its readers for the possibility that Labour might win [289].

When vote counting started in the late evening, it was very soon clear that the opinion polls had got it wrong. People woke up to newspaper headlines on Friday morning confidently claiming that *'Heath Heading for No. 10'* [290]. Wilson held on until the last moment before conceding defeat. By mid afternoon and against the odds, Edward Heath had become the new Prime Minister of the United Kingdom.

Close of play – England 1st innings 127
Rest of the World 1st innings 115 – 2, (Barlow 50*, Pollock 6*)

Day 2 – Friday 19 June

When the Rest of the World resumed their innings on Friday morning, no such surprises were expected. The first day's play had been dominated by Sobers the bowler, today it was the turn of Sobers the batman.

England was already in a position where they could not win the game. The best they could hope for was to restrict the Rest of the World's first innings lead, and then compile a huge total when it was their turn to bat again. Barlow and Pollock, the two not out overseas batsmen would not have been familiar figures to many in the crowd. Neither had played county cricket yet, but Barlow would later join and then captain Derbyshire. He was combative, had tremendous confidence and always wanted to be involved whether it was with bat or ball. John Snow, who would play against him in all five matches of the series, described him as 'a human dynamo of a player …who always seemed to be in the thick of any battle'

[291]. Though not as flamboyant as some of his South African colleagues, he was key to the side. He would end the series third in the batting averages and second in the bowling averages.

Pollock was widely regarded as South Africa's finest ever batsmen. Selected for his country at 19, by 1970 he had played 23 Test matches. All had been against England or Australia, scoring 2,256 runs at an average of 60.97. Still only 26 it is difficult to imagine what he might have achieved if his country had not been banned from Test cricket. Worryingly for England was the fact that once they had settled in Barlow and Pollock were used to building very large scores. Each had scored a double century in Test cricket, Pollock had already scored two. The second being a massive 274 against Australia just over four months ago.

By lunch time the omens did not look good. Barlow and Pollock had added a 100 runs. Neither had played any serious cricket for at least three months, and in Pollock's case he was recovering from influenza. Even so, Barlow with his determination and Pollock with his flair, showed that very good batsmen can score runs even when not totally in touch. Illingworth relied mostly on his three fast bowlers, and while not surprisingly there was the occasional missed shot, South Africa would have been the happier team at the lunch interval. Barlow the happiest of all, having reached his seventh century, and in doing so become the latest player to have his name added to the Honours' Board at Lord's. The Honours' Board displays the name of any batsman who scores a century of bowler who takes five wickets in a innings, during a Test match at Lord's.

After the break, when the crowd expected the batsmen to start to accelerate the scoring, they were surprisingly both out. Pollock was deceived by a faster delivery from Underwood, and bowled for 55. Two balls later, Barlow did not quite middle a hook shot off Illingworth, and was wonderfully caught by Underwood. A reliable fielder but not one normally known for aerobatic catches.

With the score at 237 for 4 Illingworth and Underwood were now bowling in tandem, trying to restrict the scoring until the new ball was due. The captain took it immediately and it was Ward rather than Snow who caused the problems this time. His raw pace unsettled Sobers, but he managed to adjust. His West Indian colleague Lloyd was not as lucky, underestimating the speed of a Ward delivery and being bowled. In his next over the new batsman Engineer, who had been playing attacking shots from the first ball he faced, went for the hook shot too early and was bowled. The Rest of the World had slipped from 225 for 2 to 298 for 6. And there was half and hour to the tea interval. They still had had a sizeable first innings lead but it was not yet out of sight.

That was soon to be a forlorn hope. The rest of the day's play was totally dominated by Sobers. By the time play ended for the day Sobers and Intikhab had scored 177 for the seventh wicket at better than a run a minute. Sobers was imperious, ending the day on 147 not out with Intikhab offering solid support on 56. John Woodcock of the *Times,* a respected correspondent not given to making exaggerated statements, said that he had 'seldom see Sobers bat with more relish or hit the ball harder' [292]. On the first day of the match, there had been periods when Sobers' bowling had been almost unplayable. Today after the tea interval, he had at times been impossible to bowl to. Perhaps most worrying of all for England was that towards the end of the day Sobers played a little more quietly. It seemed, the close of play total of 475 for 6 was not enough.

Close of play – Rest of the World 1st innings 475 – 6, (Sobers 147★, Intikab Alam 56★)

Day 3 – Saturday 20 June

The Saturday of Lord's Test match has always been a special occasion. If the gods are smiling, then a packed ground would be basking in glorious sunshine and watching England playing (and hopefully beating) whoever was touring that summer. The previous year it had been the West Indies. Then the gates had been closed a half an hour before play started, and a capacity crowd of 27,000 had watched England bat all day. John Hampshire in his first Test match made a 107, and England ended the day with another Yorkshireman Illingworth 97 not out, also in sight of his first Test century.

A year later, the position was very different. With the Rest of the World beginning the day already a massive 348 runs ahead on first innings, the chance of even drawing the match was now long gone. The forecast for the days ahead, was for continued sunshine, so not even rain could save

England. The object for Illingworth and his team now was purely one of pride, to bat a great deal better in their second innings than they had done in the first.

Although Sobers did not reach the heights of the previous day, he still struck some powerful blows. First Ward was the target. The day before he had been England's most impressive bowler, now he too was being punished. Underwood was then hit over long off for a massive six.

Intikhab the other not batsman overnight did not last long. Only adding another 5 runs before being bowled middle stump by Ward, He had played his part the previous evening. It must have been disheartening for the England side with the score at 496 for 7 to see Mike Procter the hard hitting all rounder walk to the wicket. He played a short cameo inning, briefly even outshining Sobers by thumping 26 runs in a eighth wicket partnership of 41, before trying another big shot against Snow and losing his off stump. At 537 for 8 Sobers threw caution to the wind and went for everything in an attempt to reach 200. He finally fell for 183, but it needed another fine catch from Underwood to see the end of him. Sobers had hit 30 fours and two sixes and he was applauded by every member of the England side as he left the field. Shortly afterwards the Rest of the World were all out for 546, a lead of 419. Nobody seriously expected them to have to bat for a second time.

There were 45 minutes left before lunch, and the immediate target for the incoming England batsmen Jones and Luckhurst was to still be there at the interval. Unfortunately, that hope only lasted one delivery. Procter opened the bowling for the Rest of the World, and as in the first innings Jones tried to cut a fast rising delivery that was too close to his body, edged it and again was caught behind by Engineer. This time for naught. It had not been a great first Test for Jones. He had to hope that he would get a second chance.

The new batsman Denness, also playing for his place, joined his county colleague. On a pitch which certainly did not have the same movement as on the first morning, the pair survived a difficult period until lunch. They never looked totally at ease especially against the pace of Procter, but with attacking fields set by Sobers there were boundaries to be had for a batsman willing to play decisive shots.

After lunch Sobers gave his seam bowlers a rest and changed to an all spin, attack with Intikhab and Gibbs coming on for a long spell in the hot sunshine. The later was bowling for the first time in the match, he had just not been needed before then, the seam bowlers had swept England up on their own in the first innings. 15 minutes into the afternoon session, Denness misread or misjudged a googly from Intikhab and was caught by Sobers for 24. This was a score which was neither good nor bad. The question was would this be enough to keep his place for the next Test match? D'Oliveira who was probably coming in too high in the batting over then built a solid partnership with Luckhurst. The Kent opener was slowly coming to terms with the challenge of facing Test level bowling. Against the spinners in particular he began to play with more confidence. One seasoned cricket correspondent was clearly impressed noting that 'I have not seen an England batsman use his feet so freely to high-class slow bowling for ages' [293].

D'Oliveira was soon playing with his usual forthright confident style. If he was under pressure this did not show. He has rarely failed in both innings of a Test match. The pair batted on until just after tea, when Luckhurst went down the wicket to Intikhab once too often and presented a juggling catch to Engineer. His 63 runs and the manner in which he made them showed that he did not look out of place at Test level. Unfortunately the incoming batsman Sharpe was out of form, and as so often happens in these situations out of luck. He was bowled, off of his pads by Sobers and would have left the field perhaps wondering if he would get any further chances to play Test cricket.

With positive drives, an upright sweep shot and a six off Gibbs, D'Oliveira continued to add runs, until he mishit a delivery from Intikhab into the covers, where the outstanding Lloyd made no mistake. His 78 runs were not going to change the outcome of the match, but they at least showed some fight. Illingworth and Knott batted out the rest of the day, ensuring that everybody would need to return on Monday. However, with England closing on 228 for 5, the outcome of the match had been decided long ago.

Close of play – Rest of the World 1st innings 546
England 2nd innings 228 – 5, (Illingworth 36★, Knott 12★)

Day 4 – Monday 22 June

On Monday 22 June 1970, the sports pages of most national newspapers were dominated by reports of the FIFA World Cup Final, which had been played the previous evening. In a pulsating match a well organised Italy had been beaten 4-1 by a Brazilian team some described as the 'The All Time Greatest' [294]. The Italians played as well as they could but in the end were not able to deal with the superior skills of the Brazilian team as a whole, and the ability of individuals like Pele and Jairzinho to produce pieces of magic. England may have had some sympathy for Italy. They too had been overwhelmed in this case the chief magician was Garry Sobers.

Illingworth and Knott walked out to resume their innings knowing that all they had left to play for was pride and individual goals. Neither was playing to keep their place in the side. Some of the more pessimistic observers expected the match to be over in half an hour or so. Illingworth was a technically sound batsmen, who never gave his wicket away. Knott was quick on his feet, a bag of energy always looking to unsettle the bowler. Together these two, not only lasted until lunch but until half an hour afterwards. Knott was then finally beaten by the tireless Gibbs, and out lbw for 39. Shortly afterwards, Illingworth followed, caught off Sobers now bowling wrist spin for an admirable 96. He had topped the England batting in both innings. The remaining three wickets fell without great trouble to Intikhab. Tail end batsmen do not normally play leg spin bowlers very well.

So by mid-afternoon the match was over. Apart from the batting of Illingworth, D'Oliveira and Knott, and the bowling of Ward there was little to cheer the England supporters. The reality was that England had been soundly beaten by an innings and 80 runs, with over a day and a half to spare. The worry was that some in the Rest of the World side like Barlow and Pollock were still clearly brushing off the cobwebs from months away from first-class cricket. If this was 'pantomime cricket', then somebody it seems had forgotten to tell Sobers and his team.

Close of play – England 2nd innings 339
Rest of the World won by an innings and 80 runs.

14

England v Rest of the World
Second Test Match
Trent Bridge, Nottingham
2nd – 7th July 1970

Ray Illingworth would have had good reasons to be worried as he reflected on England's performance in the first Test match. The brutal truth was that they had been well beaten with time to spare, by a group of players who had not played together before as a team.

Under normal circumstances, you would expect the Rest of the World to improve as they got used to local conditions and each other. If England had been beaten so easily in the first match, then there were those who were already predicting a 5-0 whitewash.

The other issue was that of attendance. Only 35,000 spectators had paid to see the first three and a half days play at Lord's. This compared to 100,000 over five days the previous summer. Unless the matches became more competitive, it was unlikely that attendance would increase.

The one man in the England team who could feel some satisfaction with his performance during the first Test was Illingworth himself. Considered a bowling all-rounder who could bat, he had been his side's top scorer in both innings, and led with confidence.

Colin Cowdrey, the man Illingworth had replaced as captain, was now match fit and scoring runs. He had made 126 and 106 not out in his last two County Championship matches. He was ready to take back his role of captain, with perhaps Illingworth as his vice-captain now that Graveney was no longer available [295]. The selectors hesitated again. They took the easier option, and at the end of the first Test announced that Illingworth had been asked to continue as captain, but only for the second Test match. As for the side he would lead, that needed a few days more thought.

The Rest of the World selectors had no such problems. At the end of the Lord's Test they announced that the side would remained unchanged, although Younis Ahmed of Surrey would replace Mushtaq Mohammad as twelfth man (mainly to allow Mushtaq to play some cricket for his county Northamptonshire).

When the England selectors and Illingworth sat down to choose a team for the second Test they were certainly not thinking of an unchanged side. Only about half the side could be certain of keeping their place. Few would have argued with putting Knott, Snow and Underwood in without much discussion. In addition, D'Oliveira was a certainty but not batting at number four. Edrich was fit again and could take his usual place as one of the opening batsmen. Cowdrey was also fit and ready to resume his normal batting position at number three. His selection of course put the two most likely candidates to captain England in Australia during the coming winter in a difficult position. They were in the same side but in effect also competing against each other.

The selectors decided that as far as specialist batsmen were concerned, Alan Jones, Mike Denness and Phil Sharpe would be dropped in favour of John Edrich, Colin Cowdrey and Keith Fletcher. Sharpe's place in the side had always been tenuous, with his outstanding ability as a slip fielder often keeping him in the side. This time though, with Cowdrey and Fletcher who were both better batsmen and specialist slip fielders available, Sharpe lost his place for the last time.

Denness would eventually return, ultimately as captain. Sadly though, after waiting for so long, the Lord's Test would turn out to be Alan Jones first and last as an England player. Nobody would dispute he had a shocker, out to a rampant Mike Procter in both innings. However, many players have started their international careers poorly, but been given another opportunity and gone on to be successful.

For example, Graham Gooch was out for nought in both innings of his first Test match against Australia at Edgbaston in 1975. He was also facing two useful bowlers in Jeff Thomson and Max Walker. Gooch was given a second chance and went on to have a remarkable career as both player and captain [296]. For Jones though, there was to be no second chance. Luckhurst the other debutant batsman at Lord's was more fortunate, his performance in the second innings had been enough to persuade the selectors that he had the potential to play at the highest level.

For the bowlers, Alan Ward had impressed with his raw pace. Some observers thought the 23 year old was the fastest bowler they had seen in the England team for a while [297]. They were looking forward to seeing the Australian batsmen struggle against him on a fast pitch in Perth. It would certainly make a change. As far as the present was concerned though, an injury to his ankle made him unavailable and he was replaced by the experienced David Brown.

The most interesting selection by far, was the choice of a bowling all-rounder to compete with Shuttleworth for the role of the third seam bowler. While D'Oliveira was capable of bowling tightly and taking the occasional wicket, he was not an automatic choice as first change bowler. At 38 he was also nearing the end of his career, and in many observers' eyes was not an automatic pick for the winter tour.

The name the selectors came up, to the surprise of some, was A. W. (Tony) Greig. The 23 year was by no means the finished article but the 6ft 7" (200 cm) South African born Sussex all-rounder, certainly did not lack confidence or enthusiasm. The previous season only John Snow had taken more wickets for Sussex in the County Championship, while at the same time Greig was only 61 runs short of also scoring a 1000 runs in the season. The England selectors saw potential for more. If he could combine his ability for destructive batting with a sounder defensive technique, and similarly become more consistent with his bowling the potential to become an outstanding all rounder was there. Their hunch would prove to be correct. Tony Greig would go on to captain both Sussex and England before becoming one of the key figures in Kerry Packer's World Series cricket venture.

The thirteen selected for the second Test were therefore Ray Illingworth (captain), John Edrich, Brian Luckhurst, Colin Cowdrey,

Dennis Amiss, Keith Fletcher, Basil D'Oliveira, Tony Greig, Alan Knott, David Brown, Derek Underwood, John Snow and Ken Shuttleworth. Dennis Amiss, who had been on standby as a replacement batsman in the previous Test, retained his position but was expected to be twelfth man again, while Shuttleworth was in the group as a standby for Greig who was recovering from a minor injury. This was a better balanced and more experienced side than the one chosen for Lord's.

After the first Test was over, Illingworth reflecting on his opponents concluded that 'This really is the best side in the world. But if we can catch them after rain, or when the wicket is doing something – as they caught us here on the first morning – we could shake them' [298]. The selectors had it seemed given up experimenting for the winter tour. Shaking the opposition was now the first priority. The Rest of the World team could have been even stronger, as there was only one Australian in the side. For a number of reasons most of McKenzie's team mates preferred a summer at home after a long year.

Day 1 – Thursday 2 July

It was a cold, grey day with the threat of rain which greeted the players when they arrived at the Trent Bridge Ground for the start of the second Test match. The blazing sunshine of Lord's seemed a world away.

The overcast weather and chill wind were more reminiscent of winter at home for most the Rest of the World players. These were so called 'English conditions' and the England bowlers should certainly have been hoping that they would get first use of it. As expected Shuttleworth and Amiss were left out of the thirteen and so Tony Greig was awarded his first Test cap.

Sobers won the toss, and while there was the possibility of a helpful pitch, after some hesitation he decided to bat first. Trevor Bailey, the retired all-rounder who was now a sports reporter for the *Financial Times*, maintained that deciding what to do when winning the toss was simple. In his typical matter of fact way he said it was straightforward 'If a captain wins the toss they bat first, or else they take a few minutes to consider it, and then bat first' [299].

Rain delayed the start of the match by seven minutes, and when Barlow and Richards walked out to bat, it was in front of a sparse crowd. The ground was less than a quarter full. This was very disappointing given this was the first time that a home Test match had not been broadcast on television since 1951. The BBC preferred the State Opening of Parliament, the first for the new Government led by Edward Heath. Dwindling attendances at Test matches would certainly not help the TCCB (Test and County Cricket Board) when it came to negotiating deals for media coverage and marketing rights for future series.

Snow and Brown opened the bowling for England, and bowled accurately but often were not full enough to allow the ball to swing in the air. They were economic without looking particularly threatening. Barlow and Richards managed a rather pedestrian 13 runs before the rain came again. This time it was much heavier and the players were off the field for 30 minutes. When they returned, Illingworth bought on his two medium pace all-rounders. It was immediately obvious that the rain had changed the character of the pitch, added life to it. With only his third delivery, D'Oliveira bowled a well directed out-swinger, which Barlow edged to first slip, Cowdrey taking the catch with his usual elegance. At lunch the Rest of the World were 40 for 1 and hoping that batting would become easier in the afternoon.

After the break, Illingworth continued to use the medium pace of D'Oliveira who was achieving swing in the air and movement off the pitch, and the less accurate but at times unplayable Greig. Between them they demolished the middle order of the Rest of the World. In Greig's second over, Kanhai misjudged a drive, edging a catch to Fletcher at second slip. Two balls later, Pollock received a delivery from D'Oliveira which pitched middle stump, moved sharply avoiding a defensive bat, and bowled one of the best batsmen in the world. The Rest of the World were 55 for 3, not great but still lots of batting to come.

Richards and the new batsman Clive Lloyd showing no signs that their team was in trouble, added 51 runs at better than a run a minute before Greig again struck with devastating effect. First he had Richards caught acrobatically down the leg side by Knott for 64, then he bowled Sobers off the under edge of his bat for 8, quickly followed by Engineer caught by Knott this time on the off side. In three overs the Rest of the World had collapsed from 106 for 3 to 126 for 6. At this point most sides would have folded, but this was no ordinary side. With players able to score runs at international level right down to number nine, a cause was rarely lost. Lloyd, with his deceptive laconic batting style, was now increasingly hitting shots of brutal power, while his partner Intikhab was providing solid support. At tea the Rest of the World were 170 for 6.

Shortly after the interval, like Barlow earlier in the day, Intikhab edged a leg cutter from D'Oliveira to Cowdrey still at first slip. Lloyd and Intikhab had added 45 runs for the seventh wicket, but still it was not over as Mike Procter was striding to the wicket. Between them, Lloyd and Procter dragged the initiative away from England. Lloyd was particularly savage on short-pitched deliveries on his leg side, and on three occasions dispatched deliveries from Brown with ease over the boundary rope for six. Not to be outdone, Procter began to inflict similar treatment on Underwood, at one point hitting him for three leg side fours in an over.

Once he reached the nineties, Lloyd suddenly became tentative, unsure whether to prod or blast teasing deliveries from Illingworth to reach his century. Eventually after a few near misses, he straight drove a delivery to the boundary to reach his fourth Test century. He continued onwards but finally ran out of partners. Procter was bowled by Brown for an entertaining and rapid 43 and McKenzie magnificently caught and bowled by Brown for 0. Finally, D'Oliveira the bowler who had taken the first wicket, took the last, when he bowled Gibbs. The Rest of the World were all out 276, five minutes before the close of play. Somewhat ironically, England's two South African born players had taken four wickets each. Lloyd who finished the day on 114 not out, had rescued the innings for the visitors, and was deservedly applauded by spectators and opposition alike as he walked off the field.

A total of 276 was an average score, but England would expect to at least match it on a wicket which had become increasingly easy during the day. In the back of Iliingworth's mind that night though, would have been the thought that they had the opposition at 126 for 6, and then they let them get away. This was not a team who would give you too many chances.

Close of play – Rest of the World 1ˢᵗ innings 276 all out

Day 2 – Friday 3 July

After the debacle of the first Test, England's bowlers would have been feeling that they had regained some credibility in bowling the Rest of the World out for a relatively moderate score. Now it was the turn of their batsmen. On paper at least, a top five of Edrich, Luckhurst, Cowdrey, Fletcher and D'Oliveira had a far more solid look about it than the line-up at Lord's.

Edrich and Luckhurst started the day facing Procter and McKenzie. Like England the day before, they bowled accurately but rarely beat the bat. Edrich played as normal, phlegmatic, unspectacular but effective. Blocking, nudging and pushing. Taking as few risks as possible, he saw the primary role of an opening batsman as that of blunting the new ball attack. Luckhurst it seemed was from the same mould. He had a sound defensive technique, and a temperament which did not seem to worry if a delivery missed the bat or if he went for a long period without scoring. He was beginning to look the part of a Test opening batsman.

As the interval approached, the openers had 78 runs on the board and in truth there had only been one chance, when Edrich had glanced a difficult catch to Procter at short leg which had been dropped. It was all looking good. With twenty minutes left of the session, Sobers called up Eddie Barlow to bowl. Barlow was a medium pace bowler, with a bustling action and supreme confidence. The sort of player who believed he could take a wicket with every ball, and frequently reminded anybody within range how lucky a batsman was still to be there.

This time Barlow backed up his optimism with results. In eight deliveries he changed the whole complexion of the morning. First he bowled Luckhurst who misjudged the length of a delivery and was yorked for 37. Cowdrey came to the wicket, scored a run from his first ball but in the next over from Barlow he was out, caught by Richards falling forward at short leg. There was some controversy as Cowdrey did not believe the ball had carried to the fielder before hitting the ground. However, the umpire had given Cowdrey out, so that was that. Edrich was now joined by Fletcher who confidently drove his first delivery for four, but the next from Barlow moved from leg to off, catching the edge of Fletcher's bat and giving Engineer a comfortable catch behind the stumps. England had slipped from 78 for none to 86 for three, and the solid start had been wasted. Leaving the field at the interval, it was clear which side would have the happier lunch.

When the afternoon session began, Barlow carried on where he had left off. It would have been a brave man indeed to suggest to Barlow that somebody else should bowl. By 2.30 pm, Edrich had been caught, edging an away swinger to the wicketkeeper and D'Oliveira had missed a delivery which kept low and been bowled. Barlow had taken all five wickets to fall.

Tony Greig strode confidently to the wicket, and not surprisingly was surrounded by seven close fielders all waiting for the nervous edge from the debutant. The new batsmen was however not known for being hesitant, and he hit the first three deliveries he received in Test cricket for 4, 3 and 4. Greig then showed his inexperience. Unwisely chasing a wide delivery from Sobers, he hit it firmly to the gully where Gibbs made a wonderful leaping catch. England were now 126 – 6, exactly the same as the Rest of the World had been the previous day. Illingworth found himself, for the third Test innings in a row, batting to give the side's score some credibility. This time his partner was Knott.

Even Barlow needed to be rested, and so Illingworth and Knott began batting more comfortably on a pitch which now held few terrors. In just over an hour, the pair added 54, before Knott hit Intikhab hard to silly mid off, where Kanhai made a difficult catch look straightforward. Brown and Underwood came and went quickly either side of the tea interval, with the first unable to deal with the pace of Procter and the second with the guile of Intikhab.

When Snow, the number eleven batsman walked out to join his captain, it was a quarter to five. England were 195 for 9, still 81 runs behind their opponent's first innings score. Illingworth, not without some luck, had battled his way to 42. The sometimes moody Snow, may well have been upset at being relegated to number 11. Whatever the reason, be played solidly and correctly right from the start. It was head down and concentrate rather than going for a few minutes of fun as a tail end slogger. Illingworth showed complete confidence in Snow, and began opening out with drives, cuts and even a hook shot or two. The difference between the two sides first innings score gradually went down. When England reached 240, a delivery from McKenzie finally caught the edge of Snow's forward defensive push. The ball flew to slip, where Barlow of all people dropped a straightforward catch.

With a few overs left in the day's play and the light deteriorating, England had reached 279 with Illingworth three runs away from a well deserved century. Sadly it was not to be. Like Lloyd the previous day, when he reached the 90s, Illingworth had gone into his shell, almost as though he was waiting until the following day when the light would be better. Finally Sobers found a way through Illingworth's defence and he was out, bowled for 97. Snow had contributed a invaluable 27 not out, and England's total of 279 gave them a first innings lead of 3 runs. They had matched the Rest of the World in bowling and batting so far in this Test. Barlow was the standout bowler for the opposition, finishing with five for 66. Illingworth had been a triumph, top scoring for England in three consecutive innings. The man who many thought was just keeping the seat warm for Cowdrey, was clearly in no mood to give it back without a fight.

Close of play – England 1st innings 279 all out

Day 3 – Saturday 4 July

With no Test cricket played on a Sunday in England until 1981, the authorities at Trent Bridge would have hoped for a sell out on the Saturday. It was the only day many people could attend and it was also the home ground of Garry Sobers the captain of Nottinghamshire. With two days of the match completed, there was also the chance of seeing the end of one side's first innings and the beginning of the other's second. This year it was a little different. The weather was gloomy and cold, attendance poor and day three of the match was beginning with each side having completed their first innings and scored almost the same number of runs. The crowd was disappointing. The people of Nottingham it seems had not yet decided whether the Rest of the World were a real Test team!.

As Barlow and Richards walked out to the wicket to begin the Rest of the World second innings, their sides objective would have been to bat as long as possible and in doing so set England a run target they could not reach. A lead of say 350 by tea on day four would be perfect. The day started on time, in spite of the grey skies, but it was not long before bad light caused a short break in play. Not surprisingly with these conditions the opening batsmen started slowly, this was already a game of attrition. The usually free scoring Richards managed only 13 runs in the first hour, at one stage less than his partner Barlow who as always gave the impression that he was there to stay, all day if possible.

Over in Swansea, the unlucky Alan Jones was also walking out to bat, but for Glamorgan in a County Championship match against Gloucestershire. By the end of the day he had scored his third century of the season but would not get another chance to bat for England [300].

In much the same way as England's first innings had started, Snow and Brown bowled accurately but rarely produced enough movement in the air or off the pitch to beat the batsman.

With twenty five minutes to lunch, Illingworth turned to his medium pace bowlers. D'Oliveira replaced Brown, and an increasingly confident Richards pulled his first deliveries for six. At the other end, Greig was bought on to replace Snow. This change produced a result almost immediately. Richards misjudged the movement in the air and was bowled. The new batsman Rohan Kanhai had been in reasonable form for his county Warwickshire, including hitting a 162 against a Sussex bowling attack headed by Snow in mid June. Today though he looked ill at ease from the first delivery and it was no surprise to see him caught behind pushing forward to D'Oliveira. Pollock was next in, and lasted one ball. Deliberately not playing a delivery but allowing it to hit his pad, under the newly introduced lbw law he was out. Maybe he had forgotten about the change in the law, but the umpire's finger was raised and he had to go. At lunch the Rest of the World had slipped from a comfortable 68 for 0 to a more uncertain 87 for 3.

After the break, Lloyd decided to attack whenever possible. The England fast bowlers were working on the theory that Lloyd was suspect against the short pitched ball. The trouble with this was that Lloyd kept depositing these deliveries further and further over the boundary rope. Illingworth quickly went back to his slower bowlers. Underwood was maybe a little fortunate, but he soon had Lloyd out for a quick fire 20. Watching all this sometimes almost unnoticed from the other end, Barlow had continued to slowly accumulate runs, scoring only 32 between lunch and tea. Even the champion all-rounder Sobers was struggling. A combination of Underwood, Greig and D'Oliveira dried run making up to such an extent that only 20 runs were added in 70 minutes. Finally Sobers driving a half volley from Greig, mishit and skied a catch for Knott behind the stumps. Engineer did not look in form, struggling with almost every delivery. It was no surprise when he was caught and bowled by Underwood for 1. At tea the Rest of the World had struggled to 154 for 6. England were definitely on top, and their opponents would need to make use of their long batting line up.

After tea, Barlow carried on as he had all day while Intikhab after settling in, started to play some shots. An hour before the close of play, and after nearly five hours at the wicket, Barlow drove a delivery from Greig to the boundary to reach his second century of the series. Intikhab continued to hit some brutal attacking shots. Illingworth took the new ball as soon as it became available. Intikhab responded by trying to hit a delivery from Brown back over his head. Not quite catching it full on the bat, he gave Brown the chance to turn and dive full length to make a great catch. The seventh wicket had produced 66 runs and at 220 for 7 for most sides the innings would have been nearing the end. Procter striding to the wicket had other ideas, and proceeded with Barlow to add an entertaining 37 runs in the last 35 minutes of the day. With the Rest of the World ending the day on 257 – 7, Illingworth knew that the first part of Monday would be crucial. Take the last three wickets quickly and England should win. Let the opposition score another 100 and there would be trouble.

Down in London SW19 another of the summer's great sporting occasions was coming to a close. The Wimbledon Lawn Tennis Championships were almost over for another year. John Newcombe had won the Men's Singles; Margaret Court the Women's Singles, and John Newcombe and Tony Roche the Men's Doubles; all Australians [301]. It was to be hoped the Ashes Test Series in the winter would be a little less one sided.

Close of play – Rest of the World 2nd innings 257 – 7,
(Barlow 123★, Procter 25★)

Day 4 – Monday 6 July

The weather on Monday was more like summer, warm with patches of sunshine. A much better day for both playing and watching cricket. Frustrating of course for all those spectators who had frozen on Saturday, the only day they could attend. Before play began, it was announced that Illingworth had been appointed captain for the third Test match, which was to be played at Edgbaston in two weeks. Either Illingworth was doing too well for Cowdrey to be appointed as captain of the winter tour, or else Cowdrey had not yet done enough to justify replacing Illingworth. Either way, the selectors were running out of time, a decision would have to be made soon.

With the ball only 12 overs old, Illingworth started with a combination of fast and medium paced bowling. His bowlers faced the age old problem; to take wickets quickly but without conceding too many runs. It was again medium pace which accounted for the first wicket. D'Oliveira caused Procter to check his drive, and in doing so offer a catch to Edrich at mid-wicket. He had only added 2 to his close of play score. 18 runs later, Greig took the key wicket of Barlow. After a cautious start he was beginning to find fluency and look dangerous again when he was late coming down on a faster delivery, and bowled for 142. Barlow left the field to a standing ovation from the small crowd, having dominated the innings. Finally, Snow took the last wicket bowling Gibbs for 1. The Rest of the World were all out 286, which set England a target of 284 to win, a total Illingworth would expect them to reach. D'Oliveira and Greig has each taken seven wickets in the match. They could not expect this to be the case on the hard, fast pitches in Australia during the winter.

Edrich and Luckhurst walked out to bat, knowing that with five and a half sessions still available and fine weather predicted for the next two days, that time was not an issue. The pitch was if anything getting easier for the batsmen, and as Snow and Brown had shown it offered almost nothing for the fast bowler. The openers' first objective was simple, to bat the 75 minutes that remained until the interval without losing a wicket. Neither risked an attacking stroke, although Edrich slashed at and fortunately missed two deliveries that Sobers had bowled across the left hander. The Rest of the World's fast bowlers, Sobers, Procter and McKenzie gave it everything but without success. At lunch England were 27 for 0. Not very exciting cricket for the spectators, but the objective not to lose a wicket had been achieved.

The afternoon session continued with the fast bowlers struggling on a lifeless pitch. Finally, when the score had reached 44, Edrich played another involuntary slash at a rising delivery. This time, it caught the edge of the bat and flew to Barlow at slip. It was almost impossible to keep Barlow out of the match, whether batting, bowling or fielding.

The new batsman Cowdrey had last played Test cricket 15 months ago in Pakistan, a country then being ripped apart by civil unrest. Having scored only 1 in the first innings he would have been aware that a failure in this innings, would not help his chances of regaining the England captaincy for the winter tour.

Whatever pressure Cowdrey may have been feeling, he did not show it. He started his innings with a 4 off McKenzie down to fine leg. He was almost immediately playing square drives, cover drives and sweep shots with his customary authority and elegance. As Swanton wrote in his newspaper report 'it is enough to say he played as though he had never been away from the Test arena' [302]. During his innings Cowdrey overtook Walter Hammond to become the highest run scorer in the history of Test cricket (Hammond managed 7, 249 in 140 Test innings, this was Cowdrey's 173rd).

Cowdrey and Luckhurst continued to build the second wicket partnership, as they would have done many times playing for Kent. Although there was the occasional half chance both batsmen were for the most part untroubled. Luckhurst though seemed to have difficulty with short pitched deliveries, particularly from Procter. Showing the tendency to duck, even before the ball had left the bowlers hand, this would need attention with Australia on the horizon.

After tea, with the new ball due, a wicket finally fell. Cowdrey was out lbw when he tried to clip a full toss to the leg side and missed. The bowler could be nobody else but Barlow. The Kent colleagues had added 120 for the second wicket, with Cowdrey making 64 [303]. Fletcher, who was also playing for a place on the winter tour, joined Luckhurst at the wicket.

There was still 40 minutes play left in the day, but these passed incident free. At the close England had reached 184 for 2, with Luckhurst on 69 and Fletcher 8. With only 100 runs needed, victory sometime before lunch the next day, looked almost inevitable.

Close of play – Rest of the World 2nd innings 286 all out
England 2nd innings 184 – 2, (Luckhurst 79★, Fletcher 8★)

Day 5 – Monday 7 July

England started the day in a position many would have thought unlikely at the start of the series. They needed 100 runs with 8 wickets in hand to win a Test match against this team of star players. The weather was good, the pitch benign and they had the whole day in which to score the required runs. It was their match to lose.

Sobers realising that it was all or nothing as far as his side were concerned, began with attacking field placings. Opening with Procter and McKenzie, they bowled flat out from the start, knowing they would not need to last the whole day whatever happened. McKenzie almost got a breakthrough in the second over when Fletcher edged a delivery close to second slip. He also fortunately played and missed two more deliveries that moved sharply away from the same bowler. Although Sobers tried different types of bowling combinations, it gradually became a matter of not if but when England would reach their target.

The England batsmen were still in a safety first mentality. After an hour they had cautiously added just 28 runs to the overnight score. Perhaps not quite believing that they could win and still looking for a banana skin or two. Luckhurst reached a 100 in only his second Test match. Although the critics may have said that it had taken nearly seven hours, England would have been in some trouble without it. Fletcher began to play with fluency, and look a Test batsman after a few uncertain performances in earlier matches. Suddenly it was as though the resistance had gone. The remaining 72 runs needed were scored at almost indecent speed in 45 minutes. Fifteen minutes before lunch England had reached 284 for 2 and achieved an unlikely but well deserved win. It was also the highest fourth innings total England had so far scored to win a Test. After 1979, when the covering of pitches during a Test match became mandatory, such totals would become run of the mill. The only sadness was that over the five days, just 16,000 spectators had turned up to watch England win a famous victory.

Close of play – England 2nd innings 284 – 2, (Luckhurst 113★, Fletcher 69★)
England won by 8 wickets.

15

England v Rest of the World
Third Test Match
Edgbaston, Birmingham
16th – 21st July 1970

Only two weeks ago a hastily assembled Rest of the World team had beaten England in less than four days at Lord's. The British press, especially the tabloids wasted little time in denouncing both the team and the series. The most outspoken, perhaps with an eye on sales, wondered whether it was worth playing the other four Tests at all.

Now England were heroes. Even the usually phlegmatic Illingworth seemed caught up in the emotion of the occasion. After receiving the £2,000 (Equivalent to £35,000 in 2020) winner's cheque, in a brief speech he said 'I don't think I have ever known an England side achieve a better or tougher win than this' [304]. Perhaps the significance of the win was slightly exaggerated, but even so England deserved credit for bowling out a talented Rest of the World line-up twice on a good pitch. Sobers was gracious in defeat, but also not impressed with his team's performance, saying 'The side which bats badly twice, deserves to be beaten' [305].

There was little time for celebration, the following day the quarter-finals of the domestic Gillette Cup knock out competition were being played. Not all of the England players were involved, but there were some fascinating contests within a number of the matches. Players who had been team mates in the Test match would be opponents the following day. For instance, in the match between Kent and Sussex, Cowdrey, Luckhurst. Knott and Underwood would be facing the bowling of Snow and Greig, while in Surrey's match against Middlesex, Edrich and Intikhab would now be on the same side. Sobers was also back captaining Nottinghamshire against Somerset, and even though he scored 96 not out, he ended up on the losing side.

The next Test match was to be played at Edgbaston, Birmingham in ten days. From England's perspective the often quoted guidance of 'don't change a winning team' seemed appropriate. It was difficult to believe that the Edgbaston pitch would be one in which England's medium pace swing bowlers, would again take the majority of the wickets. The fast bowlers Snow and Brown had done little wrong, they had just come up against a totally unresponsive pitch. With Alan Ward still injured, there were anyway no obvious replacements. The Lancastrians were championing the case for Peter Lever or Ken Shuttleworth especially with the winter tour in mind.

As far as the batting was concerned, the four specialist batsmen had all got runs in the first or second innings, with the all-rounders contributing with either bat or ball. Knott had quickly become an automatic pick as the wicketkeeper. It was no surprise when the England selectors announced an unchanged side for Edgbaston with Amiss remaining twelfth man.

There was of course still the issue of naming the captain for the winter tour. Illingworth who was in the side as a bowling all-rounder, had again paradoxically been England's highest scorer in their first innings. It was expected that the selectors would announce a decision on the England captain for the winter at the end of the next Test. The media were split on the matter. Some wondered why it was taking so long. After all Illingworth had been appointed in a caretaker capacity while Cowdrey recovered from his injury. Now that he had proved his fitness, he should resume his role as captain, with maybe Illingworth being rewarded for his success by being appointed vice-captain. Others believed that Illingworth was showing a fresh tactical insight which would be badly needed in Australia [306].

Like most top sportsmen, Sobers did not like losing and he and his fellow selector were not slow in making changes. The side for Edgbaston was announced by Freddie Brown almost as soon as the Trent Bridge match had finished. Farokh Engineer, the Indian wicketkeeper had been disappointing with the bat, scoring just three runs in three innings. His replacement, to the surprise of some, was the West Indian Deryck Murray. The 27-year-old Trinidadian was not even playing first-class cricket at the time he was selected. The previous season he had been first team wicketkeeper at Nottinghamshire, so Sobers knew him well. Murray had played in two Test series for the West Indies, but at the moment he was undertaking postgraduate study at Nottingham University and only playing club cricket with the occasional charity match for the International Cavaliers and D. H. Robbins XI [307]. It was asking a lot to step straight back into the Test match arena.

The other change was to replace Graham McKenzie with Peter Pollock. McKenzie, known by the nickname Garth because of his extreme fitness, had been the spearhead of the Australian bowling attack since making his international debut in 1961. There was now though clearly something wrong. The 29 year old fast bowler was not just out of form but lacking in energy. In the recent tour of South Africa he had taken only one wicket in four Test matches. Illingworth would have been quite happy to see McKenzie rest and return to form because he was now a team mate at Leicestershire.

Peter Pollock (the elder brother of Graeme) was in England working as a journalist. Also 29, he had initially said he did not want to be considered for the series. He too had played against Australia at the beginning of the year. Procter, Pollock and Barlow had taken 52 wickets between them in the four Test series, which South Africa had convincingly won 4-0. The three South Africans along with Sobers, were considered a world class seam bowling attack which any opposition would find difficult to handle.

Nobody could doubt the quality of England's opponents, but describing them as Rest of the World was stretching things a bit. The starting XI now consisted of five South Africans, five West Indians and one Pakistani; not really representative of the rest of the cricket playing world.

Now that England had won a Test match, the sponsors and MCC were hoping that the series would finally catch the imagination of the public, with attendances at Edgbaston an improvement on the disappointing crowds at Trent Bridge. The BBC were still not broadcasting the match on television. The British Commonwealth Games, which this time was being held in Edinburgh, opened on the first day of the Edgbaston Test and so the BBC were giving blanket coverage to this event. Of course there was still Test Match Special on Radio 3. The ball by ball commentary by Brian Johnston, John Arlott and Alan Gibson, with expert summaries by Trevor Bailey and Richie Benaud, and close of play summary by E. W. (Jim) Swanton was to many already an essential part of summer.

Day 1 – Thursday 16 July

The weather at Edgbaston was cloudy but with the forecast for sun later in the day. Most locals expected the pitch to be slow with help for the spin bowlers on the last two days. This was a toss that both captains wanted to win. Illingworth chose correctly this time and without any hesitation, elected to bat first.

The team that took the field for the Rest of the World were: Garry Sobers (Captain) Eddie Barlow, Barry Richards, Rohan Kanhai, Graeme Pollock, Clive Lloyd, Mike Procter, Deryk Murray, Intikhab Alam, Peter Pollock and Lance Gibbs. England were unchanged: Ray Illingworth (Captain) John Edrich, Brian Luckhurst, Colin Cowdrey, Keith Fletcher, Basil D'Oliveira, Tony Greig, Alan Knott, David Brown, Derek Underwood and John Snow.

Just before 11.30, Edrich and Luckhurst walked out to bat, with the ground around a third full. 7000 spectators was still not a typical attendance for the first day of a Test match at Edgbaston, but it was an improvement on Trent Bridge. The first hour of the match was frankly dull. Almost from the first delivery it was clear that the pitch was lifeless. Pollock and Procter the strike bowlers who had been so effective on the hard, fast pitches in South Africa could find neither bounce or movement to unsettle the batsmen. Sobers and Barlow could do no better, and after 70 minutes the England score had reached 50, with each player on 25. It looked like Edrich and Luckhurst were in for a long stay, and England a big total.

Sobers then came on for a second bowling spell and turned the innings on its head. Now bowling over the wicket, his first delivery moved away off the pitch and Luckhurst edged it to Murray behind the stumps. His second delivery to the new batsman Cowdrey was an in-swinger, deceiving the batsman who was out lbw. Then from the other end Pollock bowled a delivery that kept low, and Edrich edged it onto his stumps. England had slipped from 56 for 0 to 66 for 3, and there was still almost half an hour to lunch.

The two new batsmen reacted to the situation in completely different ways. Fletcher, failed to score a run but somehow managed to at least be not out at lunch. In contrast, D'Oliveira played with supreme confidence making it clear he was going to hit poor deliveries, no matter how precarious England's position might seem. Almost immediately he hit Pollock for four, and in the last over before lunch hit a delivery from Gibbs back over his head into the pavilion for six. England left the field on 76 for 3. In just a few overs they had lost the advantage that Edrich and Luckhurst had carefully built.

The interval did not help to steady things. With the second ball of the afternoon Sobers bowled an out-swinger which Fletcher, like Luckhurst earlier, edged to the wicketkeeper. D'Oliveira was joined by his in-form captain. Illingworth started a little nervously but soon settled in and began playing a support role. Meanwhile D'Oliveira just powered on ahead. He was dominating both the fast and slow bowlers without it seemed taking any risks. After 75 minutes Procter, putting everything he had into a short pitched delivery, finally managed to produce some uncomfortable bounce which Illingworth edged to the wicketkeeper. The fifth wicket stand had added 68 runs, of which D'Oliveira had made 50. The new batsman Greig, unusually for him was also uncertain, but like Illingworth he saw his role as that of a supporting batsman.

After tea, showing no signs of slowing down, D'Oliveira reached his fourth Test century. It contained 15 fours and a six, and had been a completely chanceless innings. Greig was now also beginning to play with more confidence. Half an hour before the close, D'Oliveira made his first mistake when he swung at a medium paced delivery from Lloyd. The wonderfully athletic bowler leapt into the air to take a difficult catch at the second attempt. D'Oliveira received a deserved standing ovation from the spectators as he left the field, surely there would be no doubt about him going on the winter tour now [308]. Greig, now came out of his shell and started to play attacking shots. Just after reaching his first Test fifty, he became a little too confident against Procter, and was bowled by a fast inswinging yorker.

With the score at 258 for 6, the pressure was off the batsmen probably for the first time in the day. For the remaining half hour, Knott and Brown played with spirit against tiring bowlers. As the players left the field at the close of play, Illingworth would have reasoned that while 282 for 7 was certainly not a match winning total, at lunch with the scoreboard showing 76 for 4, it could have been so much worse.

Along side the Test match, South Africa continued to make headlines in both the sporting and political arena. That evening the International Cricket Conference (ICC), who had just finished their annual two day meeting at Lord's, issued a press release. The ICC did not normally put anything but the briefest summary of their meetings into the public domain. The minutes of their meetings were usually text-book examples of brevity. This time they went out of their way to acknowledge the pressure the MCC had been under during the *Stop the Seventy Tour Campaign*. Regarding the key question of the future of Test cricket for South Africa, they sat on the fence. They noted the UK Cricket Council's statement of 19 May regarding the conditions that needed to be met before any further Test matches could take place between England and South Africa. There was though no move to make it ICC policy for all other countries. Instead, It was decided that member countries would consider the way forward individually 'and if any member wishes to put forward a proposal, it will be considered by the 1971 Conference' [309]. A classic kick the can down the road strategy.

Peter Hain had moved onto other issues related to South Africa. His focus was currently on the willingness of the Conservative Government led by Edward Heath to sell arms to South Africa. Hain was threatening 'an even more intensive campaign' to stop such sales going ahead [310]. Coincidentally the Foreign Secretary was now Sir Alec Douglas-Home. He was a previous President of the MCC and had been a key figure in the decision to resist calls for cancellation of the 1968 winter tour to South Africa [311].

Close of play – England 1st innings 282 – 7, (Knott 15★, Brown 13★)

Day 2 – Friday 17 July

Day two started, with Sobers keen to take the last three English wickets as quickly and as cheaply as possible. At the moment, barring any heroics from Alan Knott and the tail end batsmen it looked as though England might be bowled out for less than 350. On such a lifeless and relatively slow pitch that was a good effort on the part of Sobers and his bowlers. The ever competitive Sobers of course thought they should have restricted their opponents to an even lower total.

The weather was still very English, hazy with sun maybe later on. There would be no hot weather to quicken up the sluggish pitch. Even so, it was not one you would want to chase any sort of large last innings score on.

The overnight not out batsmen were Alan Knott and David Brown. Chosen as a wicketkeeper who could bat rather than a batsman who could keep wicket, Knott was already showing himself to be one the best wicketkeeper in England. He was also capable of scoring Test fifties and the occasional century.

The previous evening, the pair had batted with comparative freedom against a tiring bowling attack during the last half hour [312]. However, there was nothing easy about England's start on the second day. Sobers began using a fully charged Procter at one end and the leg spin of Intikhab at the other. That proved to be more than enough to finish England's innings. In no time at all, Procter had bowled Brown and then Knott with fast in swinging deliveries. Underwood playing an elegant on drive was well caught by Sobers, and it was all over. It had taken half an hour with England adding only twelve runs to their overnight score, finishing on 294 all out. Procter had taken all three wickets ending with five for 46.

Well as he had bowled, it had been Sobers' three wickets for 0 the previous morning that had been the crucial strike.

When Richards and Barlow came out to open the innings for the Rest of the World, both struggled. England's opening bowlers were accurate and difficult to score off. Snow in particular was unlucky, beating Richards twice in his second over but failing to find the edge of his bat. Then in his fourth over he got a delivery to move away and bowled Barlow for 4. England would have been glad to see him depart. It was just the sort of pitch on which the tenacious Barlow was capable of grinding out a big score.

Richards was joined by Rohan Kanhai. At his best, the West Indian was one of the most flamboyant cricketers in the world. Sadly for the spectators, he had been struggling so far in the series. He had started the English season in great form. Playing for Warwickshire, he was the first in the country to reach 1,000 runs. It was a source of frustration that he could not yet carry that over to the Guinness series.

The day did not look promising for him, even though Edgbaston was his home ground during the summer. The pitch was slow, the bounce low and not easy for stroke players like Richards or Kanhai to play their natural game. The period up until lunch was a mixture of near successes for both sides. The batsmen playing and missing, and then playing a delightful drive or pull shot to dispatch the ball to the boundary. At lunch the Rest of the World had fought there way to 69 for 1. Not pretty cricket, but they had not lost any more wickets.

Shortly after lunch, just as Richards was beginning to look fluent in his stroke play, he was out. Going for an elegant off-drive off Snow, he edged a catch to Greig at slip. His 47 runs had taken nearly two hours but given the conditions many batsmen would have been out for far less.

Kanhai was now joined by Graeme Pollock. Like Barlow, Pollock had not played competitive cricket since the last Test match against Australia four months ago. There was also a huge difference between the pitches he had been playing on in the South African summer, and the lifeless one he found himself on now.

If the cricket before lunch had been competitive, it now became attritional, almost deadlocked. D'Oliveira and Underwood bowled such a accurate line, that both batsmen found it almost impossible to score runs at anything more than a trickle. The crowd also became frustrated and started with some slow hand-clapping. The players were waiting for the poor delivery which never came, and as tea approached two of the most exciting batsmen in the world had taken nearly two hours to score 77 runs. Then with the last delivery before tea, Snow again got a ball to cut in off the pitch and bowled Pollock for 40. His highest score of the series so far. Chasing 296, at 157 for 3, things did not look too good for the visitors.

After tea it got no easier for the batsmen. Kanhai finally took a huge risk sweeping across the line, to hit a delivery from Illingworth on middle stump over square leg for six. This was pure frustration, and it was really no surprise when just before five o'clock Kanhai's torment ended. He drove Illingworth to mid-on, straight into the hands of Greig. With the captain coming to the wicket, the Rest of the World were in big trouble at 175 for 4. A first innings lead was beginning to seem unlikely.

Sobers though was in no mood to worry about what the pitch might or might not do. He played with aggressive intent from the first ball, not worried about the occasional play and miss. Hitting savagely, boundary after boundary, Sobers needed only 58 deliveries to reach 50. His fellow left hander, Lloyd, began to gain confidence from his captain's display and by the time the new ball was due at just past 6 pm, the Rest of the World had reached 255 for 4. Less than an hour ago, Illingworth had almost complete control of the game, now he was taking the new ball even though his bowlers were tired, in order to try and stop the torrent of runs. It did not work. In 23 minutes 44 runs were added, as the new ball was hammered for boundary after boundary [312]. As the players left the field at 6.30, the England players would have been a little disappointed. They could rightly say that they had been on top until the last ninety minutes of the day. Then despite their best efforts, the brilliance of Sobers, with increasing support from Lloyd, had snatched the initiative away from England. If Sobers and Lloyd were in for too much longer the following morning they would also take the match.

Close of play – England 1ˢᵗ innings 294 all out
Rest of the World 1ˢᵗ innings 296 – 4, (Lloyd 62*, Sobers 63*)

Day 3 – Saturday 18 July

Spectators arriving at Edgbaston the following morning had to deal with something new in the Test series; queuing and crowds. The people of Birmingham had turned out in force, and with fine weather forecast there was the anticipation of a great day's cricket ahead. At last, it really felt like the Saturday of a Test match. When Sobers and Lloyd walked out to continue their innings, they were welcomed by 12,500 noisy and enthusiastic spectators. With its high immigrant population, there was plenty of support for both sides. There was also particular cheers for Kanhai, Gibbs and Brown. Opponents today, but normally on the same side when they played county cricket for Warwickshire. This was their home ground.

Since the ball was only a few overs old, Illingworth started with his fast bowlers Snow and Brown. It soon became obvious that the pitch was even slower than the previous day and after only three overs from each of his opening bowlers he moved to Underwood and himself.

A little hesitant at first, Lloyd and Sobers were soon into their stride, and with the boisterous crowd cheering every boundary it looked like it might be a long day for England. Then with his score on 80 and a century beckoning, Sobers misjudged the length of a delivery from Illingworth and was bowled, trying to adjust his shot. Lloyd seemed temporarily unsettled by his captain's departure but then decided there was going to be no nervous nineties for him as his century got nearer. He played a booming on-drive, hitting a delivery from Greig into the crowd for six, and the next over after reaching his second century of the series, swung rather crudely across the line and was bowled for 101. The Rest of the World were 377 for 6, a lead of 83. If England could take the remaining 4 wickets cheaply, maybe they had a chance of keeping the first innings lead down to 120 or so. Still a useful lead, but not out of sight, and with the opposition batting last on what then would be a difficult pitch. Who knows? The new batsman Murray and Procter, appeared to play quietly, but by lunch had already taken the score to 418 for 6. Without playing any extravagant shots, they had already begun to close the door.

After lunch the door was shut. Procter, was technically an all-rounder but could have player in many sides as a specialist batsman or bowler. He had a well organised defence, and looked in little trouble. When he attacked it was with total commitment. He seemed to have all the shots, playing powerfully either side of the wicket. He rapidly reached 50, with all but 5 runs coming in boundaries. At the other end, Murray after an understandably hesitant start, soon looked as though he had been playing first-class cricket all season. Again the game was rapidly pulling away from England. With a century on the horizon, Procter was a little surprisingly beaten by a faster delivery from Snow and bowled for 62. The score was now 450 for 7, and the new batsman was Intikhab, another all-rounder. He also took time to play himself in while Murray was responsible for moving the score along. At tea, the Rest of the World were 519 for 7, a lead of 225. Now the game really was beginning to look out of sight.

After tea, England's play understandably started to become a bit ragged, with misfields and a few dropped catches. Murray almost inevitably reached 50, before edging a delivery from Underwood to slip. Pollock was then given time to play a few shots. Following Intikhab's dismissal, to almost certainly the biggest cheer of the day the local favourite Lance Gibbs came to the wicket. A natural number eleven batsman he proceeded to demonstrate his technique against the new ball, with each defensive stroke receiving a cheer as though it were a boundary. Finally at 5.30, Sobers decided enough was enough and declared on 563 for nine. The Rest of the World had a massive first innings lead of 269.

Edrich and Luckhurst came out to start England's second innings with fifty minutes play left in the day. They had little to gain and everything to lose. It took only six overs from Procter and Pollock, giving it everything, to confirm that this was not a pitch for fast bowlers. Batsmen could play comfortably off the front or back foot, knowing that a delivery would not rise sharply and that even a short pitched delivery would hardly get to stump height. When the spinners, Intikhab and Gibbs, were bought on to bowl it was a different story. With men round the bat and the pitch taking turn, the batsmen were suddenly under pressure. At the close of play, England had reached 19 for 0. A small triumph, but Edrich and Luckhurst were under no illusions about the difficulty of the task ahead. Monday was going to be a long, long day.

**Close of play – Rest of the World 1st innings 563 all out
England 2nd innings 19 – 0, (Edrich 3★, Luckhurst 13★)**

Day 4 – Monday 20 July

Often the Monday of a Test match can feel like a bit of an anti-climax. With most of the population returning to work, there is rarely the same buzz in the crowd or sense of anticipation that was there on Saturday. Even so as they walked out to bat, Edrich and Luckhurst were absolutely clear that their immediate target was to be there at lunch. England still trailed the Rest of the World by 250. They would need to bat the best part of the day just to erase the first inning's deficit. Tomorrow would then be about scoring enough runs to ensure England could not be beaten. A draw was realistically the best England could hope for and to achieve this they would need to bat until at least mid-afternoon on the last day.

From Sobers point of view, the lead of 250 would allow him to set very attacking fields and not worry too much about conceding runs, as long as wickets fell at regular intervals. Sobers decided to start the day with Intikhab bowling leg-spin from one end and Pollock fast seam bowling from the other. This would mean that the batsmen would find it more difficult to settle with a change in technique constantly needed.

His strategy worked. After only fifteen minutes with just a single added to the overnight score, a delivery from Intikhab bounced more than expected, and Edrich edged a catch to a close in fielder. The fielder of course was Sobers! This bought Cowdrey to the wicket, who like Illingworth later, was well aware that the England selectors were meeting that afternoon to finally decide who would lead the MCC winter tour to Australia. The bureaucracy required that the selectors recommendation be approved by the Chairman of the Cricket Council and President of the MCC, before being released to the press. Not an easy situation for either of the main candidates. Cowdrey had the added burden of having been out for 0 in the first innings.

Although this was only Luckhurst's sixth innings as an England batsman, he was beginning to look more and more at home at international level, and so was able to keep adding to the score while Cowdrey took his time to settle in. Used to batting together for Kent, the pair were beginning to look comfortable when Luckhurst was out. Trying to cut a delivery from Intikhab, he misjudged and was caught by the wicketkeeper. The new batman Fletcher, may well have been playing for a place on the winter tour. His nought in the first innings would not have helped but if he was nervous it did not show. His first two scoring shots were an on-drive off Gibbs for four, followed by an even better straight drive for six. This was the player people in county cricket were used to seeing. Fletcher and Cowdrey were still together at lunch and the attack was beginning to look less threatening. Maybe the unthinkable was possible.

After lunch, Cowdrey though not at his very best and Fletcher continued to push the score along at a healthy rate. Then with the score on 132, unexpectedly and needlessly Fletcher was run out. Playing a delivery to the off side he called Cowdrey through for a straightforward run. Cowdrey started then stopped, Fletcher was caught half way down the pitch and easily run out. Cowdrey and Fletcher had added 74 at almost a run a minute. They were certainly not batting for a draw.

The incoming batsman D'Oliveira, was perfect for this situation. While Cowdrey fretted on his part in Fletcher's dismissal, D'Oliveira was having none of it, and started as he had left off in the first innings. He was bristling with confidence from the very first ball. He dealt equally positively with pace and spin, and was particularly severe on Pollock. The bowler who along with Procter had demolished the Australians in South Africa at the beginning of the year, looked well below his best. Then again another inexplicable dismissal. Pollock bowled a long hop down the leg side, Cowdrey swung at it and edged it to Murray behind the stumps. This was by some distance the worst delivery Cowdrey had faced in his innings, and yet it caused his downfall. Out for 71, of course not a bad contribution, but England needed a big hundred from one of its higher order batsmen.

D'Oliveira was joined by Illingworth, and again England rebuilt. With an hour to go the score had advanced to 271. The first innings deficit had been erased, both batsmen were playing with confidence and they still had six wickets left. Once more hopes were rising. Then, as already had been the case so often in the series, Sobers made a crucial contribution. Bowling slow left arm he induced a rare false stroke from D'Oliveira. Out for 81, the all rounder had come so close to scoring a century in each innings of a Test match (something last achieved by an Englishman in 1947). Eight runs later, Illingworth, who had looked as confident as at any time during the series, took an unnecessary swing at a delivery from Gibbs and was bowled for 43. Finally, after a few belligerent boundaries Greig was undone by a delivery from Sobers, bowled using his other style of slow left arm bowling. A comfortable 271 for four had all too rapidly become 317 for 7. Knott and Brown held out until the close, but a win for the Rest of the World looked inevitable the next day.

Close of play – England 2nd innings 320 – 7, (Knott 16★, Brown 1★)

Day 5 – Tuesday 21 July

The final day started with England just 51 runs ahead and having only 3 wickets left in their second innings. To set the Rest of the World a challenging target, England would need to score another 120 runs at least. Unlikely, but all three results were still a possibility. No matter what happened in the coming hours, tomorrow's sports headlines would be dominated by the choice of captain for the winter tour. The cricket correspondents of the national newspapers were still divided, although Crawford White in Tuesday's *Daily Express* was already boldly declaring 'It's Illingworth – he gets the tour job' [313.]

When play resumed, it was soon apparent that taking these last three wickets was going to be far from a formality. As you would expect from a wicketkeeper, Knott was quick on his feet, and with at times almost exaggerated defensive shots, with his nose over the ball. Brown was well organised, capable of solid defence with the occasional adventurous swing to send the ball to the boundary. The pair had batted for 65 minutes with Brown on 32, when maybe his ambition got the better of him. He tried to hook Procter, and mishit a catch to Murray behind the stumps. Underwood did not have time to settle in, before Sobers bowled him with an in swinging yorker,. At 364 for 9, and with a lead of 95 an early finish still looked likely.

As with his bowling, John Snow was a man of moods. Batting at number eleven would have been something he would have taken exception to. It was soon clear that he was not going to give his wicket away by enjoying a few slog shots. With some good fortune, Knott and Snow continued to frustrate and take runs when they could They were still there at lunch, by which time England had moved on to 409.

After lunch just as thoughts of an unlikely victory were beginning to surface, it was over. Snow was bowled by, who else but Sobers, for 21. Knott was left on 50 not out, and the Rest of the World needed 141 to win.

Before they could begin the chase it started to rain, but it was only a light shower and at 2.30pm, Richards and Barlow were walking out to bat. They had three hours and ten minutes to score the runs needed for victory.

Barlow was soon out without scoring. It had not had a good match with either bat or ball, for the South African all-rounder who had done so well so far in the series. After this alarm, Richards and Kanhai settled and started to build the score. An extravagant hook shot for six by Kanhai off Brown persuaded Illingworth that the best option for taking wickets was to use himself and Underwood.

The score moved on to 72 for 1, and it was beginning to look reasonably straightforward when Richards surprisingly tried a hook shot against Underwood and was bowled for 32, and seven runs later Kanhai was also out to Underwood. It was then Illingworth's turn to taste some success, taking the wickets of Sobers and Lloyd. At 107 for 5, there was a murmur in the crowd. Graeme Pollock was not fit to bat, unless absolutely necessary. Surely England couldn't win. The new batsmen at the crease Intikhab and Procter survived a few lbw appeals against Underwood, but soon they were hitting off the runs required at pace. With less than an hour to go to the close of play, the Rest of the World reached their target, in the end winning by a comfortable 5 wickets.

It had been an entertaining match, in which England had fought hard, and at times had a chance to win. The public had suddenly also taken an interest in the series with over 30,000 paying to attend the game over the five days. For now the question on most people's lips was who had been chosen to lead MCC in Australia? A decision had at last been made.

There was a sad postscript to the game. As was normal at that time, the umpires for the series were selected and agreed in advance by the International Cricket Conference from the home country's Test Umpire's Panel. For J. S. 'Syd' Buller, one of those standing in the Third Test, the match would be his last international fixture. Just over two weeks later while officiating in the county championship fixture between Warwickshire and Nottinghamshire at Edgbaston he collapsed and died during a break in play for rain. He was only 60 but had already umpired in 35 Test matches. The fifth Test later in the summer began with a minute's silence in memory of J S 'Syd' Buller. John Woodcock writing in the *Times* echoed the thoughts of many when he wrote 'it is a fine thing to be able to say of any man that he was acknowledged as the best and fairest in his profession' [314].

Close of play – The England 2nd innings 409 all out
Rest of the World 2nd innings 141 – 5,
(Intikhab Alam 15★, Procter 25★)
Rest of the World won by 5 wickets.

16

England v Rest of the World
Fourth Test Match
Headingley, Leeds
30 July – 4 August 1970

On the afternoon of the fourth day of the Edgbaston Test match Ray Illingworth was in the England dressing room taking off his pads. Having just been bowled by Lance Gibbs he was annoyed with himself for playing a poor shot when occupation of the crease was the main objective. It was a bad example to his team.

A few moments later he was joined by Alec Bedser, the chairman of selectors, who congratulated him on his innings and then added in his usual low key manner that Illingworth was their choice to lead the MCC touring party in Australia and New Zealand [315]. Two years ago it had all looked so different. It seemed as though both his on/off international career and his domestic career were coming to an end. He was in dispute with Yorkshire for expecting more than the standard one-year playing contract. Ultimately he had little choice but to leave the county he had played for all his cricketing life. In 1968 he moved to Leicestershire where he was appointed captain. Under his guidance they were already improving, and would win their first County Championship in 1975.

Now, he had been given what most considered the toughest assignment in international cricket, the chance to win the Ashes down under. Talking to the press later he sad 'Now that it has come to me it's fantastic. It is certainly the high-spot of my career', however he was wrong, that was yet to come [316].

In contrast to Illingworth's joy, Colin Cowdrey had to deal with the bitter disappointment of once again being passed over and offered the consolation prize of the vice-captaincy. Understandably perhaps, he was not in a hurry to accept the deputy's role for the fourth time in a row. Illingworth and he were in many ways opposites. One a no nonsense northern professional cricketer from West Yorkshire the other an urbane sportsman from the green pastures of Kent. At 38 and 37, both were nearing the end of their careers but ambitious to achieve more success before retiring as players. There was also a history of disagreement between the two on a previous tour [317]. There are always matters of disagreement on overseas tours, which are usually sorted out and quickly forgotten. In a recent biography Murtagh suggests that the differences between Illingworth and Cowdrey were often exaggerated by the press [318]. The sacking of Brian Close as England captain in 1967 to be replaced by Cowdrey has caused ill feeling and reinforced views many in Yorkshire had about the MCC. This had nothing to do with Cowdrey but the north versus south arguments would be resurrected again. Nonetheless, Cowdrey was well aware that this would be his last visit as a member of a MCC touring party to Australia. Realistically, the choice was go as vice-captain or not at all.

No sooner had the match and presentations at Edgbaston been completed, then some of the players from both sides were on the move, as they would be playing cricket again the next day. The Gillette Cup one day competition had reached the semi-final stage. The competition was in its eighth year and showed no signs of losing popularity. This year Somerset were playing Lancashire at Taunton while Surrey had been drawn against Sussex at the Oval. The prize, a place in the final played before a guaranteed packed house at Lord's in the first week of September. Like the FA Cup Final in football, the Gillette Cup final in many ways signalled the end of the season, and was an occasion enjoyed by spectators and players alike.

In the match at the Taunton, Lancashire proved to be just too strong for Somerset. The home side has been given a solid start by Roy Virgin and Tony Clarkson but too many of the middle order were out cheaply, and so unable to build the big partnership necessary for a large total. Their final score of 207 was unlikely to be enough against a strong Lancashire batting line up which included Clive Lloyd and Farokh Engineer. Six of the top seven batsmen got runs and Lancashire reached their first Gillette Cup final with overs to spare.

The match at the Kennington Oval was a real nail bitter. Batting first Surrey only managed 196. John Edrich went cheaply, unaccountably not playing a shot and out lbw. Their other danger man Younis Ahmed was also out cheaply, while John Snow bowled the potentially dangerous Intikhab Alam for nought. John Snow and Tony Greig took 7 wickets between them. Although they were chasing a small total, Sussex also never found it easy to score runs. Facing a bowling attack which included Intikhab Alam , Geoff Arnold and a young Bob Willis it was a constant struggle. When they reached the last over of the game, playing in front of a huge excitable crowd, Sussex needed three runs to win. Tony Buss and John Snow were batting and Sussex looked to have the advantage. However, in the one day game this is where the nerves can take over. No runs were scored off the first two deliveries and Buss was run out from the third. The new batsman managed a single off the fifth ball, leaving Snow to score two off the last delivery. In a fervent atmosphere, Snow's last shot was misfiielded by Intikhab allowing Sussex to get the second run and win the match. This illustrated perfectly why the one-day format was here to stay.

When deciding on the side for Headingley, the selectors were still trying to meet two objectives. Firstly, they wanted to choose a side that could win and therefore take the series to a decider at the Oval. Secondly there was the need to finalise the team for the winter tour. Although the captaincy issue had been decided, there were still some places in the touring party to be filled and only two more matches in which to try potential candidates.

The touring party would most likely consist of sixteen players. Three opening batsmen, four middle order batsmen and all-rounders, two wicketkeepers, three slow bowlers and four fast bowlers. The area of biggest concern was the bowlers. Only John Snow and Alan Ward (if fit) were certainties while Derek Underwood and Ray Illingworth would be two of the three slow bowlers needed. Candidates for the remaining fast bowling positions could not be judged on anything approaching

Australian conditions in the remaining two Test matches of the summer, but the selectors had to work with what they had. In the end the decision was to drop David Brown and give an opportunity to the young Yorkshire seam bowler Chris Old. He had topped the Yorkshire bowling averages the previous season and would do so again in the present one. There were though concerns about his ability to stay fit.

For the slow bowlers, the selectors decided to give a second Yorkshireman, Don Wilson another try. The slow left arm spinner had played four Tests against India in the 1963/64 winter tour, but had not been picked for England since. Of course Illingworth would have been well aware of his capabilities, having been a county team mate until recently.

Finally, a third Yorkshireman Geoffrey Boycott was bought back having made himself unavailable for the first three matches of the summer because of his poor form. Typically, he had worked obsessively at his batting and was now scoring runs in the County Championship again. To make room for Wilson and Boycott, Edrich and Underwood were rested as they were certainties for the winter tour.

The final twelve for the fourth Test were therefore Ray Illingworth (captain}, Geoff Boycott, Brian Luckhurst, Colin Cowdrey, Keith Fletcher, Basil D'Oliveira, Tony Greig, Alan Knott, Chris Old, Don Wilson and John Snow. Mike Denness was again given twelfth man duties.

The Rest of the World selectors had less to think about. The experiment to move Peter Pollock from the Press Box at such short notice had not been a success. He had looked far below his best and the lack of match practice was evident. He was replaced by Mushtaq Mohammed the Pakistani leg-spinner all-rounder who was currently playing for Northamptonshire. Peter Pollock's brother Graeme was also a concern. He was clearly out of form and so far had not been able to demonstrate the stroke play, which made him one of the best batsmen in the world. However there was never any thought of dropping him as an agreement had been made at the beginning of the series that Barlow and Pollock, the two South Africans not currently playing county cricket, would play in all five Tests.

Day 1 – Thursday 30 July

The day began with the news that Colin Cowdrey had at last accepted the role of vice-captain on the winter tour. While Cowdrey made little public comment on his reaction to being offered the role as Illingworth's deputy, ten days of silence perhaps said it all. This was not a promising start for efforts to build a harmonious touring team but that was for the future. Now, there was a Test match to focus on and England were still in the series.

The possibility that an injury to Boycott's right hand might prevent him from playing caused some anxiety before the final teams were announced but in the end all was well. The previous weekend the pitch at Headingly had been under water, but bright sunshine and blustery winds since then had helped dry everything. The day was warm and cloudy, with a moist atmosphere and a green pitch. A large crowd had turned up to watch the first day's play. They had the added attraction of seeing an England team containing three Yorkshiremen and one exile. The captains had to consider how long these 'English conditions' would be helpful to the bowler. Garry Sobers won the toss and decided to take the risk and ask England to bat first. He was banking on his all-star attack, bowling England out cheaply before the pitch lost its venom.

The first overs of the match were as expected a battle for the batsmen, but in particular a duel between Sobers and Boycott. The Yorkshire hero had a poor record against the left arm seam of Sobers. Boycott was now right back in form and the previous weekend he had hit the highest score of his career, a spectacular 260 against Essex in the County Championship. For good measure he had also scored 98 in the Sunday League game against the same opposition.

Sobers started with three maiden overs, but Boycott was not one to fret about not scoring. It actually took eight overs play before he had a run to his name. Then having broken the shackles, Boycott opened up, driving Barlow for two fours in an over. Just when the crowd were beginning to relax, Boycott was out. He glanced a medium paced delivery from Barlow behind to the wicketkeeper for 15. There was a collective groan in the crowd. No century for Boycott today.

Cowdrey came out to bat. With the decision about the vice-captaincy made, it still seemed as though he was not fully focused. After 15 minutes he pushed tentatively at a Barlow delivery and gave Murray another catch. Out for just 1 run. The next man in was Fletcher who had unpleasant memories of his Test debut at Headingly two years ago. It had been a nightmare. The partisan crowd thought wrongly, that Fletcher was playing instead of a local man Philip Sharpe. When he dropped catches and was out for a duck in his first innings, Fletcher became subject to a torrent of abuse from the crowd. He was still bitter about this 15 years later when he published his autobiography [319].

This time, he played with a positive determination right from the start, and now both luck and the crowd were with him. His first two boundares went wide of slip but this did not deter Fletcher from playing his shots. Meanwhile Luckhurst continued in his unhurried way, maybe not a flamboyant stroke maker, but looking secure and difficult to get out. At lunch England had reached 69 for 2, and honours were more or less even. Barlow had the wickets but Sobers had created the pressure by bowling 17 overs for just 14 runs.

After the break, England lost two wickets in the first hour of the afternoon session. First Luckhurst, having played so carefully, tried to hook a slow (by his standards) bouncer from Procter, got it wrong and skied a catch to square leg. Even so, with another solid innings, and 35 runs to his name he would almost certainly be in the winter touring team. This was not D'Oliveira's day, and he was almost immediately out, caught in the gully for 2. More importantly, in taking the catch Richards wrenched his already damaged back. He would now not open the innings for the Rest of the World. However, At 91 for 4 it was England who were looking uneasy. So far Sobers gamble had paid off.

Fletcher was playing with increasing confidence, striking attractive boundaries and looking the part of a middle order England batsman. Meanwhile, his partner Illingworth, was doing what he had already done many times so far in the series, playing solidly and building yet another Test fifty. The two played like this to tea and beyond.

At five o'clock England had moved the score on to 192 for 4 and again the game was more or less level. When the new ball became available, Sobers decided to let Barlow and Procter share it, as he had already bowled more than his fair share of overs that day. Barlow the combative optimist who always wanted to be in the game, was more than happy to take the opportunity. There was now though almost no help for the bowlers from the pitch. Fletcher hit two boundaries off Barlow in the second over of the new ball, and as the score moved to 209 it looked like Fletcher was on his way to his first Test century, while maybe a century was even a possibility for Illingworth.

The dream was disturbed when Fletcher sparred at a Barlow delivery and edged it to the wicketkeeper for 89. Forty minutes later, almost unbelievably, England were all out for 222. Procter started the route by beating Greig's forward defensive shot with pure pace for 5. England were then destroyed by Barlow bowling massively swinging medium paced deliveries – his so called banana ball. In an amazing spell Barlow bowled Knott middle stump with the last ball of an over. He then bowled Old with the first ball of his next over and had Wilson caught at forward short leg for a hat trick. Snow hit the next ball for three and Barlow then deceived Illingworth who clipped a simple catch to Murray. Barlow had taken 4 wickets in five balls, and had overall figures of 7 wickets for 64. England had crashed from 209 for 4 to 222 all out.

Just to make the day complete, Barlow then came out to open the innings with Murray (Richards was not fit to bat) and between them they saw off Snow, Old and D'Oliveira to close at 20 for 0. It had been the Rest of the World's day in nearly all respects.

Close of play – England 1st innings 222 all out
Rest of the World 1st innings 20 – 0, (Barlow 12*, Murray 6*)

Day 2 – Friday 31 July

The overnight news on the injuries to Richards and Kanhai was uncertain. Richards' back injury had got worse and he would not bat in the first innings and only bat in the second if absolutely necessary. Kanhai although handicapped by his hand injury, would bat in both innings.

Barlow and Murray as a stand in opener walked out to bat under another grey sky. It was muggy and the pitch though still green offered almost no assistance to the bowlers from the very first delivery. Yesterday, when the pitch had been least helpful and assistance from the atmosphere negligible, Eddie Barlow had taken five of his seven wickets. Illingworth was hoping that Greig and D'Oliveira would have similar success.

After forty minutes Illingworth's first choice seam attack of Snow and Old was replaced by the slower Greig and D'Oliveira. The change of bowlers had an immediate effect, with batting becoming tougher. First Barlow driving at a wide delivery, hit it to Boycott at cover. Then in no time at all, Mushtaq was lbw to a delivery that came back off the wicket, and Pollock was out playing a loose shot too early in his innings. The Rest of the World had slipped from 67 for 0 to 90 for 3, with Greig taking all three wickets in seven overs. Greig was again demonstrating that he was already a useful change bowler, capable of taking wickets, but he still bowled too many poorly directed deliveries to be considered a full-time member of the bowling attack.

The Rest of the World were suddenly not in a great position. The injuries to Richards and Kanhai meant that they might be in effect, 90 for 5. Also worrying was the continuing poor form of Graeme Pollock. Five innings and he had only scored a hundred runs in total. There were many in the crowd who had been looking forward to seeing one of the best batmen in the world show his skills., but so far as in the previous Tests they had been disappointed.

After lunch, Murray who had not been fazed by his role as make-shift opening batsman, continued to anchor the innings. He was not a flamboyant stroke player like some of his colleagues, but still capable of punishing the poor delivery. His partner Lloyd, often seemed almost too languid in his approach. However when he played attacking shots he could destroy any bowler. On this occasion Lloyd never looked terribly settled. He had just begun to build an innings, when much to the delight of the Yorkshire supporters, he drove at a yorker from Old, missed it and his middle stump was spectacularly knocked out of the ground. Not a bad scalp for a first Test wicket (There was also the added bonus for the Yorkshire crowd that Lloyd played for Lancashire!). It was now 152 for 4 and Sobers was coming to the wicket. Always an important wicket, but today getting Sobers out as quickly as possible was crucial. He started quietly, clearly in safety first mode. By tea Murray was within sight of his first Test century.

Unfortunately this was not to be the case. Fifteen minutes into the evening session he tried to sweep Wilson, and the skied shot was caught by Snow at square leg for 95. He had batted for nearly five hours, not given a chance and at 220 for 5, the Rest of the World were now only 2 runs behind England's first innings score. Again it seemed that England had got themselves to a strong position, only to let it slip.

Seeing Procter coming in higher in the order because of the injuries, was not much of a consolation for England. He was soon playing handsome drives, and appeared to want to score only in boundaries. He hit 6 fours in his first half hour at the wicket, before mis-hitting the new ball. Procter was replaced by Intikhab who also played some thumping drives. All this time at the other end, Sobers in a very restrained mode was letting his all-rounders have their head. The Rest of the World were pulling away again. Not for the first time, Greig showed that he has one more piece to his armoury, luck. He persuaded Intikhab to try and hook the last ball of the day. The delivery was no more than a tired long hop, which Intikhab got totally wrong, skying a catch to Knott behind the stumps.

At the close of play the Rest of the World had moved to 309 for 7, already a lead of 87 with the restrained Sobers on 75 not out. England had not played badly, Snow in particular had beat Sobers a number of times on a pitch not suited to his bowling. Even so, when it really mattered one of the opposition's star players would deliver. With only two days gone, it already seemed that England would need plenty of luck if they were to rescue this match.

Close of play – Rest of the World 1st innings 309-7, (Sobers 75★)

Day 3 – Saturday 1 August
The Saturday of the Headingly Test match was a day, which Yorkshire cricket followers usually looked forward to with relish. A highlight in their cricket calendar, this time with the added bonus of Boycott, Old and

Wilson in the England team and even Illingworth could still be considered a Yorkshireman for the day!. Sadly the weather did not play its part, the first day of August this year was grey and murky.

In theory, the Rest of the World still had three wickets left in their first innings. In practice, it was only two. It had been decided overnight, that Richards would now only bat if absolutely necessary. So Kanhai walked out to resume the Rest of the World's innings with Sobers. It was not clear how the hand injury would affect Kanhai's ability to bat. If he was badly limited Sobers would have to hit out and get whatever runs he could. The initial overs showed that although severely limited, Kanhai was capable of staying in. There would be no outrageous attacking strokes today.

Realizing that he did not need to protect Kanhai, Sobers then used all his considerable skill to find the gaps in the field and when the opportunity arose hit savage boundaries. In half an hour, he had scored the 25 runs needed to reach his twenty third Test century (at that time only Bradman had scored more). Meanwhile Kanhai nudged and flicked singles, and just once gritted his teeth and straight drove Greig back over his head for a boundary. After 70 minutes he pushed rather than drove a delivery from D'Oliveira, only to present the bowler with a simple catch.

With Gibbs now coming out to bat, Sobers knew that he had to attack every delivery. Lance Gibbs might be a world class slow bowler, but he was also a true number eleven batsman. Illingworth, knowing exactly what options his opposite number had put three men on the boundary. Snow bowled a fast, wide delivery, Sobers flashed a drive, did not connect enough and was caught at mid wicket. He had batted just over four hours for a 114, hitting 15 fours and a six. The innings had been more workman like than flamboyant, but was exactly what the team needed. With Richards not able to bat, Sobers declared on 376 for 9. The Rest of the World had a first innings lead of 154. It seemed that the game was already theirs to lose.

When they came out to begin England's second innings, Boycott and Luckhurst had 35 minutes to bat. Their objective was simple to walk off the field together at lunch. Rather than opening the bowling with Procter, Sobers gave the ball to Barlow. He was perhaps hoping that the England batsmen would remember how Barlow had destroyed the lower order batting on the first day. Strangely, he was not as effective opening the bowling as coming on as a change bowler. There was the occasional play and miss, but these were rare. Boycott and Luckhurst had little to worry about when they left the field with England on 23 for 0.

After the break it was a different story. Sobers took over from Barlow, bowling in tandem with Procter. Although at times progress almost ground to a halt, neither batsman seemed unduly worried. Gradually they broke the shackles and no matter what combination of bowlers Sobers tried the runs started to increase. The 'new' Boycott in particular, appeared to be in the form of his life. Scoring freely he got to 64 out of 104 when he made his first (and only) mistake. He did not quite get forward enough to drive a Barlow delivery, and edged a catch to slip.

Cowdrey was met with polite applause as he walked to the wicket, with some in the crowd wondering whether this would be the last time they saw him bat for England in a Headingly Test match. This was not a match to remember for Cowdrey as almost immediately he played across a delivery from Barlow and was comprehensively bowled for his second nought of the match. At 108 for 2 England's position was fragile, and it was Barlow who had again knocked a hole in their batting. The new man in Fletcher was dropped and then beaten, and then Luckhurst was beaten. If luck had been going his away, Barlow could have had three wickets in four balls. Suddenly England seemed to be struggling, but both batsmen had the capacity to not appear worried if they played and missed. Today the luck was with them and although progress was pedestrian both were still there at tea. After the interval England continued to inch forward. With just ten minutes to go of the day and Luckhurst in sight of a century, the opener tried to play a delivery off his legs and was caught at mid-wicket for 92. It had taken four and a half hours but again Luckhurst had shown that if the situation required it, he could just occupy the crease. Inevitably the bowler was Barlow.

A day of hard combative cricket had ended with England on 204 for 3. Fifty runs ahead they had something to build on after the rest day, but as had also been shown in this series, it could also end in tears.

Close of play – Rest of the World 1st innings 376 – 9 dec
England 2nd innings 204 – 3, (Fletcher 41★ Snow 2★)

Day 4 – Monday 3 August

The 3 August was not a public holiday in England in 1970, only in Scotland. Even so 11,000 turned up to watch the fourth day's play of a Test match England had to win if they were to retain a chance of winning the Guinness Trophy.

The weather was the best of the match so far, warm and balmy and the pitch was at its best. England had a lead of 50 with three wickets left. Not a big enough lead to set a serious challenge yet. The spectators would have had different views of the overnight batsmen. Snow had been sent in as a night watchman on Saturday evening, and in many ways had done his job by still being there. Anything else was a bonus. Fletcher would be expected to add a few more runs yet, and strengthen his bid for a place on the winter tour.

John Snow usually took his batting seriously. He had been dropped to number eleven in the batting order in the last Test and this time had a chance to prove the selectors wrong. Facing a ball which was not many overs old, to his credit he lasted 40 minutes against Sobers and Barlow. When he was eventually caught at slip off a Barlow out-swinger, he may have only added 8 to his overnight score but he had eaten up valuable time, and maybe used up a little of the bowler's energy.

Fletcher seemed more tentative than he had done on Saturday evening. Maybe he was still unsure of his place on the winter tour, and aware that getting out cheaply would go against him. Maybe he was thinking of his new responsibility as his wife had given birth to their first child when he was batting on Saturday evening [320]. This time though luck was with him. He was dropped in the gully by Gibbs when he had added 12 to his overnight score but continued to play defensively. His new partner D'Oliveira, so often at his confident and belligerent best in these situations was also uncomfortable and unable to stamp his authority on the game. Progress was slow but after ninety minutes of high class swing seam bowling Sobers decided to change the attack to Procter and Lloyd.

Whether it was because the batsmen had relaxed thinking that they had ridden out the storm, almost immediately things began to happen. In Lloyd's first over, Fletcher was caught at slip for 63, an innings which had taken three and a half hours. Then from the other end, D'Oliveira was bowled by a change of pace from Procter, and two balls later Greig edged a catch to the wicket keeper. From a reasonably strong position of 257 for 4 England had slipped in just a few deliveries to 268 for 7. There was fifteen minutes to lunch. England had a lead of 114 with only three wickets left. A win for the Rest of the World before the day was over began to look a probability.

In the afternoon session Illingworth again found himself in the position of working with the tail end batsmen to add as many runs as they could to the total; and again he delivered. His partnerships with Knott and then Old helped take England's total to 376. If there is such a thing as beginner's luck, Chris Old had it in abundance, at least as far as his batting was concerned. As one reporter observed 'in making 37, Old must have been beaten 20 times' [321]. His strategy seemed to be a choice between an authentic attacking cricket shot or a big swing and miss. Illingworth, considered a bowling all-rounder, was again playing an intelligent mixture of defence and attack and made a Test fifty for the fifth time in the series. The Rest of the World now needed a more challenging 223 to win.

Barlow and Murray came out to open the bating for the Rest of the World. The objective, to win and take an unassailable lead in the Guinness Series. For England it was now all or nothing. They knew the opposition batting was weakened by injury and others were not in good form. The weather was the best it had been all match and the crowd the biggest. It was just a pity that it had taken four matches for the spectators to realise this was not exhibition cricket but tough cricket of the highest quality

Snow bowled the first over of the innings to Barlow. Not known for taking a backward step, Barlow drove two deliveries through the covers off the back foot, he then tried to repeat the shot and edged a catch to Cowdrey at second slip. Snow in the mood and bowling fast, soon had the other opener Murray out lbw with a fast delivery that cut back – 25 for 2. Inspired by Snow, and on his home ground, the debutant Old found extra pace and between them they gave Pollock and Lloyd a tough time in front of an increasingly boisterous crowd.

Illingworth then changed the pace and challenge by bringing himself and Wilson on to bowl. Off his first delivery the captain had Lloyd caught at backward short leg and came close to getting the out of form Pollock lbw. Snow came back on to bowl and with pace and movement off the pitch, comprehensively bowled Pollock with his second delivery. Intikhab was then sent in ahead of Sobers to join Mushtaq in order to keep the captain for the following day. He would not have been impressed therefore, when in the penultimate over Mushtaq tried to sweep Illingworth, missed and was out lbw. Sobers now had no choice but to come out and bat for part of at the most two overs. He was clearly annoyed because rather than play out the remaining deliveries quietly, he hit 11 runs. At the close of play the Rest of the World were 75 for 5 and it was now anybody's game.

**Close of play – England 2nd innings 376 all out
Rest of the World 2nd innings 75-5, (Intikhab 6★, Sobers 11★)**

Day 5 – Tuesday 4 August

Sobers and Intikhab came out to bat, with both sides knowing that the first hour's play would be crucial. Much had been written about the depth of the Rest of the World's batting, but today it would be properly tested. 148 runs were still needed for victory and there were doubts over the ability of Richards and Kanhai to bat, let alone score runs. England had a good chance, if they could take an early wicket, preferably that of Sobers.

Naturally the atmosphere in the ground was not as fervent as it had been the previous evening. Illingworth and Snow started, and such was the care with which Sobers began, he only scored two runs in the first half hour. Intikhab was also cautious but the robust all rounder could not resist a thumping drive every now and then if the opportunity presented itself. This also gave the England bowlers hope that Intikhab was the most likely of the two to provide a chance of a wicket. When he had added 5 to his overnight score, that chance came. Intikhab failed to get the full face of the bat to an out swinging delivery from Snow, it caught the edge and Greig at first slip dropped it. That was a chance gone and though they tried to remain positive, Illingworth knew there would not be many of these.

Sobers used the dropped catch to remind his partner, of the often used advice, just stay there and eventually the runs will come. He did as he was told, and even though Illingworth tried all permutations of his bowlers, slowly but surely the runs came. Sobers got to another Test match fifty, and the score passed 150. With lunch approaching a win for the Rest of the World began to look inevitable. Then with five minutes to go to the interval, incredibly Sobers was out. Playing forward to a good delivery from Snow, for once he did not quite get it right and edged a catch to Cowdrey at second slip. Making it look easier than it was, Cowdrey held the catch with his usual aplomb. 177 for 6, but only 49 needed. Procter joined Intikhab so there was still no problem. Illingworth made yet another change in the bowling, his tenth of the morning. Surprisingly, replacing the wicket taker Snow with the spin of Wilson. For the last over before lunch Wilson gave the delivery some flight, Intikhab could not resist it and drove the ball to the long off boundary where D'Oliveira took a well judged catch. 182 for 7 at lunch. Suddenly the momentum was with England. A game which seemed to be drifting inevitably to a win for the Rest of the World, was alive again.

After lunch, the handicapped Kanhai was joined by Richards, who was unable to bat in the first innings and was not really fit to play now. Kanhai had already given one chance, but in the second over tried to cut a delivery from Illingworth only to give Knott a catch behind the stumps. 183 for 8. Procter was now at the wicket, with the injured Richards. 40 runs still needed, and only Gibbs, a genuine number eleven batsman to come.

In his first over against Don Wilson, Richards 'appeared to edge the ball onto his pad and then into the hands of silly mid on' [322]. Those around the batsman joined Wilson in appealing for a catch. The umpire gave it not out. This was long before the days of referrals and video analysis. The umpire had given the decision not out and that was that. Of course no one will ever know for sure whether England would have gone on to win the match had Richard been given out. The chances of a Procter/Gibbs partnership scoring the forty runs still needed would have been low. Procter was of course a world class batsman, but whether he could protect Gibbs while at the same time scoring the bulk of the runs, that was a tough ask.

As it was, Richards and Procter, settled in, playing sound defensive cricket and taking no risks. Finally at just after 3.00pm Procter scored the runs needed to take his side's total to 226, and a win by two wickets. The win gave the Rest of the World a 3-1 lead with just the Test match at the Oval to come. It had been so close, and when Procter came to the wicket to join Richards, the result could have gone either way. In the end the extra batting quality the Rest of the World had in the lower order counted. A relieved Sobers said afterwards 'I thought they had done us, and I assure you I was glad to see us finally scrape through' [323]. There was something ironic that in a match being played to replace a cancelled tour by the South African national team, that the two batsmen at the crease when the winning runs were scored were white South Africans.

Close of play – Rest of the World 2nd innings 226 – 8,
(Richards 21★, Procter 22★)
Rest of the World Won by 2 Wickets

17

England v Rest of the World
Fifth Test Match
Kennington Oval, London
13th – 18th August 1970

With the series decided, the final Test match at Kennington Oval may have seemed to be of little importance. For the Rest of the World, this was probably the case, although it was still a final chance for players who had not been at their best so far to show what they could really do. The most obvious example was Graeme Pollock, who had been in poor form and since he did not play for an English County it was not clear when the British cricket supporter would have an opportunity to see him play again. There was a three-day match against a T N Pearce XI scheduled as part of the end of season Scarborough Cricket Festival. This really was more like Sunday afternoon cricket, designed to entertain holiday crowds and collect money for charity. Only Kanhai. Gibbs, Murray and Mushtaq were likely to play in this one.

For the England players, there was a much bigger prize at stake. At the end of the match on Tuesday, the party for the winter tour of Australia and New Zealand would be finalised. Most commentators would agree that Ray Illingworth, Colin Cowdrey, Geoffrey Boycott, John Edrich, Alan Knott and John Snow were certainties. This left ten spots still to be decided. For England at least, the fifth Test would be no exhibition game.

This really was the England selectors final chance to look at individual players before finalising the squad for the winter tour. The biggest difficulty they faced was that the pitch at the Kennington Oval was likely to be slow. Not the best way of finding out how a batsmen might cope in four months time on the fastest pitch in the world in Perth.

The Oval was the home ground of Surrey County Cricket Club, and so far this season five of the nine County Championship matches played there had ended in a draw. More significantly over a third of the wickets had been taken by Intikhab Alam. He would be playing for the Rest of the World rather than Surrey in this match, but again in Australia the England side would not be expecting to face much world class leg-spin bowling on a slow turning pitch.

Fast bowlers were key to any successful tour of Australia. Without a pair of hostile fast bowlers to open the attack and a good first change bowler, the chances of winning a Test series there were poor. To allow appropriate cover for injuries it was normal to include four fast bowlers in the tour party who could all open the bowling in a Test match. Snow and Ward (if fit) were two certainties but the players who would fill the other two places were still to be settled. So far in the series, David Brown had been dropped and not recalled and Ken Shuttleworth had been tried for one Test. For this final Test, it was decided to given Chris Old a second game and a little surprisingly the 30 year old, fast/medium left arm bowler Peter Lever was selected for his first Test match. For the spin bowlers, Don Wilson retained his place, to give him a further opportunity to make his claim to join Illingworth and Underwood on the tour.

As far as the batting was concerned, there was still the issue of the middle order. Fletcher had improved but could not yet be certain of his place. Sharpe and Denness had been tried but neither had done enough to keep their place in the team. In the end it was decided to give Dennis Amiss another chance. In an on/off international career, the Warwickshire batsman had so far played five Test matches. The last had been against the Australians in 1968 when he had been out for 0 in both innings. This season he was playing confidently and the only English player above him in the first-class batting averages at the moment was Geoffrey Boycott. Tony Greig was dropped to make room for Lever. He had by no means been a failure in the three Tests he had played. His knack of taking a number of wickets close together had been particularly impressive. However by dropping him the selectors were probably indicating that he was not quite ready for an overseas tour yet.

The final twelve for the fifth Test were therefore Illingworth (captain}, Geoffrey Boycott, Luckhurst, Colin Cowdrey, Keith Fletcher, Amiss, Basil D'Oliveira, Alan Knott, John Snow, Chris Old, Don Wilson and Peter Lever. It was almost certain that D'Oliveira would be twelfth man. There was little new that the selectors could learn about D'Oliveira by playing him at the Oval. It was here two years ago that his innings of 158 against the Australians had been the catalyst that had reignited the whole debate of playing South African teams chosen from only white players.

The Rest of the World selectors had no long term issues to consider. They followed the old adage 'don't change a winning side'. With Richards and Kanhai fit again, they made just one change. Lance Gibbs was having a poor series. The West Indian off-spinner, for so long such a key part of the West Indies bowling attack, had only taken three wickets in five innings. None of these had been a specialist batsman and had cost 103 runs per wicket.

He was replaced, yet again a little surprisingly by Graham McKenzie. In Australia's winter tour of South Africa, the usually prolific fast bowler seemed past his best. In the first Test of this series he looked the same, and was dropped. Returning to play county cricket with Leicestershire (captained by Illingworth) he was soon taking wickets again, and finished the season top of his county's bowling averages.

While it might have seemed strange replacing a spin bowler with a fast bowler, especially at the Oval, the rationale for the change was probably to reduce the bowling load of Sobers. He had already bowled more overs than anybody in his team, and with Intikhab and Mushtaq in the side, spin was well catered for. The Kent all rounder John Shepherd was selected in the twelve but he was almost certain to be twelfth man again.

Day 1 – Thursday 13 August

In front of 12,000 spectators, the best first day crowd of the series, Illingworth won the toss and without much hesitation decided to bat. It was the slow pitch expected and also as expected D'Oliveira was made twelfth man in order to give Amiss a chance to see what he could do. D'Oliveira would have been reasonably confident that he would be in the touring party for Australia, otherwise logic suggests he would have been playing. As expected, the Rest of the World left out Shepherd and with Richards and Kanhai fit, everybody returned to their normal position in the batting order.

Luckhurst faced the first over of the match against Procter. The young South African bowler clearly did not believe in an over or two to warm up. His third delivery was a very fast, sharply moving in-swinger, which beat Luckhurst all ends up and knocked his middle stump out of the ground. This certainly woke up any that were drifting in the warm drowsy weather. To some, Luckhurst seemed to be having problems with fast bowling again. The truth was that the delivery would have tested most of the world's opening batsmen.

Cowdrey came out to join Boycott. Cowdrey batted with the composure he usually showed no matter the conditions, while the new confident Boycott looked even more impressive and unlikely to get out. They dealt confidently with different combinations of seam bowling that Sobers offered and while the score was not rushing along, it was adequate for the first day. With 62 on the board and lunch on the horizon, Boycott made his first and last mistake. Misreading a top-spinner from Intikhab he succeeded only in providing a simple catch to Sobers close in on the leg side. Boycott was out for 24 which he would have been disappointed not to have turned into a 100 on this pitch. The new batsman Fletcher, needed an innings of confidence in order to just cross the 't' in his name with the selectors. With a score of 66 for 2 at lunch, England would have hoped that while it was nothing special there was at least something to build on.

In the afternoon, Cowdrey and Fletcher continued their partnership. Cowdrey his usual unhurried self, but still a little tentative at times.

Fletcher was the more aggressive, but in doing so the more vulnerable. At one stage the pair faced a leg spinner from either end, a rare occurrence in England. Mid-way through the session Fletcher went for a delivery from McKenzie which was well wide of his off stump and missed it. Two deliveries later he tried the same shot , but this time was not so lucky and edged a catch behind to the wicketkeeper.

Cowdrey was joined by Amiss for his opportunity to maybe snatch an Ashes place from one of the others competing for a middle order batting place. Amiss would have wanted to be positive right from the start, but it was not easy. The two leg spinners were able to bowl with close in fielders in place. Then the ever enthusiastic Procter tested him with really fast deliveries when he came back for a new spell before tea. Amiss should have been out when he reached 18. Another sharply moving delivery from Procter caught the edge of his bat, and a reasonably straightforward catch went through Pollock's hands at first slip.

Then just before tea when it looked as though luck was going with England, they got hit by a double tragedy. Cowdrey who had looked comfortable and on his way to another Test century, in reality never really dominated. On 73 he edged a delivery from Sobers to Mushtaq in the gully. In the next over Mushtaq bowled Amiss with a top spinner he was slow to react to. Again in a short period England had lost two wickets. As they left the field on 150 – 5 Illingworth and Knott knew that there were many in the crowd who expected to see the Rest of the World batting that evening.

Of course the sometimes fickle nature of cricket, meant that that just when you expected England to be bowled out they went through a whole session without losing a wicket. Illingworth was like he had been for most of the innings he had played in the series, a model of organisation. By knowing when to defend and when to attack by the close of play he had scored 47 and was almost inevitably on his way to yet another Test match fifty. Knott, constantly fidgeting but determined was the ideal partner. With only 79 runs scored in the session, it was by no means attractive cricket and the crowd began to thin towards the end. England however, had held on and while the Rest of the World would have felt the happier as they left the field at close of play, their opponents were at least still standing.

Close of play – England 1st innings 229 – 5, (Illingworth 47*, Knott 26*)

Day 2 – Friday 14 August

The local wisdom was that England would need at least 300 runs in their first innings if they were to be competitive in the match. Again the responsibility rested on Illingworth's shoulders to work with the tail end batsmen to add at least another 69 runs. He hit the first delivery he received from Intikhab to reach another Test match fifty. In doing so he became the first English man to scored six fifties in a home Test series since Denis Compton in the golden summer of 1947. What is perhaps more remarkable is that when he was chosen as captain, Illingworth was definitely a bowler who could bat a bit. At that stage in thirty Test matches he had reached fifty only once.

Today though there was to be no more. On 52 he edged Intikhab and was caught at slip by Barlow. Snow promoted in the batting order joined Knott who had now inherited the responsibility to guide the tail. Snow was no novice with the bat. He had a sound defensive technique, and he relied heavily and patiently on this. He was not looking to score quick singles but rather waiting for the bad delivery and then hitting it hard off the back foot. In this way he scored 20 with 4 boundaries in 35 minutes. Knott was also playing predominately defensive on this slow pitch, but in his case always looking for a quick single.

With the England batsmen looking increasingly comfortable against spin, Sobers bought McKenzie back into the attack. In eight deliveries, he had Snow caught at first slip for 20, and bowled Old and Wilson for 0. At 266 for 9, England looked to have fallen short. However Lever in his debut Test showed that he was better than a number eleven. First he stayed with Knott, playing defensively until the wicketkeeper reached a deserved Test fifty. Then Lever demonstrated some of his attacking shots, with a sweep and cut for four. He was eventually bowled by Barlow for 13, but the last wicket had added a useful 28 runs to take England's total to an acceptable but not spectacular 294. Certainly more than they might of hoped for when they were 150 for 5 with all their specialist batsmen out.

Richards and Barlow began the Rest of the World's reply just before lunch. They played carefully but did not show any signs of great discomfort against Snow and Old. Snow bowled fast and accurately, but as so often in the series with no great luck. Then with the score on 26, Richards playing perhaps a little too loosely, edged a delivery from Snow into his stumps.

Kanhai, now fully fit, was playing competently but with none of his famous flair shots on display. When the score reached 46, he firmly hit Wilson back down the wicket, but not finding the middle of the bat gave the bowler a difficult catch which he took so close to the ground that the square leg umpire had to adjudicate the appeal. Barlow was joined at the wicket by his fellow South African, Graeme Pollock. The champion left hander was still yet to show the English spectators what he could do.

Midway through the afternoon session Lever was finally thrown the ball by Illingworth for his first bowl in Test cricket. On 18, Pollock had a slice of luck when he edged a delivery from Lever to Cowdrey in the slips. Normally a certainty but this time the fielder was unsighted by Knott who also went for the catch, and Cowdrey dropped it. That would have been some scalp for your first wicket in Test cricket. Lever though was soon to have his reward causing Barlow to edge to Amiss at second slip, and then knocking Mushtaq's leg stump out of the ground. Sobers came to the wicket to join Pollock. At tea, the Rest of the World were a unremarkable 96 for 4, and Lever had the bowling figures of 2 for 14 from 9 overs. The English selectors would have no doubt been quietly satisfied with their surprise selection. Pollock though was looking ominous at last. He was beginning to show the sense of timing that few possess, stroking the ball effortlessly either side of the wicket. Would this be the day when he returned to form?

After tea, Sobers and Pollock, the two best left handed batsmen in world cricket at the time, gave a master class in batting. At the start, Sobers matched Pollock stroke for stroke: the comparison of cover drives and square cuts was superb entertainment. The captain though realised that this was something special and rather than compete was happy to give

Pollock the bowling at every opportunity. None of the bowlers were safe, Illingworth was pulled for six, Old viscously hooked and Wilson driven and cut brutally. Swanton thought that 'Pollock's chief glory is on the off side, and much of the off-driving and square-cutting had a sumptuous ring that made all that had gone before seem almost paltry by comparison' [324]. This indeed was something special. The pair scored 88 runs in the first hour of the session, and at just after six o'clock Pollock reached his eighth Test century. It had taken just 137 deliveries, with 75% of his runs coming in boundaries.

At the close of play the Rest of the World were 231 for 4. On paper perhaps not too bad for England, their opponents were still 63 behind. However, Pollock and Sobers were not out, and the tail of Lloyd, Procter, Murray and Intikhab was waiting.

Close of play – England 1st innings 294 all out
Rest of the World 1st innings 231 – 4, (Pollock 104★, Sobers 55★)

Day 3 – Saturday 15 August

Kennington Oval, London had long been the location of the last Test match of the English season. The Saturday of the match not surprisingly has a slight end of term feel about it. It was a final chance for friends from around the country to meet up, reflect on the season and the winter tour ahead. A crowd of at least 15,000 were already in the ground at start of play. The weather was good and there was enthusiastic support for both sides. It was just such a pity that it had taken so long for the public to realise that this was full-on Test cricket, irrespective of what those on the International Cricket Conference may eventually decide.

The neutrals in the crowd were looking for more of the wonderful batting they had seen from Pollock and Sobers the previous evening. It soon became apparent that this would not be the case. The ball was moving more off the pitch, and the batsmen who had been so dominant the previous evening, could only manage seven singles in the first half hour's play. Lever then came into the attack and this proved to be too much even for these master batsmen. In twelve overs till lunch, Lever took 3 wickets for only 14 runs. First Pollock bowled by a delivery which moved off the pitch to hit off stump, next Lloyd who had no time to settle before he was caught behind. Finally Sobers also had his off stump knocked back by a delivery which straightened. Lever's partners in this spell were Snow and Old. The first was equally challenging to the batsmen but had little luck. Old though looked lifeless and could probably see any chance he might have had of making the winter tour rapidly disappearing. At lunch the Rest of the World had crept to 299 for 7, a lead of just five runs. They had taken 31 overs to score 68, but their extraordinarily strong batting line up meant that England could not yet rest easy.

In the early afternoon, Snow finally got a wicket that his bowling had deserved, clipping Murray's off stump. Intikhab and Procter, both robust hitters, rode their luck before Intikhab hit Lever to cover point for Boycott to take a straight forward catch. With McKenzie, a genuine number eleven, coming to the wicket Procter hit out. Three fours off Lever in one over took him to a Test fifty, before Lever got his revenge in the next, giving Boycott another catch at cover. The Rest of the World were all out for 355, a lead of 61 but it might have been much worse. Lever with 7 for 83, could probably start thinking about spending the winter in Australia[325].

After the ten minute break between innings, Procter was back to open the bowling for the Rest of the World. His first delivery, a fast inswinger bowled Luckhurst for 0, for the second time in the match. Some food for thought, for the batsman who had been so reliable so far in the series.

Cowdrey joined Boycott at the wicket. Typical of the man, Cowdrey was not flustered by having to face the second ball of the innings from a rampant Procter. Radiating his usual unhurried calm, he seemed at ease straight away. Boycott was also soon playing with confidence, and between them they batted with composure to take the score to 47 in the 13 overs to tea.

After the break, the pair continued unhurried until Sobers replaced seam bowling with leg spin. It was a shock, when with his first delivery of the innings, Intikhab beat Cowdrey's back foot defensive stroke with a googly and bowled him for 31. Fletcher, still on trial, joined Boycott and together they batted until the close of play. Boycott reached another Test fifty, while

Fletcher after a careful start was playing with increasing confidence. At 118 for 2, England were now 57 runs ahead with 8 wickets in hand. The bowling of Lever and Snow backed up by the batting of Boycott, Cowdrey and Fletcher had seen England gain the advantage for the first time in the match.

>Close of play – Rest of the World 1st innings 355 all out
>England 2nd innings 118 – 2, (Boycott 54*, Fletcher 24*)

Day 4 – Monday 17 August

The day was cool and grey, a sign of approaching autumn perhaps. At the start of play as Boycott and Fletcher walked to the wicket they knew the first target was to survive the first half hour and stop the Rest of the World bowling attack building up any momentum. With only one more specialist batsman to come, England's middle order and tail was long and not very reliable (with the exception of the transformed Illingworth).

Boycott established his authority right from the start. Playing as well as he has ever done he gave no hint of any weakness, totally solid in defence and attacking with conviction when the opportunity arose. Fletcher was an able partner, although occasionally getting himself in a tangle with shot selection. A good player of spin, he tried not to let Intikhab or Mushtaq settle when they came on to bowl. No matter which combination of bowlers Sobers tried, Boycott and Fletcher played on unperturbed. Sobers even bowled spin, something he rarely did then because of a suspect shoulder. On the odd occasion when he dropped short, Boycott playing off the back foot dispatched the ball to the boundary. At one o'clock Fletcher reached fifty, and fifteen minutes later Boycott completed his seventh Test century. So well did they play, that they not only survived the first half hour but the whole session. At lunch England were 219 for 2, a lead of 158. They would have left the field confident that they had pulled the match further in England's direction.

Between lunch and tea, when England would have hoped to build on their advantage, they lost their way. Fletcher was first out, caught by Barlow in the slips off Sobers for 62. It was probably enough to secure his place on the winter tour. The next man in was Amiss who was also hoping to get a place. Unfortunately he became so preoccupied with not getting out that his contribution to the run total slowly ground to a halt.

Sobers took the new ball, and then Lloyd came on to bowl his rather innocuous looking medium pace. Like Barlow it was more dangerous than it looked. First Boycott drove at a wide delivery, which was edged to Barlow in the slips. It was Boycott's first mistake. His score of 157 had taken six and a quarter hours and contained 23 fours. An innings of 'intellect and aggression' [326] had provided the platform for England to set a serious target. Illingworth was the new batsman and in the same over, he got a delivery which jumped off the pitch at him. He tried his best to play it down but only managed to divert it to short leg where Mushtaq took a spectacular close in catch. This was a rare failure for Illingworth in the series. Again England had lost two wickets in the same over. At tea they were 302 for 5, and hoping for more.

Forty minutes into the evening session, Knott playing his favourite cut shot directed the ball from Sobers into his stumps. Amiss's difficult stay was then finally over. He had taken two hours and ten minutes to score 35 runs. An innings which probably did him more harm than good. England were now 323 for 7. Sobers and McKenzie swept away the remaining wickets, with only Snow managing a few lusty blows for a cameo 19. All out for 344, England had lost their last five wickets for 55. Even so, the Rest of the World had been set a target of 284 to win the match. Not a forgone conclusion by any means.

Barlow and Richards had fifty minutes to negotiate before the close. This was the sort of target in which Barlow's combative nature usually excelled. Today though he was beaten by the speed and movement of Snow for just 6. Richards and Kanhai then saw out the day, taking no risks what so ever. 20 runs in forty minutes said it all, the Rest of the World were determined to live to fight another day.

Close of play: – England 2nd innings 344 all out
Rest of the World 2nd innings 26 – 1, (Richards 9★, Kanhai 9★)

Day 5 – Tuesday 18 August

The last day of the series began with the Rest of the World still requiring 258 runs to win, with eight wickets remaining. This was no straightforward task on a pitch which while it had not deteriorated as much as the pessimists had expected, was occasionally behaving unpredictably and providing turn for the spinners. Wilson was only partially fit with two of the fingers of his bowling hand strapped together following a split in the webbing he had sustained earlier in the match. This may well have been a pitch for Underwood, but he was watching from the England dressing room balcony. The press would inevitably later be asking 'Why no Underwood?'. The truth was the selectors were checking on Wilson to help them decide who would be the spinner to join Underwood and Illingworth in Australia.

There was a full day available to score the required runs, but Richards hit Snow's first ball of the day for four. It soon became clear that the Rest of the World were intent on attacking the England bowlers and fielders, pushing for runs at every opportunity.

Richards was first out, advancing down the wicket to Wilson, missing and being bowled. Richards had by his standards a poor series, rarely showing what he was capable of. He went back to resume playing for Hampshire, and ended the season sixth in the first class batting averages. The five above him were Sobers, Graveney, Turner, Kanhai and Boycott. This bought one of the five, Kanhai to the wicket. He had also had a poor Test series so far, passing fifty only once in nine innings. However there were signs that he was beginning to find his touch again. In his last County Championship match playing for Warwickshire against Derbyshire he had scored a remarkable 187 not out in a first innings total of 295. Alan Ward was fit again and playing for Derbyshire. Ward took six wickets in a fast and hostile spell of bowling. All six of his victims being dismissed for either nought or one.

Kanhai had some good fortune early in his innings when he edged a delivery from Wilson just wide of Fletcher in the gully but in general it was a masterly display of batting. Meanwhile Pollock showed some of the brilliance that he displayed on Saturday, but on 28 advanced down the pitch to Illingworth, misread the length and like Richards earlier was bowled. At 92 for 3 with the languid Lloyd lopping to the wicket, England may have thought they could see a chance. However Kanhai and Lloyd each played a major innings which were perfect for the situation and removed any hope England might have had of winning. By lunch they were 177 for 3; the partnership produced 123 runs at a run a minute, before in a rare display of hesitation, Lloyd edged a delivery from the ever persevering Snow to Knott behind the stumps. With the score at 215 for 4, and with the winning post in sight it was totally appropriate that Sobers should come to the wicket. Kanhai got to a well deserved century, before giving Snow another wicket. The new batsman Mushtaq looked uncomfortable for his short stay before giving the deserving Snow his fourth wicket. Lever who had been so unplayable in the first innings, had figures of 0 for 34 in the second. Finally just before tea, Sobers clipped a ball to the third man boundary to win the Test by 4 wickets, and the series 4 – 1.

England may well have thought that the winning margin did not really reflect the difference between the two sides. However the truth was that whenever the Rest of the World where facing a difficulty, one of their side would take the responsibility of leading the fight back.

What was beyond dispute was that Garry Sobers was the still the best all-rounder in the world. He had scored more runs and taken more wickets than any player on either side and often they had been the turning point in the match [327]. Even though England had lost the series, for Ray Illingworth personally it had been a great success. His astute captaincy had kept his side competitive in most matches, he had emerged as a genuine batting all-rounder, and would now be leading England in Australia. He did not know it at the time, but there was even greater triumph to come.

Close of play – Rest of the World 2nd innings 287 – 6,
(Sobers 40★, Procter 9★)
Rest of the World won by 4 wickets
Rest of the World win the series 4 – 1

18

After the Dust had Settled

A unique Test series which had not been planned for, was now over. Hastily arranged it could have so easily been a complete disaster with exhibition cricket quickly losing the interest of dwindling crowds. Organisation had been a step into the unknown. The need to arrange a five Test series in just a few weeks was a situation Lord's had never had to deal with before. There had not been time for the usual constructive discussion, collection of feedback and reaching appropriate conclusions. The almost unreal timescale meant that many decisions literally had to be made on the spot.

Interest in the series had been slow to build, maybe because there were other major sporting events like the FIFA World Cup and Commonwealth Games vying for the sport lovers' attention. By the time the series reached the Oval, 53,000 turned up to watch over the 5 days. Respectable but still short of that normally expected for a Test match.

Following the presentation of the Guinness Trophy to Garry Sobers the winning captain and the other usual post match interviews, the two sides went their different ways. For the England players the focus was now on the upcoming winter tour of Australia and New Zealand. As already announced the tourists would be captained by Ray Illingworth with Colin Cowdrey a somewhat disappointed vice-captain. On the 19 August the selectors named the rest of the party. There were few surprises, perhaps the biggest being the inclusion of John Hampshire. He had scored a century on debut against the West Indies at Lord's in 1969, played in the following Test but not been selected for England since [328].

In March 1971 Illingworth and his team would return triumphant having beaten Australia and convincingly won the Ashes down under. He was the first person to achieve this rare feat since another Yorkshireman Sir Len Hutton in 1954/55.

As for the Rest of the World players, some such as Sobers, Gibbs, Richards and Procter rejoined their counties to finish the English season. Others like Pollock and Barlow returned to their home countries.

One issue still to be cleared up was the status of the matches themselves. The series had been sold to the sponsors, public and the television companies as Test matches. The Editor of *Wisden* later wrote that 'the cricket played that year by the two teams was some of the finest seen in England' [329]. This was also a view held by many media commentators and cricket correspondents who had watched the whole series.

Unfortunately the International Cricket Conference (ICC) held a different view, and surprised and angered many when at their meeting in 1972 they decided that the matches played in the series would be down graded from Test to first-class level. They were removed from Test records and players such as Alan Jones could no longer say that he had played for England. However, in 2020 Jones was finally officially awarded his England cap by the England and Wales Cricket Board [330]. Still, the issue over the Test status of these matches remains unresolved.

Once the series against the Rest of the World was completed, the International Cricket Conference (ICC) came under further pressure to totally isolate South Africa from international cricket by banning its Members from playing against them. The decision, as was so often the case, ended in a compromise. No blanket ban but a statement which 'recorded its earnest hope that there would soon be effective changes in South Africa which would enable that great cricketing country to take its place in international cricket' [331]. Each of the Test playing countries was left to make its own decision regarding future relations with South Africa. In most cases public opinion had already made the decision for them and it would be over twenty years before South Africa played international cricket again.

In July 1991, a now multi-racial South Africa was readmitted to the ICC, and as a result officially accepted back into the international cricket community. Ironically the Chairman of the ICC that day was Colin Cowdrey while another of those present was Dr Ali Bacher, Managing Director of the newly formed United Cricket Board of South Africa. The two would have been opposing captains, if the 1970 South African tour to England had not been cancelled.

What of Basil D'Oliveira, the man who in so many ways had been the catalyst for change? He went on to play 44 Test matches for England. This was a remarkable achievement for someone who did not play his first Test match until he was 34. He retired from first-class cricket with Worcestershire in 1980 having scored 19,490 runs and taken 551 wickets. He remained with the county as team coach, helping guide them to back to back County Championship titles in 1988 and 1989. Perhaps most poignantly of all, in 2004 it was decided that all future Test series between England and South Africa would be played for the Basil D'Oliveira Trophy [332].

The years 1968 to 1970 had certainly been turbulent, with many players and administrators in England, Pakistan and South Africa having to overcome obstacles they had never encountered before. The consequences of these two years were significant. The isolation of South Africa from international cricket took a long time to overcome, with some who would have been world class players, never having the opportunity to play Test cricket. Finally, on the morning of 10 November 1991, Andrew Hudson and Stephen Cook walked out to open their side's innings against India at Eden Gardens, Calcutta. South Africa had returned to the international cricket arena [333].

Selected Test Match Scorecards

1. Fifth Test Match, England v Australia, 22, 23, 24, 26, 27 August 1968, Kennington Oval, London. England won by 226 runs.
2. First Test Match, Pakistan v England, 21, 22, 23, 24 February 1969, Lahore Stadium, Lahore. Match drawn.
3. Second Test Match, Pakistan v England, 28 February, 1, 2, 3 March 1969, Dacca Stadium, Dacca. Match drawn.
4. Third Test Match, Pakistan v England, 6, 7, 8 March 1969, National Stadium, Karachi. Match drawn.
5. First Test Match, England v Rest of the World, 17, 19, 20, 22 June 1970, Lord's Cricket Ground, London. Rest of the World won by an innings and 80 runs.
6. Second Test Match, England v Rest of the World, 2, 3, 4, 6, 7 July 1970, Trent Bridge, Nottingham. England won by 8 wickets.
7. Third Test Match, England v Rest of the World, 16, 17, 18, 20, 21 July 1970, Edgbaston, Birmingham. Rest of the World won by 5 wickets.
8. Fourth Test match, England v Rest of the World, 30, 31 July, 1, 3, 4 August 1970, Headingley, Leeds. Rest of the World won by 2 wickets.
9. Fifth Test match, England v Rest of the World, 13, 14, 15, 17, 18 August 1970. Kennington Oval, London. Rest of the World won by 4 wickets.

Selected Test Match Scorecards

Key: ★ captain
       + wicketkeeper

FIFTH TEST MATCH - ENGLAND v AUSTRALIA
22, 23, 24, 26, 27 August 1968 at the Kennington Oval, London

Umpires	C S Elliott, A E Fagg
Toss	England won the toss and decided to bat

ENGLAND

	FIRST INNINGS		SECOND INNINGS	
J H Edrich	b Chappell	164	c Lawry b Mallett	17
C. Milburn	b Connolly	8	c Lawry b Connolly	18
E R Dexter	b Gleeson	21	b Connolly	28
★M C Cowdrey	lbw b Mallett	16	b Mallet	35
T W Graveney	c Redpath b McKenzie	63	run out	12
B L D'Oliveira	c Inverarity b Mallett	158	c Gleeson b Connolly	9
+ A P E Knott	c Jarman b Mallett	28	run out	34
R Illingworth	lbw b Connolly	8	b Gleeson	10
J A Snow	run out	4	c Sheahan b Gleeson	13
D L Underwood	not out	9	not out	1
D J Brown	c Sheahan b Gleeson	2	b Connolly	1
Extras	(1b, 11lb, 1w)	13	(3 lb)	3
Total	201.2 overs	494	59.4 overs	181

Australia Bowling	Ovrs	Mdns	Runs	Wkts	Ovrs	Mdns	Runs	Wkts
McKenzie	40	8	87	1	4	0	14	0
Connolly	57	12	127	2	22.4	2	65	4
Walters	6	2	17	0	-	-	-	-
Gleeson	41.2	8	109	2	7	2	22	2
Mallett	36	11	87	3	25	4	77	2
Chappell	21	5	54	1	-	-	-	-

Fall of Wickets

1/28 Milburn; 2/84 Dexter; 3/113 Cowdrey; 4/238 Graveney; 5/359 Edrich; 6/421 Knott; 7/458 Illingworth; 8/468 Snow; 9/489 D'Oliveira; 10/494 Brown.

1/23 Milburn; 2/53 Edrich; 3/67 Dexter; 4/90 Graveney; 5/114 D'Oliveira; 6/126 Cowdrey; 7/149 Illingworth; 8/179 Snow; 9/179 Knott; 10/181 Brown.

Result	England won by 226 runs

AUSTRALIA

	FIRST INNINGS		SECOND INNINGS	
*W M Lawry	c Knott b Snow	135	c Milburn b Brown	4
R J Inverarity	c Milburn b Snow	1	lbw b Underwood	56
I R Redpath	c Cowdrey b Snow	67	lbw b Underwood	8
I M Chappell	c Knott b Brown	10	lbw b Underwood	2
K D Walters	c Knott b Brown	5	c Knott b Underwood	1
A P Sheahan	b Illingworth	14	c Snow b Illingworth	24
+B N Jarman	st Knott b Illingworth	0	b D'Oliveira	21
G D McKenzie	b Brown	12	c Brown b Underwood	0
A A Mallett	not out	43	c Brown b Underwood	0
J W Gleeson	c Dexter b Underwood	19	b Underwood	5
A N Connolly	b Underwood	3	not out	0
Extras	(4b, 7lb, 4nb)	15	(4 lb)	4
Total	163.3 overs	324	83.3 overs	125

England Bowling	Ovrs	Mdns	Runs	Wkts	Ovrs	Mdns	Runs	Wkts
Snow	35	12	67	3	11	5	22	0
Brown	22	5	63	3	8	3	19	1
Illingworth	48	15	87	2	28	18	29	1
Underwood	54.3	21	89	2	31.3	19	50	7
D'Oliveira	4	2	3	0	5	4	1	1

Fall of Wickets

1/7 Inverarity; 2/136 Redpath; 3/151 Chappell; 4/161 Walters; 5/185 Sheahan; 6/188 Jarman; 7/237 McKenzie; 8/269 Lawry; 9/302 Gleeson; 10/324 Connolly.

1/4 Lawry; 2/13 Redpath; 3/19 Chappell; 4/29 Walters; 5/65 Sheahan; 6/110 Jarman; 7/110 Mallett; 8/110 McKenzie; 9/120 Gleeson; 10/125 Inverarity.

FIRST TEST MATCH – PAKISTAN v ENGLAND
21, 22, 23, 24 February 1969 at the Lahore Stadium, Lahore (4 day match)

Umpires   Shujauddin, Munawar Hussain

Toss   England won the toss and decided to bat

ENGLAND

	FIRST INNINGS		SECOND INNINGS	
J H Edrich	c Masood b Intikhab	54	c Majid b Masood	8
R M Prideaux	c Shafqat b Masood	9	b Majid	5
* M C Cowdrey	c Wasim b Majid	100	c Wasim b Masood	12
TW Graveney	c Iqbal b Intikhab	13	run out	12
K W R Fletcher	c Intikhab b Saeed	20	b Majid	83
B L D'Oliveira	c Ilyas b Intikhab	26	c Mushtaq b Saeed	5
+ A P E Knott	lbw b Saeed	52	b Masood	30
D L Underwood	c Intikhab b Saeed	0	c Aftab b Mushtaq	6
D J Brown	b Saeed	7	not out	44
P I Pocock	b Intikhab	12	b Saeed	1
R M H Cottam	not out	4	did not bat	
Extras	(4b, 2lb, 3nb)	9	(6b, 9lb, 4nb)	19
Total	119.1 overs	306	9 wkts dec. 84.5 overs	225

Pakistan Bowling	Ovrs	Mdns	Runs	Wkts	Ovrs	Mdns	Runs	Wkts
Asif Masood	21	5	59	1	25	4	68	3
Asif Iqbal	4	2	11	0	-	-	-	-
Majid Khan	18	8	25	1	20	5	41	2
Intikhab Alam	40.1	8	117	4	15	5	29	0
Saeed Ahmed	20	5	64	4	15.5	3	44	2
Mushtaq Mohammad	14	6	15	0	9	1	24	1
Shafqat Rana	2	0	6	0	-	-	-	-

Fall of Wickets

1/41 Prideaux; 2/92 Edrich; 3/113 Graveney; 4/182 Fletcher; 5/219 Cowdrey; 6/246 D'Oliveira; 7/257 Underwood; 8/287 Brown; 9/294 Knott; 10/306 Pocock.

1/8 Prideaux; 2/25 Edrich; 3/41 Cowdrey; 4/46 Graveney; 5/68 D'Oliveira; 6/136 Knott; 7/151 Underwood; 8/201 Fletcher; 9/225 Pocock.

Result   **Match Drawn**

PAKISTAN

	FIRST INNINGS		SECOND INNINGS	
Mohammad Ilyas	lbw b Brown	0	c Fletcher b Brown	1
Aftab Gul	c D'Oliveira b Brown	12	c Pocock b Underwood	29
*Saeed Ahmed	c Knott b D'Oliveira	18	b Cottam	39
Asif Iqbal	c D'Oliveira b Cottam	70	c and b Cottam	0
Mushtaq Mohammad	c Fletcher b Cottam	4	not out	34
Hanif Mohammad	b Brown	7	not out	23
Majid Khan	c Pocock b Underwood	18	c Pocock b Brown	68
Shafqar Rana	c Knott b Cottam	30	did not bat	
Intikhab Alam	c D'Oliveira b Pocock	12	did not bat	
+Wasim Bari	not out	14	did not bat	0
Asif Masood	b Brown	11	did not bat	5
Extras	(8b, 4lb, 1nb)	13	(3 b, 5 lb, 1 nb)	9
Total	all out 70.2 overs	209	5 wickets, 79 overs	203

England Bowling	Ovrs	Mdns	Runs	Wkts	Ovrs	Mdns	Runs	Wkts
Brown	14	0	43	3	15	4	47	2
Cottam	22.2	5	50	4	13	1	35	2
D'Oliveira	8	2	28	1	-	-	-	-
Underwood	16	4	36	1	19	8	29	1
Pocock	10	3	39	1	16	4	41	0
Fletcher	-	-	-	-	8	2	31	0
Graveney	-	-	-	-	6	0	11	0
Prideaux	-	-	-	-	2	2	0	0

Fall of Wickets

1/0 Ilyas; 2/32 Saeed; 3/32 Aftab; 4/52 Mushtaq; 5/72 Hanif; 6/119 Majid); 7/145 Iqbal; 8/176 Intikhab; 9/187 Shafqat; 10/209 Masood.

1/6 Ilyas; 2/71 Saeed; 3/71 Iqbal; 4/71 Gul; 5/156 Majid.

Selected Test Match Scorecards

SECOND TEST MATCH – PAKISTAN v ENGLAND
28 February 1, 2, 3 March 1969 at the Dacca Stadium, Dacca (4 day match)

Umpires	Shujauddin, Gulzar Mir
Toss	Pakistan won the toss and decided to bat

PAKISTAN

	FIRST INNINGS		SECOND INNINGS	
Mohammad Ilyas	c Knott b Snow	20	c Snow b Cottam	21
Salahuddin Mulla	c Brown b Snow	6	lbw b Underwood	5
*Saeed Ahmed	b Brown	19	c Knott b Underwood	33
Asif Iqbal	b Brown	44	b Underwood	16
Mushtaq Mohammad	c Cottam b Snow	52	c D'Oliveira b Underwood	31
Majid Khan	c Knott b Brown	27	not out	49
Hanif Mohammad	lbw b Snow	8	lbw b Underwood	8
Intikhab Alam	lbw b Underwood	25	not out	19
+Wasim Bari	c Knott b Cottam	14	did not bat	
Niaz Ahmed	not out	16	did not bat	
Pervez Saijad	b Cottam	2	did not bat	
Extras	(4b, 4lb, 5nb)	13	(5lb, 8nb)	13
Total	all out, 110.1 overs	246	6 wickets declared, 101 overs	195

England Bowling	Ovrs	Mdns	Runs	Wkts	Ovrs	Mdns	Runs	Wkts
Snow	25	5	70	4	12	7	15	0
Brown	23	8	51	3	6	1	18	0
Underwood	27	13	45	1	44	15	94	5
Cottam	27.1	6	52	2	30	17	43	1
D'Oliveira	8	1	15	0	9	2	12	0

Fall of Wickets

1/16 Salahuddin; 2/39 Saeed; 3/55 Ilyas; 4/123 Iqbal; 5/168 Mushtaq; 6/184 Majid; 7/186 Hanif; 8/211 Wasim; 9/237 Intikhab; 10/246 Pervez.

1/8 Salahuddin; 2/48 Ilyas); 3/50 Iqbal; 4/97 Saeed; 5/129 Mushtaq; 6/147 Hanif.

Result	**Match Drawn**

ENGLAND

	FIRST INNINGS		SECOND INNINGS	
J H Edrich	c Mushtaq b Intikhab	24	not out	12
R M Prideaux	c Hanif b Pervez	4	not out	18
T W Graveney	b Pervez	46	did not bat	
K W R Fletcher	c Hanif b Saeed	16	did not bat	
*M C Cowdrey	lbw b Pervez	7	did not bat	
B L D'Oliveira	not out	114	did not bat	
+A P E Knott	c and b Pervez	2	did not bat	
D J Brown	c Hanif b Saeed	4	did not bat	
J A Snow	c Majid b Niaz	9	did not bat	
D L Underwood	c Ilyas b Mushtaq	22	did not bat	
R M H Cottam	c Hanif b Saeed	4	did not bat	
Extras	(14b, 8lb)	22	(2 b, 1 nb)	3
Total	all out 132.4 overs	274	0 wickets, 33 overs	33

Pakistan Bowling	Ovrs	Mdns	Runs	Wkts	Ovrs	Mdns	Runs	Wkts
Niaz	10	4	20	1	2	0	2	0
Majid	11	4	15	0	-	-	-	-
Pervez	37	8	75	4	3	2	1	0
Saeed	37.4	15	59	3	3	2	4	0
Intikhab	26	7	65	1	4	0	19	0
Mushtaq	11	3	18	1	-	-	-	-
Iqbal	-	-	-	-	4	2	2	0
Hanif	-	-	-	-	-	-	-	-
Illyas	-	-	-	-	1	0	1	0

Fall of Wickets

1/17 Prideaux; 2/61 Edrich; 3/96 Fletcher; 4/100 Graveney; 5/113 Cowdrey; 6/117 Knott; 7/130 Brown; 8/170 Snow; 9/236 Underwood; 10/274 Cottam.

None

Selected Test Match Scorecards

THIRD TEST MATCH – PAKISTAN v ENGLAND
6, 7, 8 March 1969 at the National Stadium, Karachi (5 day match)

Umpires	Shujauddin, Daud Khan
Toss	England won the toss and decided to bat

ENGLAND

	FIRST INNINGS		SECOND INNINGS
C Milburn	c Wasim b Masood	139	
J H Edrich	c Saeed b Intikhab	32	
T W Graveney	b Iqbal b Intikhab	105	
*M C Cowdrey	c Hanif b Intikhab	14	
K W R Fletcher	b Mushtaq	38	
B L D'Oliveira	c Aftab b Mushtaq	16	
A P E Knott	not out	96	
J. A. Snow	b Masood	9	
D J Brown	not out	25	
D L Underwood	did not bat		
R N S Hobbs	did not bat		
Extras	(5b, 12lb, 11nb)	28	
Total	7 wickets, 175.1 overs	502	

Pakistan Bowling	Ovrs	Mdns	Runs	Wkts	Ovrs	Mdns	Runs	Wkts
Masood	28	2	94	2				
Majid	20	5	51	0				
Safraz	34	6	78	0				
Intikhab	48	4	129	3				
Saeed	22	5	53	0				
Mushtaq	23.1	5	69	2				

Fall of Wickets
1/78 Edrich; 2/234 Milburn; 3/286 Cowdrey; 4/309 Graveney; 5/360 D'Oliveira; 6/374 Fletcher; 7/427 Snow.

Result	Match Drawn - Riots Forced Play to be Abandoned on Third Day Series Result - All three Tests matches drawn.

FIRST TEST MATCH - ENGLAND v REST OF THE WORLD
17, 19, 20, 22 June 1970 at Lord's Cricket Ground, London

Umpires	J. S. Buller, A. E. Fagg
Toss	England won the toss and decided to bat

ENGLAND

	FIRST INNINGS		SECOND INNINGS	
B W Luckhurst	c Richards b Sobers	1	c Engineer b Intikhab	67
A Jones	c Engineer b Procter	5	c Engineer b Procter	0
M H Denness	c Barlow b McKenzie	13	c Sobers b Intikhab	24
B L D'Oliveira	c Engineer b Sobers	0	c Lloyd b Intikhab	78
P J Sharpe	c Barlow b Sobers	4	b Sobers	2
* R Illingworth	c Engineer b Sobers	63	c Barlow b Sobers	94
+ A P E Knott	c Kanhai b Sobers	2	lbw b Gibbs	39
J A Snow	c Engineer b Sobers	2	b Intikhab	10
D L Underwood	c Lloyd b Barlow	19	c Kanhai b Intikhab	7
A Ward	c Sobers b McKenzie	11	st Engineer b Intikhab	0
K Shuttleworth	not out	1	not out	0
Extras	(5lb, 1nb)	6	(4b, 8lb, 6 nb)	18
Total	all out, 55.1 overs	127	all out, 174 overs	339

Rest of the World Bowling	Ovrs	Mdns	Runs	Wkts	Ovrs	Mdns	Runs	Wkts
McKenzie	16.1	3	43	2	15	8	25	0
Procter	13	6	20	1	15	4	36	1
Sobers	20	11	21	6	31	13	43	2
Barlow	4	0	26	1	7	2	10	0
Intikhab Alam	2	0	11	0	54	24	113	6
Lloyd	-	-	-	-	1	0	3	0
Gibbs	-	-	-	-	51	17	91	1

Fall of Wickets

1/5 Jones; 2/17 Luckhurst, 3/23 D'Oliveira; 4/23 Denness; 5/29 Sharpe; 6/31 Knott; 7/44 Snow; 8/94 Underwood; 9/125 Illingworth; 10/127 Ward.

1/0 Jones; 2/39 Denness; 3/140 Luckhurst; 4/148 Sharpe; 5/196 D'Oliveira; 6/313 Knott; 7/323 Illingworth; 8/334 Underwood ; 9/338 Ward; 10/339

Result   Rest of the World won by an innings and 80 runs

REST OF THE WORLD

	FIRST INNINGS		SECOND INNINGS
B A Richards	c Sharpe b Ward	35	
E J Barlow	c Underwood b Illingworth	119	
R B Kanhai	c Knott b D'Oliveira	21	
R. G. Pollock	b Underwood	55	
C. H. Lloyd	b Ward	20	
*G. S. Sobers	c Underwood b Snow	183	
+F. M. Engineer	b Ward	2	
Intikhab Alam	b Ward	61	
M. J. Procter	b Snow	26	
G. D. McKenzie	c Snow b Underwood	0	
L. R. Gibbs	not out	2	
Extras	(10b, 5lb, 7nb)	22	
Total	all out, 154.5 overs	546	

England Bowling	Ovrs	Mdns	Runs	Wkts	Ovrs	Mdns	Runs
Snow	27	7	109	2			
Ward	33	4	121	4			
Shuttleworth	21	2	85	0			
D'Oliveira	18	5	45	1			
Underwood	25.5	8	81	2			
Illingworth	30	8	83	1			

Fall of Wickets

1/69 Richards; 2/106 Kanhai;
3/237 Pollock; 4/237 Barlow;
5/293 Lloyd; 6/298 Engineer;
7/496 Intikhab; 8/537 Procter;
9/544 Sobers; 10/546 McKenzie.

SECOND TEST MATCH - ENGLAND v REST OF THE WORLD
2, 3, 4, 6 and 7 July 1970 Trent Bridge, Nottingham

Umpires	C. S. Elliot, A. E. Fagg
Toss	Rest of the World won the toss and decided to bat

REST OF THE WORLD

	FIRST INNINGS		SECOND INNINGS	
B A Richards	c Knott b Greig	64	b Greig	30
E J Barlow	c Cowdrey b D'Oliveira	11	b Greig	142
R B Kanhai	c Fletcher b Greig	6	c Knott b D'Oliveira	6
R G Pollock	b D'Oliveira	2	lbw b D'Oliveira	0
C H Lloyd	not out	114	b Underwood	20
* G S Sobers	b Greig	8	c Knott b Greig	18
+ F M Engineer	c Knott b Greig	0	c and b Underwood	1
Intikhab Alam	c Cowdrey b D'Oliveira	12	c and b Brown	23
M J Procter	b Brown	43	c Edrich b D'Oliveira	27
G D McKenzie	c and b Brown	0	not out	6
L R Gibbs	b D'Oliveira	1	b Snow	1
Extras	(4b, 9lb 2nb)	15	(2b, 8lb, 2nb)	12
Total	all out, 83.4 overs	276	all out 107.2 overs	286

England Bowling	Ovrs	Mdns	Runs	Wkts	Ovrs	Mdns	Runs	Wkts
Snow	20	5	58	0	19.2	2	64	1
Brown	15	1	64	2	13	0	41	1
D'Oliveira	17.4	3	43	4	26	9	63	3
Greig	18	3	59	4	23	7	71	3
Underwood	9	4	25	0	26	13	35	2
Illingworth	4	2	12	0	-	-	-	-

Fall of Wickets

1/31 Barlow; 2/46 Kanhai; 3/55 Pollock; 4/106 Richards; 5/126 Sobers; 6/126 Engineer; 7/172 Intikhab; 8/259 Procter; 9/267 McKenzie; 10/276 Gibbs.

1/68 Richards; 2/87 Kanhai; 3/87 Pollock; 4/112 Lloyd; 5/141 Sobers; 6/154 Engineer; 7/220 Intikhab; 8/263 Procter; 9/281 Barlow; 10/286 Gibbs.

Result	**England won by 8 wickets**

ENGLAND

	FIRST INNINGS		SECOND INNINGS	
J H Edrich	c Engineer b Barlow	39	c Barlow b McKenzie	17
B W Luckhurst	b Barlow	37	not out	113
M C Cowdrey	c Richards b Barlow	1	lbw b Barlow	64
K W R Fletcher	c Engineer b Barlow	4	not out	69
B L D'Oliveira	b Barlow	16	did not bat	
*R Illingworth	b Sobers	97	did not bat	
A W Greig	c Gibbs b Sobers	14	did not bat	
+ A P E Knott	c Kanhai b Intikhab	21	did not bat	
D J Brown	b Procter	3	did not bat	
D L Underwood	c Sobers b Intikhab	2	did not bat	
J A Snow	not out	27	did not bat	
Extras	(1b, 7lb, 10nb)	18	(14lb, 4nb, 3w)	21
Total	all out, 103.5 overs	279	2 wickets, 135.2 overs	284

Rest of the World Bowling

	Ovrs	Mdns	Runs	Wkts	Ovrs	Mdns	Runs	Wkts
Procter	17	6	42	1	20	9	23	0
McKenzie	21	3	60	0	24	8	53	1
Sobers	20.5	3	49	2	18	7	24	0
Gibbs	6	3	8	0	31	10	40	0
Barlow	20	5	66	5	14	4	20	1
Intikhab	19	3	36	2	27	9	94	0
Kanhai					1	0	4	0
Pollock					0.2	0	5	0

Fall of Wickets

1/78 Luckhurst; 2/82 Cowdrey, 3/86 Fletcher; 4/106 Edrich; 5/109 D'Oliveira; 6/126 Greig; 7/179 Knott; 8/191 Brown; 9/195 Underwood; 10/279 Illingworth.

1/44 Edrich; 2/164 Cowdrey.

THIRD TEST MATCH - ENGLAND v REST OF THE WORLD
16, 17, 18, 20 and 21 July 1970 at Edgbaston, Birmingham

Umpires	A. E. Fagg and A. E. G. Rhodes
Toss	England won the toss and decided to bat

ENGLAND

	FIRST INNINGS		SECOND INNINGS	
J H Edrich	b Pollock P M	37	c Sobers b Intikhab	3
B W Luckhurst	c Murray b Sobers	28	c Murray b Intikhab	35
M C Cowdrey	lbw b Sobers	0	c Murray b Pollock P.	71
K W R Fletcher	c Murray b Sobers	0	run out	27
B L D'Oliveira	c and b Lloyd	110	c Barlow b Sobers	81
*R. Illingworth	c Murray b Procter	15	b Gibbs	43
A W Greig	b Procter	55	c and b Sobers	22
+A P E Knott	b Procter	21	not out	50
D J Brown	b Procter	13	c Murray b Procter	32
D L Underwood	c Sobers b Procter	1	b Sobers	0
J A Snow	not out	3	b Sobers	21
Extras	(7lb , 4nb)	11	(14b, 10lb)	24
Total	all out, 115.1 overs	294	all out, 205.5 overs	409

Rest of the World Bowling	Ovrs	Mdns	Runs	Wkts	Ovrs	Mdns	Runs	Wkts
Procter	24.1	7	46	5	22	10	26	1
Pollock P. M.	15	1	62	1	18	5	48	1
Barlow	11	2	28	0	9	2	26	0
Sobers	20	11	38	3	51.5	20	89	4
Intikhab Alam	19	4	45	0	63	29	116	2
Gibbs	19	5	41	0	42	16	80	1
Lloyd	7	1	23	1	-	-	-	-

Fall of Wickets

1/56 Luckhurst; 2/56 Cowdrey, 3/66 Edrich; 4/76 Fletcher; 5/134 Illingworth; 6/244 D'Oliveira; 7/258 Greig; 8/282 Brown; 9/290 Knott; 10/294 Underwood.

1/20 Edrich; 2/58 Luckhurst; 3/132 Fletcher; 4/193 Cowdrey; 5/271 D'Oliveira; 6/279 Illingworth; 7/317 Greig; 8/364 Brown; 9/364 Underwood; 10/409 Snow.

Result	Rest of the World won by 5 wickets

Selected Test Match Scorecards

REST OF THE WORLD

	FIRST INNINGS		SECOND INNINGS	
E J Barlow	b Snow	4	c Knott b Snow	0
B A Richards	c Greig b Snow	47	b Underwood	32
R B Kanhai	c Greig b Illingworth	71	c and b Underwood	37
R G Pollock	b Snow	40	did not bat	
C H Lloyd	b Illingworth	101	b Illingworth	20
*G S Sobers	b Illingworth	80	lbw b Illingworth	7
M J Procter	b Snow	62	not out	25
+D L Murray	c Fletcher b Underwood	62	did not bat	
Intikhab Alam	c Knott b Illingworth	45	not out	15
P M Pollock	not out	23	did not bat	
L R Gibbs	not out	3	did not bat	
Extras	(10b, 13lb, 2nb)	25	(1b, 4lb)	5
Total	9 wickets declared, 187 overs	563	5 wickets, 43 overs	141

England Bowling	Ovrs	Mdns	Runs	Wkts	Ovrs	Mdns	Runs	Wkts
Snow	38	6	124	4	7	2	10	1
Brown	14	2	65	0	7	2	23	0
Greig	16	0	58	0	-	-	-	-
D'Oliveira	24	8	58	0	-	-	-	-
Underwood	44	17	90	1	15	2	52	2
Illingworth	49	13	131	4	14	4	41	2
Fletcher	2	0	12	0	-	-	-	-

Fall of Wickets

1/7 Barlow; 2/80 Richards; 3/157 Pollock G M; 4/175 Kanhai; 5/350 Sobers; 6/377 Lloyd; 7/450 Procter; 8/526 Murray; 9/538 Intikhab.

1/3 Barlow; 2/72 Richards; 3/79 Kanhai; 4/100 Sobers; 5/107 Lloyd.

FOURTH TEST MATCH - ENGLAND v REST OF THE WORLD
30, 31 July 1, 3 and 4 August 1970 at Headingly, Leeds

Umpires   A E Fagg and A E G Rhodes

Toss   Rest of the World won the toss and decided to field

ENGLAND

	FIRST INNINGS		SECOND INNINGS	
G Boycott	c Murray b Barlow	15	c Pollock b Barlow	64
B W Luckhurst	c Intikhab b Procter	35	c Gibbs b Barlow	92
M C Cowdrey	c Murray b Barlow	1	b Barlow	0
K W R Fletcher	c Murray b Barlow	89	c Barlow b Lloyd	63
B L D'Oliveira	c Richards b Procter	2	b Procter	21
* R. Illingworth	c Murray b Barlow	58	b Intikhab	54
A W Greig	b Procter	5	c Murray b Lloyd	0
+ A P E Knott	b Barlow	0	c Procter b Barlow	11
C M Old	b Barlow	0	c Murray b Gibbs	37
D Wilson	c and b Barlow	0	not out	6
J A Snow	not out	3	c Procter b Barlow	10
Extras	(4b, 7lb, 3nb)	14	(3b, 8lb, 6nb, 1w)	18
Total	all out, 95.4 overs	222	all out, 168.5 overs	376

Rest of the World Bowling	Ovrs	Mdns	Runs	Wkts	Ovrs	Mdns	Runs	Wkts
Procter	21	7	47	3	40	14	67	1
Sobers	20	11	24	0	34	9	65	0
Barlow	22.4	6	64	7	32	8	78	5
Gibbs	5	0	16	0	13	2	31	1
Intikhab Alam	5	2	15	0	18.5	6	28	1
Mushtaq Mohammad	12	4	27	0	14	4	44	0
Lloyd	10	2	15	0	17	7	45	2

Fall of Wickets

1/37 Boycott; 2/43 Cowdrey, 3/81 Luckhurst; 4/91 D'Oliveira; 5/209 Fletcher; 6/218 Greig; 7/219 Knott; 8/219 Old; 9/219 Wilson; 10/222 Illingworth.

1/104 Boycott; 2/108 Cowdrey; 3/194 Luckhurst; 4/227 Snow – night watchman; 5/257 Fletcher; 6/267 D'Oliveira; 7/268 Greig; 8/300 Knott; 9/360 Old; 10/376 Illingworth.

Result   Rest of the World won by 2 wickets

REST OF THE WORLD

	FIRST INNINGS		SECOND INNINGS	
E J Barlow	c Boycott b Greig	37	c Cowdrey b Snow	6
+D L Murray	c Snow b Wilson	95	lbw b Snow	10
Mushtaq Mohammad	lbw b Greig	4	lbw b Illingworth	14
R G Pollock	c Knott b Greig	3	b Snow	8
C H Lloyd	b Old	35	c Luckhurst b Illingworth	20
*G S Sobers	c Knott b Snow	114	c Cowdrey b Snow	59
M J Procter	c Knott b Old	27	not out	22
Intikhab Alam	c Knott b Greig	15	c D'Oliveira b Wilson	54
R B Kanhai	c and b D'Oliveira	26	c Knott b Illingworth	4
L R Gibbs	not out	0	did not bat	-
B A Richards	did not bat	-	not out	21
Extras	(11lb, 6nb, 1w)	20	(4b, 1lb)	8
Total	9 wickets declared, 138.1 overs	376	8 wickets, 93.5 overs	226

England Bowling

	Ovrs	Mdns	Runs	Wkts	Ovrs	Mdns	Runs	Wkts
Snow	28.1	7	80	1	27.5	5	82	4
Old	27	5	70	2	13	5	35	0
D'Oliveira	24	10	52	1	11	6	17	0
Greig	31	6	86	4	3	0	14	0
Wilson	20	5	48	1	18	9	29	1
Illingworth	8	2	20	0	21	8	41	3

Fall of Wickets

1/67 Barlow; 2/84 Mushtaq; 3/90 Pollock; 4/152 Lloyd; 5/220 Sobers; 6/280 Lloyd; 7/309 Murray; 8/376 Procter; 9/376 Intikhab.

1/6 Barlow; 2/25 Murray; 3/49 Lloyd; 4/58 Pollock; 5/62 Mushtaq; 6/177 Sobers; 7/182 Intikhab; 8/183 Kanhai.

FIFTH TEST MATCH - ENGLAND v REST OF THE WORLD
13, 14, 15, 17 and 18 August 1970 at Kennington Oval, London

Umpires   C S Elliott and A E Fagg

Toss   England won the toss and decided to bat

ENGLAND

	FIRST INNINGS		SECOND INNINGS	
B W Luckhurst	b Procter	0	b Procter	0
G Boycott	c Sobers b Intikhab	24	c Barlow b Lloyd	157
M C Cowdrey	c Sobers b Barlow	73	b Intikhab	31
K W R Fletcher	c Murray b McKenzie	25	c Barlow b Sobers	63
D L Amiss	b Mushtaq	24	c Murray b Lloyd	35
*R. Illingworth	c Barlow b Intikhab	52	c Mushtaq b Lloyd	0
+A P E Knott	not out	51	b Sobers	15
J A Snow	c Barlow b McKenzie	20	c Mushtaq b Sobers	19
C M Old	b McKenzie	0	b McKenzie	5
D Wilson	b McKenzie	0	b McKenzie	1
P Lever	b Barlow	13	not out	0
Extras	(2b, 7lb, 3nb)	12	(3b, 19lb, 3nb)	18
Total	all out, 147.2 overs	294	all out, 150.1 overs	344

Rest of the World Bowling	Ovrs	Mdns	Runs	Wkts	Ovrs	Mdns	Runs	Wkts
Procter	20	10	22	1	19	9	30	1
McKenzie	24	7	51	4	22.1	2	51	2
Barlow	16.2	2	36	1	16	2	42	0
Sobers	15	5	18	1	42	15	81	3
Intikhab Alam	44	14	92	2	32	8	87	1
Mushtaq Mohammad	28	10	63	1	1	0	1	0
Lloyd	-	-	-	-	18	3	34	3

Fall of Wickets

1/0 Luckhurst; 2/62 Cowdrey; 3/113 Fletcher; 4/150 Boycott; 5/150 Illingworth; 6/236 Amiss; 7/266 Snow; 8/266 Old; 9/266 Wilson; 10/294 Lever.

1/0 Luckhurst; 2/71 Cowdrey; 3/225 Fletcher; 4/289 Boycott; 5/289 Illingworth; 6/319 Knott; 7/323 Amiss 8/343 Snow; 9/343 Old; 10/344 Wilson.

Result   Rest of the World won by 4 wickets and won the Series 4 – 1

Selected Test Match Scorecards

REST OF THE WORLD

	FIRST INNINGS		SECOND INNINGS	
E J Barlow	c Amiss b Lever	28	b Snow	6
B A Richards	b Snow	14	b Wilson	14
R. B Kanhai	c and b Wilson	13	c Fletcher b Snow	100
R G Pollock	b Lever	114	b Illingworth	28
Mushtaq Mohammad	b Lever	3	c Fletcher b Snow	8
* G S Sobers	b Lever	79	not out	40
C H Lloyd	c Knott b Lever	2	c Knott b Snow	68
M J Procter	b Boycott b Lever	51	not out	9
+ D L Murray	b Snow	5	did not bat	
Intikhab Alam	c Boycott b Lever	15	did not bat	
G D McKenzie	not out	4	did not bat	
Extras	(14lb,13nb)	27	(2b, 8lb, 3nb, 1w)	14
Total	all out, 118.5 overs	355	6 wickets, 87.1 overs	287

England Bowling	Ovrs	Mdns	Runs	Wkts	Ovrs	Mdns	Runs	Wkts
Snow	32	8	73	2	23	6	81	4
Old	21	4	57	0	7	0	22	0
Wilson	18	5	58	1	24	8	70	1
Lever	32.5	9	83	7	10.1	2	34	0
Illingworth	15	3	57	0	23	5	66	1

Fall of Wickets

1/26 Richards; 2/46 Kanhai; 3/92 Barlow; 4/96 Mushtaq; 5/261 Pollock; 6/267 Lloyd; 7/280 Sobers; 8/310 Murray; 9/338 Intikhab; 10/355 Procter.

1/7 Barlow; 2/41 Richards; 3/92 Pollock; 4/215 Lloyd; 5/241 Kanhai; 6/265 Mushtaq.

Selected Photographs and Credits

Figure 1 – The 1968 Australian Tourists. Reproduced with kind permission of the Roger Mann Picture Library.

Figure 2 – The MCC Tourists, Ceylon and Pakistan 1969. Reproduced with kind permission of the Roger Mann Picture Library.

Figure 3 – The England team for the first Test match against the Rest of the World, Lord's, London, 1970. Reproduced with kind permission of the Roger Mann Picture Library.

Figure 4 – The Rest of the World team for the fourth Test match against England, Headingley, Leeds, 1970. Reproduced with kind permission of P A Images/Alamy.

Figure 5 – Ray Illingworth and Garry Sobers with the Guinness Trophy, 1970. Reproduced with kind permission of the Roger Mann Picture Library.

Book Cover Design – Danuta Thorn

Figure 1
1968 Australian Tourists

Standing (L to R) A E James (Physiotherapist), E W Freeman, R J Inverarity, A A Mallett, L E Truman (Treasurer), D A Renneberg, A P Sheahan, L R Joslin, J W Gleeson, D Sherwood (Scorer)

Seated (L to R) I M Chappell, I R Redpath, N J N Hawke, R M Cowper, W M Lawry (Captain) R J Parish), G D McKenzie, A N Connolly, K D Walters, H B Taber. Missing from photograph B N Jarman (Vice-Captain)

Figure 2
MCC Tourists to Ceylon (Sri Lanka) and Pakistan 1969

Standing (L to R) B W Thomas (Physiotherapist), J A Snow, P I Pocock, R M Prideaux, R M H Cottam, D L Underwood, K W R Fletcher, A P E Knott, R N S Hobbs

Sitting (L to R) D L Brown, B L D'Oliveira, T W Graveney (Vice-Captain), M C Cowdrey (Captain), L E G Ames (Manager), J H Edrich, J T Murray. I J Jones (returned home), C Milburn (yet to join)

Figure 3
England team, first Test match against the Rest of the World, Lord's, London, 1970

Standing (L to R) A Jones, B W Luckhurst, D L Underwood, A Ward, K Shuttleworth, M H Denness

Sitting (L to R) B L D'Oliveira, J A Snow, R Illingworth (Captain), P J Sharpe, A P E Knott

Figure 4
Rest of the World team, fourth Test match against England, Headingly, Leeds, 1970

Standing (L to R) D L Murray, B A Richards, C H Lloyd, M J Procter, Intikhab Alam, Mushtaq Mohammad

Sitting (L to R) R B Kanhai, E J Barlow, G S Sobers (Captain), L R Gibbs, R G Pollock

Selected Photographs and Credits

Figure 5
**Ray Illingworth and Garry Sobers
with the Guinness Trophy, 1970**

Notes on Sources

Prologue
1. Arlott, J., *Two Summers at the Tests,* (London: Pavilion Books Ltd, 1986) p. v

Chapter 1 – English Cricket is Absolutely Fine
2. Morrow, L., *1968: The Year That Shaped a Generation*, (New York: Time Inc, 2018) p. 4
3. Cardus, N., *English Cricket,* (London: Collins, 1946) p. 9
4. Oslear, D., *Wisden The Laws of Cricket,* (London: Ebury Press, 2000)
5. Nash, J. H. (Ed.), *Yorkshire County Cricket Club, Seventieth Annual Report,* (Leeds: Yorkshire County Cricket Club Committee, 1968) pp. 9 – 16
6. Anon., *Surrey County Cricket Club Year Book For 1969,* (Reigate: Constitutional Press, 1969) p. 7
7. Edrich, J., *Runs in the Family,* (London: Stanley Paul, 1969) p. 12
8. Anon., *Surrey County Cricket Club Year Book For 1969,* (Reigate: Constitutional Press, 1969) p. 7
9. Fletcher, K., *Captain's Innings,* (London: Stanley Paul, 1983) p. 32
10. Swanton, E. W., 'Illingworth and Dexter miss tour', *The Daily Telegraph,* 26 August 1968, p. 5

11. Illingworth, R. and Mosely, D., *Yorkshire and Back*, (London: Queen Anne Press, 1980) p. 104
12. Barrington, K., *Playing it Straight*, (London: Stanley Paul, 1968) p. 146
13. Haigh, G., *The Cricket War: The Story of Kerry Packer's World Series Cricket*, (London: John Wisden, 1993)
14. Calthorpe, H., 'Illingworth 14 – 64 As Yorkshire Triumph', *The Daily Telegraph*, 8 September 196, p. 12
15. Lewis, T., *Double Century,* (London: Hodder & Stoughton, 1987) p. 318
16. *Wisden Cricketers' Almanack,* 106th edn, ed. by Preston, N., (London: Sporting Handbooks Ltd, 1969) p.1020

Chapter 2 – Yet Another Ashes Series

17. O'Reilly, B., 'Best available – but doubts left', *The Sydney Morning Herald*, 29 February 1968, p. 13
18. Woodcock, J., 'No generous gestures by Lawry', *The Times*, 26 April 1968, p. 17
19. D'Oliveira, B and Murphy, P., *Time to Declare – An Autobiography*, (London: J. M. Dent and Sons, 1980) p. 24
20. Barry Knight – a cricketing odyssey. See:-
    <https://sites.google.com/site/bodaciouscom/the-d-oliveira-affair-40-years-on/barry-knight>
21. D'Oliveira, B and Murphy, P., *Time to Declare – An Autobiography*, (London: J. M. Dent and Sons, 1980) p. 63
22. Cowdrey, C., *Colin Cowdrey M.C.C.,* (London: Hodder and Stoughton, 1976) p. 195
23. Anon., 'Jolly for Dolly', *The Guardian*, 24 August 1968, p. 8

Chapter 3 – A Friendship Under Strain

24. Hamalengwa, M., Flinterman, C. and Dankwa, E., *The International Law of Human Rights in Africa – Basic Documents and Annotated Bibliography*, (Dordrecht: Martinus Nijhoff Publishers, 1988) p. 134
25. Geldenhuys, D.,*The Diplomacy of Isolation: South African Foreign Policy Making*, (Basingstoke: Palgrave Macmillan, 1984) p. 217
26. United Nations Security Council Resolution S/RES/134 (1960). See:-
    <http://www.un.org/en/sc/documents/resolutions/1960.shtml>

27. Guidance Memorandum 271, Foreign Office and Commonwealth Office, London, 19 September 1966, PREM 13/1211, National Archives, London
28. Anon., 'Mr Vorster is S. Africa's choice', *The Times*, 14 September 1966, p. 1
29. D'Oliveira, B and Murphy, P., *Time to Declare – An Autobiography*, (London: J. M. Dent and Sons, 1980) Fig. 12, between pp. 36 – 37
30. Anon., 'Milburn and D'Oliveira in England Twelve', *The Times*, 30 May 1966, p. 3
31. Swanton, E. W., 'Welcome to McGrew and his Team', *The Daily Telegraph*, 8 April 1960, p. 2
32. Anon.,'Playing Politics', *The Daily Telegraph*, 24 June 1965, p. 18
33. Wilson, P., 'Too many Davids – and too few Goliaths', *Daily Mirror*, 23 July 1965, p. 23
34. Chalke, S., *Tom Cartwright – The Flame Still Burns,* (Bath: Fairfield Books, 2007) p. 119
35. Brearley, M., 'Basil D'Oliveira retained his dignity at the centre of the storm', *The Guardian*, 19 November 2011
36. Minutes of MCC Committee Meeting, 26 January 1968, MCC Archive, Lord's Cricket Ground, London
37. Melford, M., 'South Africa may come back to ICC', *The Daily Telegraph*, 6 January 1967, p. 13
38. Anon., 'D'Oliveira thanks England', *The Guardian*, 28 January 1967, p. 9
39. Anon., 'Minister Adamant "Dolly" Will Not Tour S.A.', *Sunday Express*, 22 January 1967
40. Letter from J. N. Elam, British Embassy, Cape Town to C. E. Pestell, Foreign Office, London, 3 February 1967. FCO 25/709, National Archives, London
41. House of Commons Debate (30 January 1967) Vol. 740, Columns 33 – 36. See:- <http://hansard.millbanksystems.com/commons/1967/jan/30/marylebone-cricket-club-south-african>
42. Howell, D., *Made in Birmingham – The Memoirs of Denis Howell*, (London: Queen Anne Press, 1990) p. 200
43. Allen, D. R., *Arlott – The Authorised Biography,* (London: Harper Collins, 1994) p. 142

44. Anon., 'S. Africa Warned On MCC Tour.', *The Daily Telegraph*, 31 January 1967, p. 1
45. Anon., 'MCC Say 'No' To Colour Bar Cricket', *Daily Mirror*, 31 January 1967, p. 1
46. House of Assembly Debates, Republic of South Africa, Columns 3959 – 3968, 11 April 1967
47. ibid
48. Reason, J., 'D'Oliveira allows no controversy', *The Daily Telegraph*, 4 March 1967, p. 4

Chapter 4 – Cricket and Politics Clash

49. D'Oliveira, B., *An Autobiography*, (London: Collins, 1968)
    D'Oliveira, B., *The D'Oliveira Affair*, (London: Collins, 1969)
    D'Oliveira, B and Murphy, P., *Time to Declare – An Autobiography*, (London: J. M. Dent and Sons, 1980)
50. Melford. M., 'The D'Oliveira Case'. In *Wisden Cricketers' Almanack*, 106th edn, ed by Preston, N., (London: Sporting Handbooks Ltd, 1969) pp. 74 – 79
51. Oborne, P., *Basil D'Oliveira – Cricket and Conspiracy*, (London: Little Brown, 2004)
52. Murray, B and Merrett, C., Caught Behind – Race and Politics in Springbok Cricket, (Johannesburg: Witts University Press, 2004)
53. Evans, R., 'Dropping Dolly: The D'Oliveira affair 50 years on', *The Nightwatchman*, No 6, Summer 2014.
54. Arlott, J., 'The D'Oliveira Decision', *The Guardian*, 29 August 1968, p. 13
55. Oborne, P., *Basil D'Oliveira – Cricket and Conspiracy*, (London: Little Brown, 2004) p. 94
56. D'Oliveira, B and Murphy, P., *Time to Declare – An Autobiography*, (London: J. M. Dent and Sons, 1980) p. 58
57. Letter from S. C. Griffith, Secretary of the MCC to D. C. Bursnall, Secretary of South African Cricket Association, 5 January 1968, MCC Archive, Lord's Cricket Ground, London
58. Minutes of MCC Committee Meeting, 21 March 1968, MCC Archive, Lord's Cricket Ground, London
59. Sheppard, D., *Steps Along Hope Street – My Life in Cricket, the Church and the Inner City,* (London: Hodder and Stoughton, 2002) p. 86

60. Cobham, C., 'Viscount Cobham clarifies his position', *The Cricketer*, Vol. 50, No. 4, (1969), p. 8
61. Ezard, J., 'D'Oliveira ban was known to two selectors', *The Guardian*, 11 April 1969, p. 1 and p. 20
62. Swanton, E. W., 'Test century puts tour in jeopardy', *The Daily Telegraph*, 24 August 1968, p. 6
63. Minutes of MCC Selection Sub-Committee Meeting, 27 August 1968, MCC Archive, Lord's Cricket Ground, London
64. Minutes of MCC Committee Meeting, 28 August 1968, MCC Archive, Lord's Cricket Ground, London
65. Brearley, M., *On Cricket,* (London: Constable, 2018) pp. 135 – 145
66. Anon., 'MCC explain their selections', *The Guardian*, 29 August 1968, p. 13
67. Evans, R., 'Dropping Dolly: The D'Oliveira affair 50 years on', *The Nightwatchman*, No 6, Summer 2014.
68. D'Oliveira, B and Murphy, P., *Time to Declare – An Autobiography*, (London: J. M. Dent and Sons, 1980) p. 70
69. Wilson, P., 'This Despicable Affair', *Daily Mirror*, 29 August 1968, pp. 1-2
70. Taylor, C., 'Hero D'Oliveira is Left Out', *Sun*, 29 August 1968, pp. 1
71. Ross, A., 'This sad illusion that cricket is only a game', *The Observer*, 1 September 1968, pp. 9
72. Arlott, J., 'The D'Oliveira Decision', *The Guardian*, 29 August 1968, p. 13
73. Swanton, E. W., 'MCC Ignore D'Oliveira and Milburn', *The Daily Telegraph*, 29 August 1968, p. 12
74. Woodcock, J., 'D'Oliveira fails to get place on tour', *The Times*, 29 August 1968, p. 10
75. Dexter, E. R., 'Dolly! Honest Bungling', *Sunday Mirror*, 1 September 1968, p. 31
76. ibid p. 31
77. Parkinson, M., 'That day in the Long Room at Lord's the selectors didn't know what they were doing', *The Sunday Times*, 1 September 1968, p. 10
78. Heywood, C., 'Valid grounds', *The Times*, 31 August 1968, p. 7
79. Madgwick, D., 'D'Oliveira and the MCC', *The Guardian*, 31 August 1968, p. 6

80. Personal Notices, *The Times*, 4 September 1968, p. 19
81. Anon., 'Colin Cowdrey defends South African tour decision', *Financial Times*, 9 September 1968, p. 18
82. Minutes of MCC Committee Meeting, 12 September 1968, MCC Archive, Lord's Cricket Ground, London
83. Minutes of MCC Selection Sub-Committee Meeting, 16 September 1968, MCC Archive, Lord's Cricket Ground, London
84. Note from Sir John Nicholls, British Embassy, Cape Town to Commonwealth Office, London, 17 September 1968. FCO 25/709, National Archives, London
85. Murray, B. K., 'Politics and cricket: the D'Oliveira affair of 1968'., *Journal of Southern African Studies'*, Vol 27, No. 4 (Dec 2001), pp. 667 – 684
86. Chettle, G. A., 'Editorial'. In *South African Cricket Annual*, Vol. XVI, ed by Chettle, G. A., (Durban: South African Cricket Association, 1969) p. 7
87. Minutes of MCC Committee Meeting, 24 September 1968, MCC Archive, Lord's Cricket Ground, London
88. Letter from S, C, Griffith, MCC to H G Wareham, SACA, 25 September 1968, MCC Archive, Lord's Cricket Ground, London
89. Minutes of MCC Committee Meeting, 24 September 1968, MCC Archive, Lord's Cricket Ground, London
90. Email from Charles Barr to Richard Thorn, 21 March 2018
91. Brearley, M., 'Basil D'Oliveira retained his dignity at the centre of the storm', *The Observer*, 20 November 2011, p. 7
92. Swanton, E. W., 'Honourable defeat for Sheppard party in historic debate', *The Daily Telegraph*, 6 December 1968, p. 14
93. Sheppard, D., *Steps Along Hope Street – My Life in Cricket, the Church and the Inner City*, (London: Hodder & Stoughton, 2002) p. 88
94. Letter from J. A. Pugh, Central and Southern Africa Department Foreign and Commonwealth Office to John Clift, Home Office, London, 6 Oct 1969. FCO 45/310, National Archives, London
95. Ali, T., *Uprising in Pakistan*, (London: Verso, 2018) pp. 17-24

Chapter 5 – Island Sojourn

96. Castle, B., In place of conciliation'. *The Observer*, 28 May 1972, p. 8
97. Swanton, E. W., 'South Africa's 1970 Tour Confirmed by MCC Council', *The Daily Telegraph*, 23 January 1969, p. 15
98. Anon, 'In Brief', *The Times*, 21 January 1969, p. 2
99. Cowdrey, M. C., *M.C.C. – The Autobiography of a Cricketer*, (London: Hodder and Stoughton, 1976)
100. Biography, Geoffrey Boycott: The World of Cricket See http://wwwboycott.gnbcommunications.net
101. Woodcock. J., 'Ken Barrington – The Accumulator'. In *Wisden Cricketers' Almanack*, 107th edn, ed by Preston, N., (London: Sporting Handbooks Ltd, 1970) pp. 106 – 118
102. Allen, D.R. (Ed.), *Arlott on Cricket*, (London: Willow Books, 1984) p. 272
103. Tour Agreement between individual cricketers and Marylebone Cricket Club, MCC/CR1/5/1/104/1, MCC Archive, Lord's Cricket Ground, London
104. Anon, 'Pakistan a pointer to chances against the West Indies', *The Guardian*, 22 January 1969, p. 14
105. ibid p.14
106. Arasaratnam, S., 'After independence', *The Guardian*, 31 May 1968, p. 7
107. Bailey, P., *A Guide to First Class Cricket Matches Played in Sri Lanka*, (Nottingham: Association of Cricket Statisticians, 1987) p. 7
108. Haigh, G. and Frith, D., *Inside Story: Unlocking Australian Cricket's Archives,* (Melbourne: News Custom Publishing, 2007) p. 154
109. ICC Classification of Official Cricket. See < http://resources.pulse.icc-cricket.com >
110. Email from Andrew Hignell, Association of Cricket Statisticians to Richard Thorn, 3 May 2018
111. Graveney, T., *Cricket Over Forty*, (London: Pelham Books, 1970) p. 69
112. Anon., 'MCC in Ceylon'. *The Cricketer*, Vol. 33, No. 1, (1952), p. 106
113. See the on-line cricket database Cricket Archive. Home page: http://cricketacrhive.com

114. See the on-line cricket database Cricket Archive. http://cricketarchive.com/Archive/Scorecards/27/27227.html
115. Anon, 'Tailenders punish MCC', *The Guardian*, 29 January 1969, p. 16
116. Hignell, A. K., 'Profile of Jeff Jones', Cricket Archive On-line, 2007. See:- https://cricketarchive.com/Archive/Articles/0/753.html
117. Melford, M.,'This Tour of Sharp Contrasts', *The Cricketer*, Vol. 50, No. 1 (1969), pp. 12-13 and 15
118. Thawfeeq, S., 'Cricket the Reid Way', The Nation, 4th July 2010, On-line edition, see <http://www.nation.lk/2010/07/04/sports5.htm>
119. Graveney, T., *Cricket Over Forty*, (London: Pelham Books, 1970) p. 70
120. Woodcock, J., 'Riots put tour in jeopardy'. *The Times*, 30 January 1969, p. 11
121. Anon., '11 more deaths in Pakistan surge of violence' *The Times*, 28 January 1969, p. 5
122. Snow, J., *Cricket Rebel*, (London: Hamlyn, 1976) p. 67

Chapter 6 – Uncertainty

123. Fletcher, K., *Captain's Innings*, (London: Stanley Paul, 1983) p. 42
124. Fergusson, N., *Empire,* (London: Penguin Books, 2003) p. 356
125. Khan, Y., *The Great Partition*, (New Haven: Yale University Press, 2017, 2nd Edn.)
126. Letter from Sir Cyril Pickard, British High Commission, Rawalpindi to Sir John Johnston, FCO, London, 3 February 1969. FCO 37/467, National Archives, London.
127. Telegram from Sir Cyril Pickard, British High Commission, Rawalpindi to FCO, London, 3 February 1969. FCO 37/467, National Archives, London.
128. Letter from Sir Cyril Pickard, British High Commission, Rawalpindi to Sir Peter Wilkinson, FCO, London, 3 February 1969. FCO 37/468, National Archives, London.
129. Anon, 'Future Test Tours', *The Times*, 29 June 1950, p. 9
130. Oborne, P., *Wounded Tiger: The History of Cricket in Pakistan*, (London: Simon & Schuster, 2014) p. 16

131. Samiuddin, O., *The Unquiet Ones: A History of Pakistan Cricket*, (Uttar Pradesh: Harper Sport, 2014) pp. 54 – 65
132. Anon, 'Imperial Cricket Conference: Pakistani Efforts to Secure Admission', *The Times*, 2 June 1950, p. 5
133. Kardar, A. H., 'Cricket in Pakistan', *The Times*, 13 February 1952, p. 8
134. Smith, L., 'M.C.C. in India and Pakistan: Reflections on a Dismal Tour', *The Cricketer Spring Annual 1962,* pp 16 – 32
135. Melford, M., 'MCC agree to new tour fixtures with only two Tests', *The Daily Telegraph*, 4 February 1969, p. 13
136. Hazelhurst, P., 'Pakistan Minister says emergency to end soon', *The Times*, 8 February 1969, p. 6
137. Anon., 'MCC may play E Pakistan Test', *The Sunday Times*, 9 February 1969, p. 23
138. Graveney, T., *Cricket Over Forty*, (London: Pelham Books, 1970) p. 71
139. ibid p. 71
140. Telegram from S C 'Billy' Griffith to Les Ames 17 February 1969 MCC/SEC/3/68 Secretaries' Telegrams 1966-69

Chapter 7 – The First Test Match

141. Ali, T., *Uprising in Pakistan*, (London: Verso, 2018) pp. 87-88
142. Hazlehurst, P., 'Eight more die as anti-Ayum riots sweep Dacca', *The Times*, 20 February 1969, p. 6
143. Melford, M., 'MCC Make Check on Milburn', *The Daily Telegraph*, 19 February 1969, p. 13
144. Anon., 'Hobbs left out of England party', *The Times*, 21 February 1969, p. 12
145. Ahmad, B. (ed), *Board of Control for Cricket in Pakistan – Cricket Annual 1968 – 1969*, (Rawalpindi: Ferossons, 1970) pp. 46 – 58
146. Chandler, M., 'The Forgotten Tour' , *Cricketweb.Net*, 28 November 2010. See <http//www.cricketweb.net/the-forgotten-tour/>
147. Melford, M., 'England doubtful on Snow', *The Daily Telegraph*, 21 February 1969, p. 13
148. Snow, J., *Cricket Rebel*, (London: Hamlyn, 1976) p. 70-71
149. Laker, P., 'Control Mob – Or We Pull Out of Test – Ultimatum by Ames', *Daily Mirror*, 22 February 1969, p. 26

150. Peel, M., *The Last Roman: A Biography of Colin Cowdrey*, (London: Andre Deutsch, 1999) p. 177-184
151. Melford, M., 'Ames Test Warning: Control Crowd or Match is Off', *The Daily Telegraph*, 22 February 1969, p. 9
152. Hazlehurst, P., 'President Ayub to Give Up Office', *The Times*, 22 February 1969, p. 1
153. Anon., 'Rev David Sheppard appointed bishop', *The Times*, 24 February 1969, p. 1
154. Laker, P., England Walk Off As Battle Rages, *Daily Mirror*, 25 February 1969, p. 30

Chapter 8 – The Second Test Match

155. Ali, T., *Uprising in Pakistan*, (London: Verso, 2018) pp. 139 – 140
156. Smith, M., 'The East-West gap widens', *Financial Times*, 19 May 1969, p. 9
157. Ali, T., *Uprising in Pakistan*, (London: Verso, 2018) pp. xi – xii
158. Graveney, T., *The Heart of Cricket*, (London: Arthur Barker, 1983) p. 63
159. Fletcher, K., *Captain's Innings*, (London: Stanley Paul, 1983) p. 45
160. Woodcock, J., 'Control Entrusted to Students', *The Times*, 28 February 1969, p. 13
161. Peel, M., *Cricketing Falstaff: A Biography of Colin Milburn*, (London: Andre Deutsch, 1998) pp. 129 – 130
162. Woodcock, J., 'Sluggish Pakistan rile crowd as Test opens', *The Times*, 1 March 1969, p. 7
163. Smith, P., 'D'Oliveira to the Rescue – but Another Draw'. *Playfair Cricket Monthly*, Vol. IX, No. 12, (1969), pp. 6-7
164. Robinson, R., *The Wildest Tests*, (London: Pelham Books, 1972) p. 102
165. Mukherjee, A., 'Roger Prideaux – South Africans were born to play sport', *Cricket Country*, 20 July 2016. See: <http://www.cricketcountry.com>
166. D'Oliveira, B and Murphy, P., *Time to Declare – An Autobiography*, (London: J. M. Dent and Sons, 1980) p. 83
167. Anon., 'Dismal end to the second Test', *The Guardian*, 4 March 1969, p. 16

168. ibid p.16
169. Butt, Q., *Sporting Wickets: Eye witness accounts of the tours of M.C.C. and New Zealand to Pakistan in 1969*, (Rawalpindi: Ferozsons Ltd, 1970) p. 58

Chapter 9 – The Third Test Match

170. King, C., 'Unbeliever Among the Mighty', *The Sunday Times*, 2 March 1969, pp. 49-50
171. Hazelhurst, P., 'Tariq Ali assesses a revolt', *The Times*, 1 March 1969, p. 9
172. Report by T. D. O'Leary, British High Commission, Rawalpindi to Sir John Johnston, FCO, London, 3 March 1969. FCO 37/468, National Archives, London.
173. Graveney, T., *The Heart of Cricket*, (London: Arthur Barker, 1983) p. 66
174. Fletcher, K., *Captain's Innings*, (London: Stanley Paul, 1983) p. 47
175. Woodcock, J., 'England add leg spinner to list', *The Times*, 6 March 1969, p. 11
176. Telegram from S. C. Griffith, Secretary of the MCC to Leslie Ames, MCC Tour Manager, 6 March 1969, File MCC/CR1/5/1/107, MCC Archive, Lord's Cricket Ground, London
177. Anon., 'Test in ruins, but Tom Graveney is superb', *The Guardian*, 8 March 1969, p. 16
178. ibid p.16
179. Cowdrey, M. C., *M.C.C. – The Autobiography of a Cricketer*, (London: Hodder and Stoughton, 1976)
180. Melford, M., 'MCC Home After Pakistan Rioters Force Tour to End', *The Daily Telegraph*, 10 March 1969, p. 11
181. Melford, M., 'The Futile Tour', *The Cricketer*, Vol. 50, No. 2, (1969), pp. 6-7
182. Anon., 'End of the Tour', *The Times*, 10 March 1969, p. 9

Chapter 10 – It Might All Just Go Away

183. Wellings, E. M., 'M.C.C. in Ceylon and Pakistan 1968-69'. In *Wisden Cricketers' Almanack*, 107th edn, ed by Preston, N., (London: Sporting Handbooks Ltd, 1970) pp. 913 – 924
184. Close, B., *Close to Cricket* (London: Stanley Paul, 1968)

185. Cowdrey, M. C., *M.C.C. – The Autobiography of a Cricketer*, (London: Hodder and Stoughton, 1976) p. 206
186. Letter from M. A. Robb, British Embassy, Cape Town to W. Wilson, Southern African Department, FCO, London, 28 March 1969. FCO 45/310, National Archives, London.
187. Manning, J. L., 'Why I offered Dolly £40,000 by 'Tiny'', *Daily Mail*, 4 April 1969. In FCO45/310, National Archives, London.
188. Hennessy, J., 'The sporting conscience', *The Times*, 5 April 1969, p. 8
189. Hennessy, J., 'D'Oliveira disclosure by Lord Cobham', *The Times*, 7 April 1969, p. 1
190. Anon., 'The Cobham disclosure', *The Cricketer*, Vol. 50, No. 2, (1969), p. 4
191. Wilson, P., 'MCC – the muddled czars of cricket', *Daily Mirror*, 10 April 1969, p. 29
192. Clarke, K., 'MCC admits warnings on D'Oliveira', *The Daily Telegraph*, 11 April 1969, p. 1
193. Todd, R., 'MCC: We kept quiet on Dolly', *Daily Mirror*, 11 April 1969, p. 32
194. House of Assembly Debates, Republic of South Africa, Columns 4403 – 4408, 21 April 1969
195. Swanton, E. W., 'S. African tour invitation stands say MCC Council', *The Daily Telegraph*, 2 May 1969, p. 13
196. Bailey, T., 'Manchester win Cup in an entertaining game', *Financial Times*, 28 April 1969, p. 3
197. *Daily Express*, 28 April 1969, p. 22
198. ibid p. 12
199. Melford, M., 'Sunday Cricket starts a TV rumpus', *The Cricketer*, Vol. 9, No. 6, (1968), p. 13
200. Griffith, S. C., 'Sunday Cricket and Television in 1969', *Playfair Cricketer*, Vol. 49, No. 11, (1968), pp. 16 and 18
201. Peel, M., *Cricketing Falstaff – A Biography of Colin Milburn*, (London: Andre Deutsch, 1998) p. 138
202. Anon., 'Milburn says he will play on with one eye', *The Observer*, 25 May 1969, p. 1
203. Arlott, J., 'Cricket still needs Colin Milburn', *The Guardian*, 26 May 1969, p. 13

204. Peel, M., *The Last Roman – A Biography of Colin Cowdrey*, (London: Andre Deutsch, 1999) p. 161
205. Anon., 'Illingworth, the exile, to captain England', *The Guardian*, 4 June 1969, p. 1
206. D'Oliveira, B and Murphy, P., *Time to Declare – An Autobiography*, (London: J. M. Dent and Sons, 1980) p. 83
207. Knott, A., *It's Knott Cricket*, (London: MacMillan, 1985) p. 44
208. Graveney, T., *Cricket Over Forty*, (London: Pelham Books, 1970) pp. 84-87
209. Marson, P., 'Graveney banned for three Tests', *The Times*, 20 June 1969, p. 1
210. Ross, A., 'The folly of too much, too late', *The Observer*, 6 July 1969, p. 19
211. Anon., 'Race protest halts cricket match', *The Times*, 10 July 1969, p. 1
212. Hain, P., *Don't Play with Apartheid*, (London: George Allen & Unwin, 1971) pp. 116-117
213. Anon., 'Race protest halts cricket match', *The Times*, 10 July 1969, p. 1
214. Arlott, J., 'Sobers' finest bowling', *The Guardian*, 14 July 1969, p. 17
215. Carey, M., 'New Zealand's captain gives fair warning', *The Guardian*, 11 June 1969, p. 20

Chapter 11 – Stop the Seventy Tour

216. Anon., 'Threat to cricket', *The Times*, 21 January 1969, p. 2
217. Anon., 'South African cricket team boycott urged', *Daily Telegraph*, 24 June 1969, p. 19
218. Anon., 'Inflated opposition for S. African Cricketers', *Sunday Telegraph*, 27 June 1969, p. 1
219. Stokes, C., 'Springboks facing chaos', *The Guardian*, 11 September 1969, p. 11
220. Hain, P., *Outside In*, (Biteback Publishing, 2020) Kindle edition, Location 1114 of 11163
221. Rowe, M., *Tour de Farce*, (Cardiff: Association of Cricket Statisticians and Historians, 2020), p. 67
222. Eriksen, E. R., Memorandum to the MCC Council, MCC/CR1/5/2/52, MCC Archive, Lord's Cricket Ground, London

Notes on Sources

223. Stokes, C., 'Springboks facing chaos', *The Guardian*, 11 September 1969, p. 11
224. Hain, P., *Outside In*, (Biteback Publishing, 2012) Kindle edition, Location 1252 of 11163
225. Letter from W. Wilson, Central and Southern African Department, FCO to Sir J. Nicholls, British Embassy, Cape Town, 25 April 1969. FCO 45/311, National Archives, London.
226. Letter from R. A. James, Home Office to J. A. Pugh, Central and Southern African Department, FCO, 9 October 1969. FCO 45/312, National Archives, London.
227. ibid
228. Memorandum from Lord Chalfont, FCO to W. Wilson, Central and Southern African Department, FCO. 23 October 1969. FCO 45/312, National Archives, London.
229. Reason, J., 'Springboks Arrive With Oxford Game Still In doubt', *The Daily Telegraph*, 31 October 1969, p. 24
230. Anon., 'S. Africans' game today at Twickenham', *The Guardian*, 5 November 1969, p. 1
231. Anon., 'Coach trips to Springbok protest', *The Guardian*, 5 November 1969, p. 1
232. Anon., 'Police pack halts rugby protest', *The Guardian*, 6 November 1969, p. 1
233. Hain, P., *Don't Play with Apartheid*, (London: George Allen & Unwin, 1971) pp. 197
234. Anon., 'Threat to step up Springbok protests', *The Daily Telegraph*, 24 December 1969, p. 2
235. Haigh, G. and Frith, D., *Inside Story: Unlocking Australian Cricket's Archives,* (Melbourne: News Custom Publishing, 2007) p. 155
236. Collins, T., *The Oval World: A Global History of Rugby*, (London : Bloomsbury Sport, 2015)
237. Anon., 'Springboks Chief Tells of Bomb Death Fear', *The Daily Telegraph*, 2 February 1970, p. 13
238. Letter from R. A. James, Home Office to W. Wilson, Central and Southern African Department, FCO, 21 November 1969. FCO 45/313, National Archives, London.
239. Anon., 'Stop Springbok Cricket Tour, Says Clubs', *The Daily Telegraph*, 9 December 1969, p. 3

240. ibid, p. 3
241. Murray, B. and Merrett, C., *Caught Behind: Race and Politics in Springbok Cricket* (Johannesburg: Wits University Press, 2004) p. 124
242. Rais, G., 'S. Africans' Cricket Tour Is On', *The Daily Telegraph*, 12 December 1969, p. 1
243. Note by Sir John Waldron, Commissioner of Police, 12 December 1969, Minute Sheet 477, p1. MEPO 31/30, National Archives, London.
244. Anon., 'No deviation from apartheid', *The Guardian*, 1 January 1970, p. 1
245. McGilvray, A., *McGilvray: the Game is Not The Same,* (Sydney: ABC, 1985) p. 172
246. Mallett, A., *Spin Out*, (Hawthorn: Gary Sparke, 1977) pp. 65 – 70
247. Anon., 'Not cricket, not good sense', *The Guardian*, 21 January 1970, p. 10
248. Warman, C., 'Wicket dug up as anti-apartheid campaign opens', *The Times*, 21 January 1970, p. 12
249. ibid, p. 12
250. Hain, P., *Outside In*, (Biteback Publishing, 2012) Kindle edition, Location 1258 of 11163
251. Notes of meeting chaired by the Home Secretary in preparation for a meeting with the Cricket Council, 27 January 1969. FCO 45/1728, National Archives, London.
252. Warman, C., 'S African tour cut to 12 matches', *The Times*, 13 February 1970, p. 1
253. Why the 70 Tour. Leaflet produced by the cricket council. FCO 45/729, National Archives, London.
254. Report on Stop the Seventy Tour, Special Branch, Metropolitan Police, 7 April 1970. MEPO 31/30, National Archives, London.
255. Warman, C., 'Big majority vote for tour to go on', *The Times*, 20 May 1970, p. 1
256. South African Cricket Tour – Note for the Record, 21 May 1970. PREM 13/3499, National Archives, London.
257. Details of meeting between the Home Secretary and Cricket Council held on 21 May 1970 (Note written 29 May 1970). FCO 45/729, National Archives, London.

258. Letter from Maurice Allom, Chairman, Cricket Council to James Callaghan, Home Secretary, 22 May 1970. PREM 13/3499, National Archives, London.

Chapter 12 – So What Now?

259. Rosenwater. I., 'The South African Tour Dispute'. In *Wisden Cricketers' Almanack*, 108th edn, ed by Preston, N., (London: Sporting Handbooks Ltd, 1971) pp. 137 – 138
260. Lake, M., 'Terse finish to long game', *The Guardian*, 27 May 1970, p. 1
261. Rosenwater. I., 'The South African Tour Dispute'. In *Wisden Cricketers' Almanack*, 108th edn, ed by Preston, N., (London: Sporting Handbooks Ltd, 1971) pp. 141
262. Rais, G., 'Discourtesy regretted', *The Daily Telegraph*, 23 May 1970, p. 1
263. Bourne, J., 'Cricket Council reluctantly cancels Springbok tour', *Financial Times*, 23 May 1970, p. 1
264. *The Times*, 23 May 1970, p. 1
265. *Daily Mirror*, 23 May 1970, p. 1
266. *The Guardian*, 23 May 1970, p. 1
267. Anon., 'Let Violence Celebrate', *The Daily Telegraph*, 23 May 1970, p. 10
268. Anon., 'Triumph of the Demo', *Daily Express*, 23 May 1970, p. 6
269. Anon., 'The right decision at last', *The Guardian*, 23 May 1970, p. 10
270. ibid p.10
271. Rayern Allen, D., *Arlott on Cricket: His Writings on the Game*, (London: Willow Books, 1984) pp. 217 – 220
272. Arlott, J., 'Why I'm off the air', *Guardian*, 17 April 1970, p. 12
273. Fay, S. and Rynaston, D. *Arlott, Swanton and the Soul of English Cricket*, (London: Bloomsbury Publishing) Kindle edition. Location 2909 of 11163.
274. Hill, A., *Peter May*, (London: Andre Deutsch, 1996) p. 166-167
275. Cabinet Papers and Minutes 17 May 1970, CAB 128/45/23, National Archives, London
276. Letter from M. S. Berthoud, British Embassy, Pretoria to J. E. C. Macrae, Central and Southern African Department, FCO, 26 May 1970. FCO 45/729, National Archives, London.

277. Anon., 'Vorster says Britain gave in to blackmail', *The Times*, 25 May 1970, p. 4
278. Letter from J. E. C. Macrae, Central and Southern African Department, FCO to Bruce W Middleton, Offices of the High Commission, New Zealand House, London, 2 June 1970. FCO 45/729, National Archives, London.
279. Letter from R. A. James, Home Office to J. A. Pugh, Central and Southern African Department, FCO, 9 October 1969. FCO 45/312, National Archives, London.

Chapter 13 – The First Test Match

280. Swanton, E. W., 'Seven in Line to Lead MCC', *The Daily Telegraph*, 3 June 1970, p. 26
281. Arlott, J., 'Illingworth captains England', *The Guardian*, 6 June 1970, p. 19
282. Anon., 'Cowdrey's Get-Fit Plans', *The Daily Telegraph*, 2 June 1970, p. 28
283. Anon., 'Brown leads selectors', *The Daily Telegraph*, 2 June 1970, p. 28
284. Arlott, J., 'Illingworth captains England', *The Guardian*, 6 June 1970, p. 19
285. *Wisden Cricketers' Almanack*, 108th edn, ed by Preston, N., (London: Sporting Handbooks Ltd, 1971) p. 424
286. Anon., 'England Out of World Cup', The Guardian, 15 June 1970, p. 1 and p. 19
287. Woodcock, J., 'England's batting too bad to be true', *The Times*, 18 June 1970, p. 15
288. White, C., 'Sobered! – Dismal England crash to Gary's pace'. Batting too bad to be true', *The Daily Express*, 18 June 1970, p. 20
289. Anon., 'Gallup puts Labour 7 pc ahead', *The Daily Telegraph*, 18 June 1970, p. 1
290. Boyne, H. B., 'Big swing to Conservatives – Heath heading for no. 10', *The Daily Telegraph*, 19 June 1970, p. 1
291. Snow, J., *Cricket Rebel*, (London: Hamlyn, 1976) p. 85
292. Woodcock, J., 'Sobers (147) once more humbles England', *The Times*, 20 June 1970, p. 9
293. Swanton, E. W., 'The best ever', *The Daily Telegraph*, 22 June 1970, p. 28

294. James, B., 'The All Time Greatest', *The Daily Telegraph*, 22 June 1970, p. 1

Chapter 14 – The Second Test Match

295. White, C., 'Ton-up Cowdrey is needed now', *The Daily Express*, 23 June 1970, p. 16
296. Lee, A., 'Graham Gooch retires from the line of fire', *The Times*, 21 July 1997, p. 31
297. Chandler, M., 'A Tale of What Might Have Been ', *Cricketweb. Net*, 25 October 2013. See <https//www.cricketweb.net/a-tale-of-what-might-have-been />
298. Swanton, E. W., 'Stronger England can erase memory of Lord's crash', *The Daily Telegraph*, 2 July 1970, p. 34
299. Bailey, T., *Wickets, Catches and the Odd Run*, (London: Willow Books, 1986)
300. Delaney, T, 'At last it's the genuine Alan Jones', *The Sunday Times*, 5 July 1970, p. 19
301. Ballantine, J., 'A gambler's panache wins it for Newcombe'. The Sunday Times. 5 July 1970, p. 16
302. Swanton, E. W., Kent stand puts England in sight of victory', *The Daily Telegraph*, 7 July 1970, p. 28
303. Woodcock, J., 'Kent pair raise hopes of an England win', *The Times*, 7 July 1970, p.8

Chapter 15 – The Third Test Match

304. White, C., 'England's greatest victory say Illy', *The Daily Express*, 8 July 1970, p. 13
305. Anon., 'What They Said', *The Daily Telegraph*, 8 July 1970, p. 30
306. Woodcock, J., MCC tour captaincy problem, *The Times*, 6 July 1970, p. 11
307. Anon., Test Call for Peter Pollock', *The Guardian*, 9 July 1970, p. 19
308. Swanton, E. W., 'D'Oliveira Century Rescues England From Sobers', *The Daily Telegraph*, 17 July 1970, p. 30
309. Melford, M., 'MCC Pay Tribute to the MCC', *The Daily Telegraph*, 17 July 1970, p. 30
310. Anon., 'S. Africa Arms For Navy Only – Hain threatens a bigger campaign', *The Daily Telegraph*, 27 July 1970, p. 1

311. Boyd, F., 'Arms sales disturbs 30 Tory MPs', *The Daily Telegraph*, 17 July 1970, p. 1
312. Arlott, J., 'Sobers and Lloyd the Aggressors, *The Guardian*, 18 July 1970, p. 15
313. White, C., 'It's Illingworth – he gets the tour job', *Daily Express*, 21 July 1970, p. 12
314. Woodcock, J., ' Chance of riches rejected', *The Times*, 14 August 1970, p. 9

Chapter 16 – The Fourth Test Match
315. Illingworth, R. and Mosely, D., *Yorkshire and Back*, (London: Queen Anne Press, 1980) pp. 73-74
316. Anon., 'I'm glad its all over', *Daily Express*, 22 July 1970, p. 12
317. Illingworth, R. and Mosely, D., *Yorkshire and Back*, (London: Queen Anne Press, 1980) pp. 63-64
318. Murtagh, A., *Gentleman and Player*, (Durrington: Pitch Publishing, 2017) Kindle edition. Location 5122 of 5980
319. Fletcher, K., *Captain's Innings*, (London: Stanley Paul, 1983) pp. 34 – 39
320. ibid p. 35
321. Woodcock, J., 'Snow and Illingworth Revive Hopes', *The Times*, 4 August 1970, p. 9
322. Snow, J., *Cricket Rebel*, (London: Hamlyn, 1976) p. 84
323. White, C., 'Gary Sobers' verdict: England can beat Aussies, *Daily Express*, 5 August 1970, p. 12

Chapter 17 – The Fifth Test Match
324. Swanton, E. W., 'Sobers & Pollock race away with 88 in an hour'. *The Daily Telegraph*, 15 August 1970, p. 14
325. Arlott, J., 'Lever nudges selectors', *The Guardian*, 15 August 1970, p. 15
326. Arlott, J., 'Boycott at his best: an innings of intellect and aggression'. *The Guardian*, 18 August 1970, p. 17
327. Woolridge, I., 'Gary Sobers: Cricketers of the Century tribute', *Wisden*, 20 July 2019. See <https://wisden.com/almanack/garry-sobers-all-rounder>

Chapter 18 – After the Dust has Settled

328. Swanton, E. W., 'Selectors bank on experience in no-surprises 16', *The Daily Telegraph*, 20 August 1970, p. 21
329. Preston, N., 'Moving the goalposts – Notes by the Editor' Wisden Cricketers' Almanack, 127th edn, ed by Preston, N., (London: Sporting Handbooks Ltd, 1980)
330. Marks, V., 'Fifty year itch scratched: Glamorgan's Alan Jones gets his England cap at last'. *The Guardian*, 17 June 2020
331. Woodcock, J., 'Conference of compromises', *The Times,* 21 July 1971. p. 8
332. Wisden Cricket Info staff, 'D'Oliveira Honoured by South Africa', 19 August 2004
    See: <https://www.espncricinfo.com/story/id/2342018>
333. Engel, M., 'South Africa Falters After Small Step', *The Guardian,* 11 November 1991. p. 22

Acknowledgements

For anybody researching and writing about English cricket, there is really only one place to start and that is the MCC Library and Archive at Lord's Cricket Ground. I am grateful to Neil Robinson for granting me access to both the library and outstanding collection of archive material. I would like to also thank Robert Curphey, the Archive and Library Manager, for answering my many questions and emails over the last three years. His responses were always detailed, friendly and much appreciated.

I wish to acknowledge and thank those who have helped me search for material and provided information. I am particularly indebted to Sarah Minney, Consultant Genealogist for again using her skill and knowledge of the UK National Archives to retrieve so much fascinating material on the politics of South Africa, apartheid and sport. Thanks also to Dr Andrew Hignell, Professor Charles Barr, Professor Ruzari Abdul Rahim and Professor Bob Green, for answering questions and/or providing information. Mark Rowe kindly provided me with a copy of his fascinating recent book *Tour De Farce*.

I am grateful to Robin Parkes for reading through my manuscript and for his suggested changes and incisive comments. Thanks also to Peter Adams for his comments on structure and his enthusiastic support in general.

Acknowledgements

My long time friend, academic colleague and fellow author, Professor Peter Sydenham continues to inspire, through our weekly far ranging Skype conversations. Similarly Professor Ashu Sharma with his knowledge of Asian culture and cricket has been a constant source of advice and of course friendship. Dr Daryl Cornish, cricket lover and enthusiast about anything sport related also gave useful feedback on cricket and South Africa. Any errors remaining are my responsibility.

My wife Danusia has been an integral part of this project from the very start. As a critical audience for each section of the book as it was written and rewritten, her perceptive comments and observations considerably improved what I thought was already finished. She has also been chief cheerleader and without her encouragement this book would still be a growing pile of papers on my desk.

Finally, many times during the writing of this book a quotation from Rousseau's *Les Confessions* came to mind:

> 'I realise very well that the reader has no great need to know all this, but I need to tell him'.

Having got this far, I hope the cricket loving reader realises that they did need to know this after all.

Richard Thorn
January 2021

About the Author

Richard Thorn is a former Head of Computing and Engineering at the University of West London; Victoria University, Melbourne and the University of Derby. A Professor of Measurement Systems he published a number of books on measurement science and engineering during his career. Now that he is retired he can spend his time researching and writing on subjects he did not have time for when working. Cricket is one of those at the top of the list.

Index

Abdul Kardar, 76
African Resistance Movement, 152
Aftab Gul, 89, 92, 107, 120, 121
Ahmed, Tofail, 105
Allen, G. O. B. 'Gubby', 38, 41, 43, 154
Allom, Maurice, 160, 166, 167
Amerasinghe, Daya, 67, 68
Ames, Leslie, 38, 40, 61, 66, 67, 69, 70, 74, 77, 81, 83, 84, 87, 88, 94, 104, 105, 106, 119, 122 - 126, 130, 131, 183
Amiss, Dennis, 16, 18, 196, 209, 241 - 244, 246, 250
Anti-Apartheid Movement (AAM), 28, 29, 149, 152, 157
Arlott, John, xii, 17, 28, 33,38, 46, 59, 138, 139, 145, 174, 211
Arnold, Geoff, 226
Arundel Castle Cricket Ground, 134
Asif Iqbal, 83, 89, 90, 92, 96, 107, 121
Asif Masood, 89, 90, 92, 107, 120, 121
Bacher, Dr Ali, 161, 164. 255

Bahawalpur, 77 - 80
Bailey, Trevor, 196, 211
Bangladesh, x
Barber, Bob, 16, 18
Barlow, Eddie, 162, 164, 183, 196, 187, 188, 192, 197 - 205, 210, 211, 215, 222, 227 - 236, 245, 246, 249, 250, 254
Barr, Professor Charles, 47, 51
Barrington, Ken, 9, 16, 18, 19, 20, 43, 44, 59, 60, 61, 119, 145, 147
Basil D'Oliveira Trophy, 255
Bedser, Alec, 15, 38, 224
Benaud, Richie, 32, 211
Bhutto, Zulfikar Ali, 80, 86, 87, 118
Birkenshaw, Jack, 138, 139
Blair, Philbert, 134
Board of Control for Cricket in Pakistan (BCCP), 70, 75, 77, 84, 104, 125
Bombay, x, 161
Booth, Roy, 27
Bornman, Corrie, 155, 157

Boycott, Geoffrey (Later Sir Geoffrey), 16, 18, 19, 20, 39, 43, 44, 59, 60, 61, 141 - 145, 182, 227, 228, 231- 234, 240, 242, 243, 248 - 251

Brearley, Mike, 30, 43, 52

Brown, David, 15, 17, 19, 20, 43, 60, 68, 80, 88, 91, 95 - 101, 107 - 110, 112, 120, 125, 130, 141, 144, 182, 195 - 198, 200, 202 - 204, 209 211, 213, 214, 217, 221, 222, 227, 241

Brown, Freddie, 183, 210,

Brutus, Dennis, 153

Buller, J. S. 'Syd', 223

Butcher, Basil, 141, 143, 145, 146

Calcutta, x, 73, 255

Callaghan MP, Rt. Hon. James, 156, 163, 166, 173

Campaign Against Race Discrimination in Sport, 28

Cardus, Sir Neville, 4

Carr, Donald, 38, 42,

Cartwright, Tom, 30. 45, 48, 49,

Castle MP, Rt. Hon. Barbara, 57

Ceylon, x, 13, 51, 52, 54, 58, 61 - 70, 76, 159, 161

Chalfont, Lord Alun, 155

Chappell, Ian, 14, 19, 21, 182

Close, Brian, 48, 130, 140, 148, 225

Cobham, Viscount Charles, 41, 42, 132

Colombo, 60, 61, 62, 65, 66, 67, 68, 70, 184

Compton, Denis, 32, 245

Connolly, Alan, 14,

Constantine, Sir Learie, 30

Cook, Stephen, 255

Cottam, Bob, 43, 60, 65 - 67, 79, 81, 88, 91, 95 - 97, 100, 101, 107, 110, 113 - 115, 120, 130

County Championship, 5, 9, 10, 49, 89, 136, 138, 147, 148, 179, 182, 183, 193, 195, 202, 223, 224, 227, 228, 241, 251, 255

Court, Margaret, 203

Cowdrey, Colin (Later Lord Cowdrey), 16, 18 - 20, 38. - 40, 43, 44, 47 - 50, 60, 61, 65, 67 - 70, 73, 74, 77, 79, 81 - 88, 91 - 93, 95 - 100, 104 - 107, 109 - 112, 114, 116, 120 - 124, 129 - 131, 139, 145, 147, 148, 181, 182, 193 - 195, 197 - 199, 201, 204, 205, 209, 211, 212, 219, 220, 225, 227- 229, 234, 236, 238, 240, 242 - 244, 246, 248, 249, 253, 255

Cowper, Bob, 14

Cricket Council, 13, 58, 63, 133, 149, 153, 158, 159, 163, 164, 166, 167, 171 - 177, 213, 219,

Dacca, x, 70, 71, 77, 81, 83, 84, 85, 87, 88, 94, 102 - 107, 110, 117, 119, 120

Dacca Stadium, 103, 107, 106

Daily News Trophy, 64

Denness, Mike, 182, 183, 190, 191, 194, 227, 241

Dexter, Ted, 46. 74, 76, 107, 139

D'Oliveira, Basil, xii, 16 - 22, 25, 27, 28, 31- 50, 53, 54, 58, 60, 63, 68, 78 - 81, 88, 93 - 98, 106, 107, 112 - 115, 119, 120, 126, 129 - 132, 139, 140 - 142, 144, 183, 185, 186, 191, 192, 194 - 200, 202 - 204, 211 - 213, 215, 220, 221, 227, 229 - 231, 233, 235, 238, 242, 243, 255

Donovan Andree Trophy, 64

Douglas-Home, Sir Alec, (Later Baron Home of the Hirsel), 41, 42, 52, 132

Index

Dowling, Graham, 146
Eaks, Louis, 163
East Pakistan, x, 70, 73, 74, 81, 82, 83, 86, 103, 104, 107, 117, 118
Eden Gardens Cricket Ground, Calcutta, 255
Edgbaston Cricket Ground, Birmingham, 8, 171, 195, 204, 208, 209, 210
Edrich, Bill, 6
Edrich, John, xii, 6 - 8, 16, 18, 19 - 21, 39, 43, 44, 60, 68, 69, 79, 80, 88, 91, 92, 98, 107, 111, 115, 116, 120, 121, 139, 141, 142, 144, 146, 182, 185, 194, 195, 199, 200, 204, 205, 209, 211, 212, 218, 219, 226, 227, 240
Edwards, Michael, 7, 8, 174
Engineer, Farokh, 178, 183, 185, 189, 190, 191, 197, 199, 203, 210, 226
Ennals, MP, David (later Lord Ennals), 150,
Eriksen, E. R. 'Ronnie', 153
FIFA World Cup 1970, 28, 192, 253
Fletcher, Keith, 8, 44, 45, 60, 68, 71, 79, 88, 93, 96, 98 - 100, 107, 111, 119, 120, 130, 139, 144, 194, 196, 197, 199, 205 - 207, 211, 212, 220, 227, 229, 230, 234, 235, 241 - 244, 248, 249, 251
Gibbs, Lance, 141, 183, 191, 192, 198, 200, 204, 211, 212, 217, 218, 220, 221, 224, 233, 235, 238, 240, 242, 254
Gibson, Alan, 211
Gifford, Norman, 27
Gilligan, Arthur, 38, 41, 63
Gleeson, John, 15
Gooch, Graham, 195

Graveney, Tom, 16, 18, 19, 20, 39, 40, 43, 44, 45, 60, 65, 68, 69, 78, 79, 80, 81, 84, 88, 91, 93, 98, 100, 101, 104, 107, 111, 112, 119, 120, 121, 122, 123, 130, 139, 140, 141, 142, 145, 147, 182, 194, 251
Green, David, 45
Greig, Tony, 195 - 197, 200, 202 - 204, 209, 211 - 213, 215 - 217, 221, 226, 227, 230 - 233, 236, 237, 242
Griffith, Charlie, 88, 133
Griffith, S. C. 'Billy', 12, 31, 33, 38, 40, 41, 43, 44, 58, 84, 122, 131, 154, 159, 160, 166, 171, 172, 177, 178
Hain, Adelaine, 151, 152
Hain, Peter (Later Rt. Hon. Lord Hain), 58, 144, 150 - 158, 160, 161, 165, 173, 213
Hain, Walter, 151, 152
Hall, Wes, 88, 133
Hammond, Walter, 59, 205
Hanif Mohammad, 78, 80, 81, 89, 93, 96, 101, 109, 110, 111, 113, 114, 115, 119, 121, 122, 123
Harman, Roger, 7, 8
Harris, John, 151, 152
Hawke, Neil, 14
Headingley Cricket Ground, Leeds, 20, 144, 145, 171, 224, 226
Heath MP, Rt. Hon. Edward, 175, 187, 197, 213,
Higgs, Ken, 16, 18, 20, 42
Hobbs, Robin, 60, 66, 67, 79, 80, 88, 119, 120, 121
Horton, Martin, 27
Hudson, Andrew, 255
Hudson, Robert, xii

305

Howell MP, Rt. Hon. Denis, 12, 33, 131, 132, 154, 155
Hutton, Sir Leonard, 59, 254
Illingworth, Ray, 9, 10, 20, 42, 138, 140, 141, 143 - 148, 181, 182, 185, 186, 188 - 198, 200 - 204, 208 - 213, 216, 217, 219 - 222, 224 - 231, 233, 236 - 238, 240 - 254
Insole, Doug, 15, 38, 41, 43, 44
International Cavaliers, 11, 134, 136, 210
ICC - International Cricket Conference/ Imperial Cricket Conference/ International Cricket Council, 13, 51, 63, 64, 74, 75, 76, 136, 213, 254, 255
Intikhab Alam, 83, 89, 90, 92, 93, 95, 97, 98, 110, 111, 121, 123, 183, 189 - 192, 198, 200, 203, 209, 211, 214, 218 - 220, 222, 223, 226, 232, 237, 238, 241 - 245, 247 - 249
Isaacs, Wilfred, 144, 153, 154
Jarman, Barry, 14, 21
Jinnah, Mohammad Ali, 117
Johnston, Brian, 211
Jones, Alan, 44, 182, 185, 190, 194, 195, 202, 254
Jones, Jeff, 42 - 44, 48, 49, 60, 66 - 68
Kanhai, Rohan, 133, 183, 186, 197, 200, 202, 211, 215 - 217, 222, 230, 231, 233, 237 238, 240, 242, 243, 246, 250 - 252
Karachi, 65, 70, 71, 73, 76, 77, 78, 79, 80, 84, 86, 89, 96, 116, 117, 119, 120, 122, 124, 126, 1
Kay, John, 17
Kennington Oval, London, xi, 6, 147, 226, 240, 241, 247

Kenyon, Don, 15, 38
Khan, President Ayub, 69, 73, 77, 82, 86, 94, 118, 126
Khan, Nawab, 75,
Knight, Barry, 18, 19, 20, 138, 140, 141, 144, 146
Kolkata, x
Knott, Alan, 16, 18 - 20, 43, 60, 68, 79, 83, 88, 93 - 99, 107, 109, 112, 115, 120, 124, 125, 130, 140, 141, 144, 183, 186, 191, 192, 194, 196, 197, 200, 203, 209, 211, 213, 214, 221, 222, 227, 230, 232, 236, 238, 240, 242, 244, 245, 246, 250, 252,
Lahore, 70, 73, 75, 77, 78, 80, 82, 81, 84, 85
Lahore Stadium, 86, 88, 90
Lawry, Bill, xi, 14, 15, 18, 21, 58, 87, 161, 182
Le Roux, Pieter, 32, 33
Lever, Peter, 183, 219, 241, 242, 245 - 249, 252
Lillee, Dennis, 7, 93
Lloyd, Clive, 134, 141, 145, 178, 183, 186, 188, 191, 197 198, 201, 202, 211, 213, 216, 217, 222, 226, 231, 235, 236, 247, 248, 250, 252
Lloyd, David, 94
Lock, Tony, 8, 106
Lord's Cricket Ground, London, xiii, 4, 7, 11, 13, 17, 18, 19, 21, 29, 30, 36, 38, 58, 74, 77, 81, 82, 84, 122, 126, 129, 131, 132, 135, 142, 143, 144, 146, 148, 149, 150, 159, 164, 171, 177, 178, 181, 182, 184, 188, 189, 193, 194, 195, 196, 199, 213, 225, 253, 254

Index

Luckhurst, Brian, 182, 185, 190, 191, 195, 199, 204 - 207, 209, 211, 212, 218 - 220, 227, 229, 233, 234, 242, 243, 248
Lyallpur, x, 77, 78, 80, 81
Majid Khan, 89, 90, 92, 93, 96, 98, 99, 100, 101, 107, 109, 110, 111, 115, 121, 124
Malan, Dr Daniel, 24
Mandela, Nelson, 151
Marylebone Cricket Club (MCC), 4, 12 - 15, 21, 27 - 29, 31- 33, 36, 38 - 48, 50 - 54, 58, 59, 61 - 71, 74, 76 - 84, 87, 94, 103, 105, 117, 118, 122, 124, 129, 131, 132, 138, 139, 154, 155, 158 - 160, 164, 176, 177, 179, 181- 183, 211, 213, 214, 219, 223 - 225
May, Peter, 15, 16, 38, 41, 42,
Mbeki, Thabo, 153
MCC Advisory County Cricket Committee, 5, 15,
MCC Committee, 4, 13, 15, 29, 30, 31, 33, 41, 43, 44, 47, 50 - 53, 80, 129, 132
MCC Cricket Council (later Cricket Council) 12, 58, 133, 149, 153, 158, 159, 163, 164, 166, 167, 171 - 177, 213, 219
MCC Selection Sub-Committee xiii, 21, 41, 43, 49
McGilvray, Alan, xii, 161
McKenzie, Graham, 14, 138, 162, 183, 185, 196, 198, 199, 200, 204 - 206, 210, 242, 244, 245, 248, 250
McLean, Roy, 32
Melford, Michael, 31, 37, 68, 90, 126
Merrett, Christopher, 37

Middleton Cricket Club, 17, 81
Milburn, Colin, 18,19, 20, 27, 28, 44, 45, 60, 105, 106, 119, 120, 121, 122, 123, 130, 138, 139, 140, 141, 145, 147
Mohammad Ilyas, 89, 95, 100, 107, 108
Mountbatten, Lord Louis, 72
Multan, 80
Munawar Hussain, 91
Murray, Bruce, 37
Murray, Deryck, 210 - 212, 217, 218, 220, 221 229 - 232, 236, 240, 247, 248
Murray, John, 43, 60, 79, 88, 174
Mushtaq Mohammad, 79, 89, 90, 96, 99, 102, 107, 109, 111, 113 - 115, 121, 194, 227, 231, 237, 240, 242, 244, 246, 249, 250, 252
National Awami Party / Awami League, 86, 118
National Cricket Association, (NCA), 12
National Stadium Karachi, 117, 120
Niaz Ahmed, 106, 107, 110, 111, 113, 120
Nicholls, Sir John, 49
Nurse, Seymour, 133
Oborne, Peter, 37, 40,
Old, Chris, 227, 230 - 232, 236, 241, 242, 246 - 248
Old Trafford Cricket Ground, Manchester, 16, 17, 19, 27, 138, 141, 142
Oostuizen, M., J., 'Tienie', 48
Pakistan People's Party, 86, 89
Parkinson, Michael, 46
Pervez Saijad, 106, 107, 110 -113, 120
Piachaud, James, 68
Pickard, Sir Cyril, 73, 74

Player's County League, 11, 135, 116, 119, 148, 228
Pocock, Pat, 16, 18, 19, 43, 60, 66, 68, 79, 83, 88, 95, 96, 97, 100, 101, 107, 119, 130
Pollock, Graeme, 211, 215, 216, 222, 227, 231, 236, 237, 240, 244, 246, 247, 251, 254
Pollock, Peter, 211, 212, 218, 219, 220, 227
Prideaux, Roger, 20, 43 - 45, 60, 68, 69, 79, 83, 88, 91, 92, 98, 100, 107, 111, 116, 119, 120, 130, 139
Procter, Mike, 161, 162, 164, 183, 185, 186, 190, 194, 198 - 200, 203 - 206, 211 - 214, 217, 218, 220 - 223, 229, 230, 232 - 236, 238, 239, 243, 244, 247, 248, 252, 254
Professional Cricketers' Association, 5, 7, 174
Quaid-e-Azam Trophy, 89
Radcliffe, Sir Cyril, 72
Rahman, Sheikh Mujibur, 86, 87, 118
Rajaratnam, Ameresh, 67
Redpath, Ian, xi, 18, 21, 162
Reid, B., G., 'Buddy', 67 - 69
Rhoades, Cedric, 178
Rhodesia, x, 41, 131, 175, 176
Richards, Barry, 134, 161, 162, 164, 183, 186, 197, 199, 201, 202, 211, 215, 222, 229 - 231, 233, 237 - 239, 242, 243, 246, 250, 251, 254
Robert Senanayake Trophy, 64
Roche, Tony, 203
Ross, Alan, 45
Saeed Ahmed, 78, 80, 81, 89 - 91, 93, 95, 96, 98 - 100, 107, 108, 111 - 115, 121 - 124,

Safraz Nawaz, 83, 120, 121
Salahuddin Mulla, 106 - 108,114, 120
Saravanamutti Trophy, 64
Sellers, A. Brian, 9
Shafqat Rana, 89, 107, 120, 121
Sheppard, Rev David (later Bishop of Liverpool), 29, 52, 53, 99, 132, 165
Shillingford, Grayson, 134, 143
South African Cricket Association (SACA), 13, 29, 31, 37, 40, 44, 50, 53, 58, 133, 160, 166, 167, 172, 174
Shackleton, Derek, 8
Sharpe, Philip, 140, 141, 143, 144, 146, 183, 186, 191, 194, 229. 241
Sharpville Massacre, 25, 149
Sheahan, Paul, 15
Shujauddin Siddiqi, 91
Shuttleworth, Ken, 182, 183, 195, 196, 209, 241
Smith, Leslie, 76
Smith, Mike, 61
Smith, Peter, 107,
Snow, John, 9, 16, 19, 20, 43, 60, 65, 68, 79, 80, 87, 88, 91, 106 - 110, 112, 113, 120, 124, 125, 130, 141, 144, 182, 183, 186 - 188, 190, 194 - 197, 200 - 202, 204, 209, 211, 215 - 218, 222, 226, 227, 230 - 238, 240 - 242, 245, 246, 248 - 252
Sobers, Garry (Later Sir Garry), 17, 133, 134, 137, 141, 143, 145, 146, 154, 183, 185, 186 - 192, 196, 197, 199 - 201, 203, 204, 206, 208, 209 - 212, 214 - 219, 221, 222, 228, 229, 231 - 235, 237 - 239, 242 - 254
Sports Arena, 155
Stop the Seventy Tour (STST), 148, 149, 150, 153, 173, 213, 214

Index

Student Action Committee, 89, 104, 105, 108, 117, 157
Swanton, E. W., 'Jim', 46, 53, 181, 205, 211, 247
Tallent, John, 158
Tennekoon, Anura, 69
Test and County Cricket Board (TCCB), 12, 158, 159, 178, 179, 197
The White Swan, Fleet Street, 150
Thomson, Jeff, 7, 90, 195
Thorpe MP, Rt. Hon. Jeremy, 153
Tissera, Michael, 65 - 68
Trent Bridge Ground, Nottingham, 8, 107, 193, 196, 201, 210, 211
Tsafendas, Dimitri, 26
Turner, Ken, 138, 147, 251
Twickenham Stadium, 156
Underwood, Derek, 16, 17, 19, 20, 43, 60, 68, 79 - 81, 88, 95, 96, 98, 100, 101, 107, 109, 113 - 115, 120, 130, 141, 143, 144, 146, 147, 183, 185, 186, 188, 190, 194, 196, 198, 200, 202, 203, 209, 211, 214, 215, 217, 218, 221, 222, 226, 227, 241, 251
Verwoerd, Dr Hendrik, 23 - 26
Vorster, Bathazar Johannes 'John', 26 - 28, 33, 34, 40, 41, 44, 48 - 50, 132, 151, 160, 175, 176
Waldron, Sir John, 160
Walker, Max, 195
Walters, Doug, 15, 19, 88
Ward, Alan, 147, 182, 183, 186, 188, 190, 195, 209, 226, 241
Wasim Bari, 89, 97, 107, 121
West Indian Campaign Against Apartheid Cricket, 165
West Pakistan, x, 54, 70, 73, 74, 82, 83, 86, 87, 103, 118,
Why the 70s Tour? Leaflet, 164
Willis, Bob, 226
Wilson, Don, 44, 227, 230, 232, 233, 236, 238, 241, 242, 245, 246, 247, 251
Wilson MP, Rt. Hon. Harold, 4, 12, 57, 152, 165, 166, 171, 175, 187,
Wilson, Peter, 30, 112
Wisden Cricketers' Almanack, 3, 37, 63, 130, 254,
Woodcock, John,
Younis, Ahmed, 194, 226
Zaheer Abbas, 83
Zimbabwe, x, 41, 176